Nancy Drew and
Her Sister Sleuths

Nancy Drew and Her Sister Sleuths

Essays on the Fiction of Girl Detectives

Edited by
MICHAEL G. CORNELIUS
and MELANIE E. GREGG

McFarland & Company, Inc., Publishers
Jefferson, North Carolina, and London

Documents from the Stratemeyer Syndicate Records (1932–1984) in
the Manuscripts and Archives Division appear courtesy of the New
York Public Library, Astor, Lenox, and Tilden Foundations, and the
Beinecke Library, Yale University. Reprinted with permission of
Simon and Schuster, Inc. Nancy Drew is a registered trademark of
Simon and Schuster, Inc.

LIBRARY OF CONGRESS CATALOGUING-IN-PUBLICATION DATA

Nancy Drew and her sister sleuths : essays on the fiction of girl
    detectives / edited by Michael G. Cornelius and Melanie E. Gregg.
        p.   cm.
    Includes bibliographical references and index.

    ISBN 978-0-7864-3995-9
    softcover : 50# alkaline paper ∞

    1. Detective and mystery stories, American — History and criticism.
2. Drew, Nancy (Fictitious character)   3. Women detectives in
literature.   4. Teenage girls in literature.   I. Cornelius, Michael G.
II. Gregg, Melanie E.
PS374.D4N36   2008
813'.08720992827 — dc22   2008030002

British Library cataloguing data are available

On the cover: stairway ©2008 Shutterstock; girl detective
©2008 Pictures Now

Manufactured in the United States of America

McFarland & Company, Inc., Publishers
  Box 611, Jefferson, North Carolina 28640
  www.mcfarlandpub.com

I'd like to dedicate this book to Joe and to the many wonderful scholars and dedicated fans who have helped keep Nancy Drew and her kin alive for so many years, especially Kate Emburg, who introduced me to this happy world many years ago, and Jenn Fisher and Garrett Lothe, who do so much to keep me informed.

— Michael G. Cornelius

I'd like to dedicate this book to my brother, who got me hooked, three yellow-spines at a time.

— Melanie E. Gregg

Acknowledgments

I would like to acknowledge the excellent work of all the contributors to this project, as well as all the presenters at the "Nancy Drew and Girl Sleuths" conference held at Wilson College in February 2007; the ideas and thoughts presented there inspired many a piece in this text. I'd like to thank all the members of the Wilson College family for their support and the assistance they proffered. Special thanks must go to my co-editor, Melanie E. Gregg, for her hard work and for always being "across the hall." I would also be remiss if I did not thank the many authors who created all those wonderful mysteries that still provide me with hours of entertainment to this day.

— Michael G. Cornelius

I would like to express my thanks to all of the contributors to this volume for their participation in this project. I am especially grateful to my friend and colleague Michael G. Cornelius for his determination to see this project through to publication. The expertise, dedication, and humor he brought to the work made this a particularly enjoyable collaboration. Full credit for the successful realization of this project goes to him.

— Melanie E. Gregg

Table of Contents

Introduction: The Mystery of the Moll Dick*

Michael G. Cornelius

"But girls can be just as smart as boys, and there's no reason why women detectives shouldn't be even better than men."
— *The Gatehouse Mystery*, Julie Campbell

In the first edition of *The Gatehouse Mystery* (copyright 1954), the third book in the wildly popular Trixie Belden girl detective series, thirteen-year-old Trixie and her best friend Honey Wheeler, having already successfully solved two mysteries, declare that they wish to be private detectives when they grow up. In reply, Jim Frayne, an older boy whose inheritance Trixie restored in the first book and who has been adopted by a wealthy, loving family in the second, also thanks to Trixie's efforts, "hoots," and jokes that she would then be a "Moll Dick" (42). Kathleen Chamberlain notes that the "point of Jim's mocking response seems clear: we're supposed to recognize the gender and age transgressions — perhaps even the gender contradictions — inherent in the very idea of a *girl* detective" (Chamberlain). Indeed, the very phrase "Moll Dick" reflects the gender contradiction inherent in the figure of the girl sleuth. The word "moll," first recorded in English in the fourteenth century, meaning "soft" or "mild," was used during Renaissance times to mean a girl or woman. The word was especially used to refer to a prostitute or, sometimes, a woman

*The author would like to thank Kathleen Chamberlain for suggesting the title of this introduction, and Leona W. Fisher for suggesting the epigraph.

1

of villainous repute, as in the case of Mary Frith (c. 1584–1659), a notorious thief in London who went by the nickname of Moll Cutpurse. Later, in the nineteenth century, the term came to refer to a female companion or girlfriend, especially the girlfriend of a gangster or mobster.

Contradictory to "moll's" feminine connotations, the word "dick" has generally reflected masculine definitions. First recorded in English in 1553, "Dick" derived from a diminutive of the common name Richard and referred to any generic boy or man, as in the expression "Tom, Dick, or Harry." The word was so staunchly male-centric that by 1891 it was recorded as a slang word for the male genitalia, a usage commonplace to this day. It was not until 1908 that Joseph M. Sullivan, in his compendium *Criminal Slang*, recorded the slang usage of "dick" to mean a cop or detective. This version of the word became especially popular in the genre of hard-boiled detective novels and film, and the word remained familiar in that particular context until the latter half of the twentieth century.

Thus the phrase that Jim Frayne uses to laughingly describe Trixie Belden's career ambition, "Moll Dick," literally means "girl boy." Though Freud would certainly have a field day with the penis envy implications inherent in labeling an entire class of literary characters "girl boy," the essential opposition intrinsic in the phrase neatly describes the perplexing figure of the girl sleuth. The girl sleuth is fearless but cautious; she is intelligent but undereducated; she is bold but decorous; she is physical yet cerebral; she is unbound yet always contained. The girl sleuth navigates the world of adults with the greatest of ease; police chiefs flock to her for aid, and criminals are generally subdued with a minimum of fuss and muss. However, she remains ever young, always eager to attend a dance or go to the malt shop with a "special" friend. The girl sleuth is impossibly feminine, perfectly appointed and impeccably dressed, yet she is also downright feminist, barging through barriers that her adult female counterparts would not get through for decades to come. She enjoys a cadre of loyal friends but often prefers to act alone, saving the denouement of the mystery solely for herself.

Many scholars have often described this dichotomy of dueling characteristics inherent to girl sleuths as being particularly male or particularly female. For these critics, many of the qualities that are largely unique to the girl sleuth character — her independence, her puissance, her sense of justice, her fearlessness — are those qualities that are more often described as emanating from traditional masculine realms. More feminine characteristics — her gentility, her compassion, her dedication to appearance —

are often viewed negatively, not as weaknesses, but as qualities that do not distinguish the characters beyond other examples of girl-driven literary creations of the twentieth century.

The confusion of gender roles that the figure of the girl sleuth manifests is often remarked upon, sometimes even by the sleuth herself. Judy Bolton, for example, says of herself that she "sometimes ... wish[es] I were a boy.... A detective.... A great one who goes into all kinds of dangers" (Sutton 53). The fact that Judy is a "great" detective has seemingly not only escaped her notice, but also the notice of the patriarchal world around her. Ann Eliasberg has written, "Interestingly, a psychoanalyst ... discovered ... that Nancy Drew's image satisfies the young girl's daydream that 'maybe I can be a boy'" (Eliasberg 38). This is echoed by P. M. Carlson, who, in the critical introduction to a reprint of the 1930 text of the Nancy Drew book *The Bungalow Mystery*, stirringly writes, "Yes, we're female, but we too can hunt down truth! We can fight for justice! We too can have adventures! We can do it!" (iii).

Critics such as Patricia Craig and Mary Cadogan have commented on the seeming masculinity of both the work and the characteristics inherent in the girl sleuth. Yet this reading seems limited by an anti-feminist perspective. Perhaps when Nancy Drew first appeared in 1930 critics lacked the feminist terminology so apt for describing Nancy — even the generally conservative Harriet Stratemeyer Adams, who ran the Stratemeyer Syndicate from 1930 and was instrumental in Nancy's rise to cultural phenomenon, has admitted the girl sleuth "was ahead of her time" (Rehak 272). In her important work *The Girl Sleuth*, Bobbie Ann Mason writes that Nancy Drew "manages the almost impossible feat of being wholesomely 'feminine'— glamorous, gracious, stylish, tactful — while also proving herself strong, resourceful, and bold" (49). Although strength and resourcefulness were often considered masculine attributes in 1930, the women's movement soon claimed these characteristics as their own — and Nancy Drew as one of their own, too: "No one knew that Nancy Drew would be adored by little girls for thirty years, and then, just as it seemed her power was waning, deified by women's libbers who recognized her as one of their own" (Rehak xii).

This prelude to feminism — this amalgamation of the qualities perceived to be finest in both boys and girls — this ability to inhabit and succeed in realms traditionally ascribed to men — this potent combination of will, desire, intelligence, and a healthy dash of fearlessness — it is these qualities that make the girl sleuth as popular as she is. In describing Nancy

Drew, Betsy Caprio calls her a modern day Joan of Arc, a truly fitting comparison (7). Like Nancy and her many sister sleuths, Joan inhabited masculine realms, often showing up the boys at their own games, achieving successes that society never thought possible for girls. Yet whereas Joan was punished for her temerity, Nancy and her detective chums are lauded and rewarded for their detective efforts. Of course, their only desired reward is another mystery to solve, which always appears in the form of another book or sequel.

In many ways, the gender-based contradiction inherent in the young female sleuth — the "girl boy" — suggests perhaps the best reason for the continuing appeal of this enduring literary figure. Led by the cultural revolution that is Nancy Drew, girl detectives from Judy Bolton and the Dana Girls to Vicki Barr, Cherry Ames, Connie Blair, Penny Parker, Penny Nicholls, Shirley Flight, Linda Carlton, Linda Craig, and dozens of others have been finding lost wills, exorcising haunted attics, and bringing nefarious adult male criminals to justice for almost eighty years, all while expertly coiffed and rarely ever chipping a nail or batting an eye. The spectacular popularity of the girl sleuth has long been documented; their ranks and sales figures may wax and wane, but the girl detective remains one of the more stalwart literary creations of the twentieth century. Their hemlines, hair-dos, and detective methods may change, but girl sleuths themselves never go out of style. Karen Plunkett-Powell has suggested that the popularity of Nancy Drew in particular "is a product of engaging, fast-paced texts, perfect historical timing, healthy publishing economics, exceptionally strong responses from readers, and of special note, visual impact" (6). Peggy Herz has noted the Stratemeyer Syndicate's use of a highly successful and adaptable formula as key to its success, a formula she described as "good mystery and lots of action, with some educational material" (8). The remarkable record of the Stratemeyer Syndicate — which not only produced girl sleuths like Nancy Drew and the Dana Girls but dozens of other successful series, including the Bobbsey Twins, the Hardy Boys, Bomba the Jungle Boy, the Motor Girls, Ted Scott, Kay Tracey, Honey Bunch, the Happy Hollisters, Linda Craig, and Christopher Cool, Teen Agent, just to name a few — certainly belies the success of their stock approach.

It is Nancy Drew who remains the iconic representation of the girl sleuth for most Americans today. She has moved beyond the pages of juvenile fiction and into the consciousness of American popular culture; references to her abound, in novels, television shows, and films. Calling someone a "Nancy Drew" is an immediately-understood reference to a snoop, a sleuth, a detective. Few other figures have so dominated their genre as effectively as Nancy. In turn, the characteristics associated with Nancy Drew have become typical for the teenaged girl detective. Like most girl sleuths who followed her, Nancy is pretty, popular, intelligent, and good at just about everything she tries, a natural-born leader. Nancy is motherless, living with her father and housekeeper; numerous other girl sleuths, such as the Dana Girls, Kay Tracey, and Penny Parker, have only one or no surviving parents. Nancy was born into an upper-class household and wants for nothing; even the Depression does not impact her sleuthing for a moment. Most girl sleuths that have succeeded her are also similarly privileged; if not wealthy, they certainly do not have to wonder how their new car or trip abroad will be paid for. Like most girl sleuths, Nancy never ages, never has a birthday, never engages in a serious romantic relationship (Ned Nickerson has been Nancy's boyfriend since the early 1930s, but he didn't get kissed until the 1990s). She is timeless and eternal, still a teenager solving mysteries in her sporty blue car nearly eighty years after her introduction. Sure, the car has changed — from a roadster to a coupe to a hybrid — but the essential characteristics of the car's driver have remained relatively unchanged, and most girl sleuths that have followed Nancy have sought to emulate her fine example.

Yet for every girl sleuth who seems a replica of Nancy Drew, another became popular because of how different she is from America's number-one teenage detective. Judy Bolton aged and married in her series, negating that Drew-like sense of timelessness; her adventures were based in actual locales, further grounding the character into reality. Trixie Belden was significantly younger than Nancy and had trouble with her schoolwork. Her family worried about their finances, and Trixie "enjoyed" the burden of family (mother, father, three brothers, assorted aunts and uncles) from which Nancy and many others had been freed. Cherry Ames and Vicki Barr had careers as nurse and flight attendant, respectively, in addition to solving crimes, adding the twin burdens of fiscal and occupational responsibility to their busy sleuthing schedules. These few examples make it seem apparent that there must be something beyond a "tried-and-true" syndicate formula that explains the enormous appeal of Nancy and her ilk. Ultimately, what one is left with is the mystery of the moll dick — the debutante detective, the paradox in pumps, the "girl boy" who solves crimes and sells millions and millions of books.

The paradoxical aspects of the girl sleuth were a significant part of what drew dozens of scholars, critics, and fans to share their own thoughts on the confounding figure of the girl dick at the "Nancy Drew and Girl Sleuths: Past, Present, and Future" conference held at Wilson College in Chambersburg, Pennsylvania, in February of 2007. The conference theme of "Past, Present, and Future" perfectly highlighted the various questions posed by the papers presented at the conference. As conference organizer, I hoped that by examining the origins of the girl sleuth figure, her present condition and her future possibilities, and by focusing on the most far-reaching girl dick of all, those assembled might begin to understand exactly how and why the character of the girl sleuth in popular literature has taken hold in ways that are not mirrored by other literary figures or in other genres. Indeed, the merging of juvenilia and girl sleuths seems a proverbial match made in heaven, one that has been copied by other literary figures, with varying success, and in other mediums, often with less success. Although the conference ultimately reached no longstanding conclusions about exactly what makes girl sleuths tick, the papers presented there, and in this collection, do strive to examine the conditions under which girl sleuths have molded and shaped the culture that they have inhabited for the last eighty years.

Solving mysteries remains the essential and defining act of the girl sleuth, and solving mysteries is what each of the authors represented in this collection strives to do. As a thorough-going representation of the popular culture of their day, girl sleuths perfectly reflect the past, present, and future of the society they are born into. Thus these characters' relationships with the past, present, and future bear scrutiny. For example, many readers and critics have lauded these series for their adherence to "old-fashioned" values and for their nostalgic outlook on contemporary life. In the recent Warner Bros. *Nancy Drew* motion picture, Nancy defends her style of dress by saying, "I like old things" (*Nancy Drew*). This line succinctly encapsulates the backwards-glancing perspective of many girl sleuths, whose desire to right wrongs and restore order reflects what many cynics cite as a value normally viewed as being beyond the general purview of teenagers. Still, girl sleuths are ever progressive and forward-thinking, demanding justice for all, embracing new roles for women in the workplace and the home, and leading the charge — whether they knew it or not — for women's liberation. It is this combination of past and future that empowers girl sleuths as perfect representations of their own present. They embody the best in girls, the highest of their hopes, dreams, and ambitions, and the noblest aspect of our own society. What a world we would live in if there were only more sleuths like Nancy Drew, Judy Bolton, or

Vicki Barr running around, helping others, solving mysteries, saving the day, and setting an example for all of us to emulate.

The meeting of past, present, and future in the girl sleuth reflects very much the goals of this collection, of examining this potent figure from a variety of temporal, cultural, and critical perspectives. Perhaps the past is the best place to start, in the oft-repeated, semi-legendary, and at times disputed origins of the most famous girl sleuth of all. To that end, the collection opens with James D. Keeline's essay, "The Nancy Drew *Myth*tery Stories," which examines the origins of Nancy Drew and the Stratemeyer Syndicate. Keeline's goal is not to repeat the histories that have already been written, but to correct them. Using archival research and numerous primary Stratemeyer sources, Keeline is able to examine which of the more famous myths surrounding the founding of the syndicate and the origin of Nancy Drew are true, and either ratify or debunk them, giving readers a valuable historical insight into the real beginnings of the best-selling girl detective of all. Linda K. Karell also looks at Nancy's origin, specifically her authorship, in "Originator, Writer, Editor, Hack: Carolyn Keene and Changing Definitions of Authorship." While even the most casual Nancy Drew fan has come to realize that Carolyn Keene is only a pseudonym, Karell looks not only at the people who actually wrote the Nancy Drew mysteries but examines how the relationship between the syndicate, which provided extensive outlines of each story, and the ghostwriter impacts our own notions of authorship and the concept that one person must have created a particular character or text. Indeed, Karell juxtaposes the common desire for a "real" author of the series against the impossibility of knowing where the author of an extensive outline ends and the author of a ghostwritten text commences.

Melanie E. Gregg looks at Nancy's translators. The Drew books have been translated into more than twenty-five different languages; sometimes the texts are translated quite faithfully, and sometimes the books are rewritten wholly to adapt to a particular culture or context. For example, Danish Nancy Drew titles tend to be faithful adaptations of the series, while Malaysian Nancy Drew books would be hardly recognizable to readers of the original English titles. In "Alice Roy, Détective: Nancy Drew in French Translation," Gregg uses the French translations of the series as a case study to explore how the Drew books were adapted and modified for a French audience, focusing especially on the alteration of characters, a critical examination that raises significant questions and adds much to our knowledge of how the Drew texts were translated across various cultures and how the famous character has been presented to and received by non–English speaking societies.

Leona W. Fisher's "Race and Xenophobia in the Nancy Drew Novels: 'What kind of society...?'" considers the pervasiveness of white privilege and white "supremacy" in the Drew series. Although critics have long professed the Drew books of the 1930s and 1940s to be racist and ethnically biased, Fisher here demonstrates that while the representation of African Americans and other minority groups has changed in the series, the bias against them has not. Fisher persuasively argues that Nancy's present has become largely a whitewashed world, a society very different from — but no better than — the openly racist attitudes espoused in the early 1930s texts. My own essay, "'They blinded her with science': Science Fiction and Technology in Nancy Drew," looks at the failure of the Drew books and girl sleuths in general to embrace technology and, by extension, education. Examining a series of Drew books from the late 1960s through the mid–1970s, I explore the relationship between technology and gender in the series, demonstrating that the use of hard science renders Nancy impotent, forcing the books' male characters, who always have a better grasp of the mechanics of any scientific tool or process, to step in and solve at least part of the mystery themselves. This essay demonstrates Nancy's unease with a future rife with technology that threatens to make her own existence perhaps obsolete, a relationship that does not improve even in the twenty-first century.

While Nancy Drew remains the most widely known and studied girl sleuth of all time, she was neither the first nor the only girl sleuth solving mysteries. In many ways, those series freed from the crushing success of the Drew paradigm often reveal more insight about the genre and the culture into which these girl sleuths were written. Fred Erisman's "Linda Carlton: Flying Sleuth/Sleuthing Flier" introduces the reader to the Linda Carlton mysteries, a five-volume series about a girl sleuth who happens to fly planes; or, as Erisman persuasively argues, about a girl flyer who happens to solve mysteries. Erisman examines the identity of the girl pilot/girl sleuth, suggesting that, in the end, the girl flyer is usually more aviatrix than detective. In a similar vein, H. Alan Pickrell, in "The Girl Sleuths of Melody Lane," explores one of the odder girl sleuth series of all time: the Lillian Garis–penned Melody Lane series, named not after an eponymous sleuth but rather after the section of town in which the books are (partially) set. This prompts Pickrell to ask, "What defines a girl sleuth series?"; this is a question he continually re-examines as he details the varying aspects of the Melody Lane series that may or may not constitute their wholeness as a unified series of books.

Larger detective series, sometimes containing dozens and dozens of entries, often go through serious shifts in perspective and representation. As the years and decades pass, the books sometimes change as well, modifying how the girl sleuth is perceived by new generations of readers. Critics and fans have often chided the Cherry Ames series for its propensity to land Cherry in a new job in every edition (*Department Store Nurse, Jungle Nurse, Cruise Nurse, Dude Ranch Nurse, Flight Nurse*), thus condemning this particular girl sleuth to a never-ending cycle of similar tales. Yet Anita G. Gorman and Leslie Robertson Mateer argue in "Measuring Up to the Task: Cherry Ames as Nurse and Sleuth" that the Cherry Ames series actually falls into several distinct and evolving textual identities. Gorman and Mateer track and classify the various changes in the Cherry Ames books and suggest categories of classifications that posit the series into various epochs based on authorship, the representation of various characters, and Cherry's own relationships with her career, men, and mystery in the works.

Conversely, some series never really adapt to the world around them, and remain relatively static and stolid for their entire run. One such series is the Trixie Belden series, and Steven J. Zani argues in "Puzzles, Paternity, and Privilege: The Mysterious Function(s) of the Family in Trixie Belden" that this famous series contains a family dynamic wholly different from other girl sleuth books, and that this dynamic acts as an identity-marker for the series itself. Zani stresses that the purpose of mystery-solving in the series is to ensure that familial units function and thrive in the happiest ways possible, and that the mysteries in the series are only a means to the end of familial reunification. The focus on family distinguishes the Trixie Belden series from other series, creating a unique yet wildly popular chapter in girls' series lore.

Girl sleuths are not just a figment of the past, as Marla Harris and Glenna Andrade demonstrate in their respective essays. In "Not Nancy Drew but Not Clueless: Embodying the Teen Girl Sleuth in the Twenty-First Century," Harris examines such contemporary girl detectives as Lulu Dark, Veronica Mars, and Ingrid Levin-Hill, showing how these series have adapted themselves to (post)modern times and how they both reflect and burlesque the values espoused in more classic series like Nancy Drew. Andrade's essay, "Hermione Granger as Girl Sleuth," looks at the central female character in the popular Harry Potter series as a representation of the famous girl sleuth figure, a representation that is often at odds with the male-centric, fantasy-genre world of Harry Potter himself. Andrade explores Hermione's detective instincts and skills in the early Potter novels and shows how the character and her detection are forced to take a backseat in later books, demonstrating the tension inherent in merging the girl sleuth with the fantasy hero on the same page.

The last essay in the collection, "The Teen Sleuth Manifesto," is included as much for its critical value as its entertainment value. Authors Melissa Favara and Allison Schuette-Hoffman combine cultural criticism, critical encomium, and stand-up comedy to explore the impact of Nancy Drew and her friends on the generations of girls who grew up worshipping the girl sleuth. Part Valentine to Nancy and her kin, part chide for some of the series' more disturbing aspects, and all endlessly entertaining, "Teen Sleuth Manifesto" represents, in many ways, the culmination of this study, a work both critical and effusive, reminding readers that all of the authors in this collection began as fans, curled up in a special reading corner with only a flashlight and a mystery book to while away the hours during a warm summer night or fierce winter storm.

In the third Nancy Drew mystery story, *The Bungalow Mystery*, the narrator modestly understates of the world's most formidable junior sleuth, "Nancy Drew had a talent for unearthing mysteries" (12). Yet for all the mysteries Nancy and her many sister sleuths have solved, it is the mysteries that they leave with us — why are girl sleuths so popular? what legacy have they left us with? what will girls sleuths look like in the twenty-first century and beyond? — that truly will endure. It seems fitting that the ultimate legacy of the girl sleuth is a secret, the "mystery of the moll dick," and yet, here in these pages, we hope to have uncovered clues to help elucidate at least some aspects of the mysterious figure that is the teenage girl sleuth.

Works Cited

Caprio, Betsy. *Girl Sleuth on the Couch: The Mystery of Nancy Drew*. Trabuco Canyon, CA: Source Books, 1992.

Carlson, P. M. "Introduction." In *The Bungalow Mystery*. Carolyn Keene. New York: Applewood Books, 1991.

Craig, Patricia, and Mary Cadogan. *The Lady Investigates: Women Detectives and Spies in Fiction*. New York: St. Martin's, 1981.

Eliasberg, Ann. "Are You Hurting Your Daughter Without Knowing It?" *Family Circle* (February 1971): 38+.

Herz, Peggy. *Nancy Drew and the Hardy Boys.* New York: Scholastic Books, 1977.

Keene, Carolyn. *The Bungalow Mystery.* New York: Grosset and Dunlap, 1930.

Mason, Bobbie Ann. *The Girl Sleuth.* Athens: University of Georgia Press, 1975.

Nancy Drew. Dir. Andrew Fleming. Perf. Emma Roberts, Max Thieriot, Josh Flitter. Warner Bros., 2007.

Plunkett-Powell, Karen. *The Nancy Drew Scrapbook.* New York: St. Martin's Press, 1993.

Rehak, Melanie. *Girl Sleuth: Nancy Drew and the Women Who Created Her.* Orlando: Harcourt, 2005.

Sutton, Margaret. *The Vanishing Shadow.* New York: Grosset and Dunlap, 1932.

The Nancy Drew
*Myth*tery Stories

James D. Keeline

When a librarian from the University of Arkansas once inquired about Carolyn Keene, the author of *The Password to Larkspur Lane* (Grosset and Dunlap, 1933), she received an extraordinary answer:

> In reply, I must bring to your attention the fact that there are many people in official, political, or professional life who have the urge to write books, especially for young people, but who for various reasons deem it inadvisable to attach their own names to their stories. Owing to a like situation, the real identity of Carolyn Keene must remain a mystery....
> Very sincerely yours,
> Secretary to Miss Carolyn Keene (17 January 1936)

As this letter indicates, the origins of the Nancy Drew series are, in many ways, more mysterious than the cases she solved, since the Stratemeyer Syndicate, and more recently Simon and Schuster, didn't care to reveal too many details about the production of the books and the multiple identities of "Carolyn Keene." This deliberate mysteriousness has had an interesting result. In the more than seventy-five years since the series began, there have been a large number of articles published in newspapers and magazines about Nancy Drew and the Stratemeyer Syndicate. Yet the majority of these contain factual errors, wishful thinking, or carefully-crafted stories for public consumption. Thus the purpose of this study is to provide a brief history of the Stratemeyer Syndicate and the origins of the Nancy Drew series and help straighten out some of these myths along the way.

Edward Stratemeyer

As with most stories, it is useful here to begin at the beginning. The Stratemeyer Syndicate was founded in 1905 by Edward Stratemeyer. He was born in Elizabeth, New Jersey, to German immigrant parents on October 4, 1862. Relatively little is known about his childhood beyond a collection of often-repeated facts and brief statements which appear in the many articles that mention him, though many of these are, in fact, errors. Repeated often enough, these errors take on the illusion of truth.

Many biographical dictionary entries produced after his death supply a middle initial of "L" (Masterson 5) or occasionally "T." However, his daughter, Harriet Stratemeyer Adams, wrote in a 1940 letter to the publisher L.C. Page, regarding a copyright renewal, that Edward had no middle name (12 December 1940). His older brothers all had middle names. Harriet's personal assistant, Nancy Axelrad, related that Harriet did not have a middle name either, and when she tried to add one as a youth, Edward scolded her for not being satisfied with the name she was given. The mistaken middle initial has continued to be used by some sources today (Commire; Burke).

Edward's father, Henry Julius Stratemeyer, according to some accounts, arrived in the U.S. in 1848 and soon afterward went to California to participate in the gold rush. Genealogical records confirm that he was naturalized as a U.S. citizen in 1848, but his obituary ("Henry") says he came to the U.S. in 1837, the same year as his younger brother, George Edward Stratemeyer. He is listed in the 1850 U.S. census for El Dorado County, California, as a miner, although his name is misspelled as "Stratmore." Edward learned details of Sutter's Mill and the Mokelumne River area from his father and worked it into his story called "One Boy in a Thousand" ("One"), which was published in book form as *Oliver Bright's Search* (Merriam, 1895), as he mentions in the preface for the revised edition (Lee and Shepard, 1899) of that volume:

> In conclusion, the author would say a word in regard to the scenes in the mining districts of California. These were drawn very largely from the narratives of a close and dear relative who spent much time out there, going as an Argonaut of '49, and to whom the vicinity of Sutter's Mill and the Mokelumne River became as an open book, not only then but later on. To write down these descriptions was, therefore, not only a work of interest, but of love [iv].

Some articles indicate that Henry returned to New Jersey unsuccessful in the gold fields (Masterson 5). However, he must have had at least some small success. The 1850 Census gave the value of his estate at $1,500, much higher than that of other people mentioned on the same page (1850 Census). When Harriet Stratemeyer married Russell Vroom Adams, the "bride's wedding ring was made from a nugget of gold dug in 1849 in California by her grandfather," Henry Julius Stratemeyer ("Adams-Stratemeyer").

Henry returned from California in 1851 and established a tobacco store in downtown Elizabeth, New Jersey, near one of the railroad stations. A short time later his brother George died in a cholera outbreak in 1854. Henry helped settle the estate and later married his brother's widow, with whom he had three more children, including Edward, another son, and a daughter, in addition to the three sons from her first marriage.

Edward attended the public schools of Elizabeth and is said to have been the valedictorian of his class. In fairness, it should be noted that there were only three students in the Class of 1879 at Public School No. 3. The principal of his high school, W.D. Heyer, guided Edward in some additional studies for a couple of years ("Life").

The beginning of Stratemeyer's writing career is often summed up in the now mythical "brown wrapping paper" story: while clerking in his father's tobacco store, he tore off a piece of brown wrapping paper and wrote a story in pencil that was sent into and accepted by *Golden Days.* When he showed the $75 check to his father, he was encouraged to write more of them. This became his first published story, "Victor Horton's Idea," serialized beginning in November 1889.

Like many stories told about Edward and the syndicate, this idealized tale has several points in error. First, this story was written at home, according to his own literary account book, not in any of his family members' stores. Several other stories he wrote afterward were written in his brother Maurice's store (Stratemeyer "Literary").

Second, a first draft was actually written in pencil on yellow paper with a pseudonym, "Arthur M. Winfield," below the title. However, he set the manuscript aside for some length of time before it was revised and recopied in ink on good paper (Lawrence) for submission to James Elverson of *Golden Days.*

Josephine Lawrence, a reporter for the *Newark Sunday Call* who later became a syndicate ghostwriter, interviewed Edward and preserved an early version of the story:

> "It ran about eighteen thousand words," said its author reminiscently, "and my father told me I was wasting my time and might better be doing

something useful. I had to send that story out, however, and I finally selected the editors of *Golden Days,* a young people's weekly published in Philadelphia, to judge it. When I received a letter telling me they were reading it and asking what I would take for it I was elated. I wanted more than anything else to see it in print! The editors of *Golden Days* sent me a check for $75 for the story...."

"If I hadn't wanted to use the money I would have framed that check!" he confessed whimsically. "Well, I took it uptown, where my father was in business, and found him reading his newspaper.

"'Look at this!' I said.

"My father looked at the slip of paper and pushed up his glasses.

"'Why, it's a check made out to you!'

"'They paid me that for writing a story!' I explained proudly.

"'Paid you that for writing a story?' repeated my father. 'Well you'd better write a lot more for them!'" [Lawrence].

While it is fair to say that "Victor Horton's Idea" was Statemeyer's first professional sale, it is far from his earliest writing, including writing for pay. Extant examples include stories typeset (if not published) as early as August 1876 ("Revenge"), when he was still 14 and before he graduated from high school. He was identified as the "publisher" of a booklet in 1878 called *A Tale of a Lumberman. As Told by Himself.* In the first three months of 1883 he published three issues of a story paper called *Our American Boys.*

There is also some confusion about his first published book. Edward had written a good number of long stories for *Golden Days* and for *The Argosy,* along with some other publications. When he wanted to offer stories for book publication, he tried to buy back some of his serials. The editor of *Golden Days* would not sell Stratemeyer's stories back but Frank A. Munsey, editor of *The Argosy,* did, and several of these were published in book form. The first of these serials published in book form was *Richard Dare's Venture* (Merriam, 1894). After his experience in unsuccessfully buying back stories from *Golden Days,* Stratemeyer was more careful to sell only first serial rights for his stories. It was one of several lessons that guided the policies he established for his syndicate in later years.

Some of his stories were brought out in book form by the publishers to whom he sold the serials. For example, several books issued by Street and Smith in the hardcover Boys' Own Library (later under the David McKay imprint) were not owned by Stratemeyer at the time. These were published using his personal pen names of Arthur M. Winfield and Captain Ralph Bonehill. The publisher's advertisements associated Stratemeyer with these two pen names, causing him a great deal of frustration, since he was trying to separate them in the minds of the public and the publishing industry.

Another lesson involved writing specifically for book publication. The first book Stratemeyer wrote specifically for book publication was not *Under Dewey at Manila* (Lee and Shepard, 1898), as reported in several sources. He began writing several works before *Under Dewey*. For example, he wrote a story as "Lost in Cuba" on speculation in August 1897; it was later published in book form as *When Santiago Fell* (Mershon, 1899). He wrote "Young Gold Hunters in Alaska," which was published as *To Alaska for Gold* (Lee and Shepard, 1898).

The first book he wrote under contract with a publisher was *The Minute Boys of Lexington* (1898) for Estes and Lauriat. This book and its sequel were sold outright, something Edward regretted later on when the publisher continued the Minute Boys series Stratemeyer began by using another writer, James Otis, to add several more volumes. The publisher then advertised the series using both names, and Stratemeyer felt that this indicated that he co-wrote the stories with Otis, thereby harming his reputation. However, since the stories were sold outright, he had little recourse. Stratemeyer never had warm feelings for Otis as a result of this event.

Under Dewey is sometimes characterized as being written as a generic story of two boys on a naval vessel and rewritten in a rush upon the request of the publisher, Lee and Shepard (Brinser 206). According to Stratemeyer's "Literary Account Books," the story was written in June 1898, *after* the historic events of May 1, 1898, which are described in the story. Thus the story was inspired directly by the events as described in the newspapers; it was not rewritten from an existing tale.

Further, much has been made about the sales success of this book. *Under Dewey* had good sales, but not extraordinary ones. A royalty statement from February 1899, which included the holiday sales of this book in its first year, listed just over 6,000 copies sold in the six-month period. This was the highest figure for the extant royalty statements; sales quickly dropped to dozens of copies. The very specific setting for the story limited the period when it would be a strong seller. Edward seems to have learned from this, since most of his later books tried to capture a timeless quality, and many of these books far outsold *Under Dewey at Manila*.

The Rover Boys series was, by far, the best selling group of books actually written by Stratemeyer. The early volumes were published by Mershon under a range of prices. When the series was published by Grosset and Dunlap, beginning in 1908, they hit their stride sales-wise and sold one million copies by 1912, as related in a letter to Grosset and Dunlap suggesting that a line be added to the dust jacket flap to commemorate this sales achievement for the entire series (19 April 1912).

This popular series was issued under Stratemeyer's "Arthur M. Winfield" pseudonym. When describing the origin of the name, he gave credit to his mother for "Winfield" to describe his desired success and the name "Arthur" being similar to "author," his chosen field. In the account published in an issue of *Grosset and Dunlap's Business Promoter* (November 1914) and reprinted in *Life* (9 July 1925), Stratemeyer said that he selected "M" as a middle initial and determined that it stood for "thousands" — the numbers he wanted to sell — since "M" is the Roman numeral for 1,000. Not long after telling this version, the cumulative sales for the Rover Boys exceeded 2 million, and later versions of the tale transfer credit for the middle initial to his mother, Anna, as well as indicating that "M" stood for "millions" (Lawrence).

When recounting this tale, most articles associate the creation of this pen name with the beginning of the Rover Boys series in 1899. However, it was used much earlier, including on the first draft of "Victor Horton's Idea" on yellow paper (1888), on the poem "He Will Remember Me" (1889), and on the manuscript for the short story "Crele" (January 1885).

Around the same time that the Rover Boys series was begun, Stratemeyer was asked by Lee and Shepard's editor to write the final volume in "Oliver Optic's" Blue and Gray on Land series, *An Undivided Union* (1899), since the author of the other books, William T. Adams, had just died. Another contemporary of Adams, Horatio Alger, Jr., found that with his health failing, he was unable to complete some books he was working on. He wrote to Stratemeyer and asked him to finish up the stories: "I have been wondering if you can't help me. I have a story two thirds written, but am in a state of nervous breakdown and not only can't write, but can't invent the rest of the story for some time to come. I think of all of the juvenile writers you can write most like me" (26 October 1897).

The story was split and issued as two different pieces in 1900, after Alger died the previous year. After Alger's death, the rights to his books and estate went to his sister, Olive Augusta Cheney, and Stratemeyer negotiated with her for use of manuscripts, plays, and short stories to be developed into books. Stratemeyer wrote a total of eleven "Alger completions," so called because they were credited on the title page with Alger's name above and the phrase "Completed by Arthur M. Winfield" in smaller type below. Edward also wrote a biographical article about Alger for *Golden Hours Junior* in October 1901 ("Gallery").

Stratemeyer Syndicate

In one of his letters to Cheney (22 November 1900), Stratemeyer described how he expected to act more as a literary agent, purchasing stories to be issued in book form, and spend less time writing himself. This was the germ of the idea that became known as the Stratemeyer Syndicate.

Edward faced the problem that many nineteenth-century authors faced: publishers wanted to be the sole source of a writer's output, yet those same publishers could only comfortably issue a few books a year. In the periodical world, this was sometimes resolved by issuing some stories under the author's real name while others, running at the same time, were issued under pseudonyms. This is a practice that carried well into the twentieth century. Robert Heinlein, for example, had some of his stories appear under the "Anson MacDonald" name when other stories under his own name were running in the same publication.

Around the same time that Edward was beginning the Old Glory series with *Under Dewey,* he began a similar series for a cheaper publisher, Mershon, the company that was issuing the Rover Boys series. This similar series was published under his "Captain Ralph Bonehill" pen name. This tactic was no secret to his main publisher, Lee and Shepard, and Stratemeyer often complained that the sales of these more expensive books did not earn him as much income as the cheaper books issued by Mershon. Prior to this, Edward sold most books on a 10 percent royalty basis. The royalties based on the Mershon retail prices were less than 10 percent, and the books themselves were cheaper, but since they sold more copies, Stratemeyer earned more.

These factors, along with changes in the copyright laws, created a confluence of events that made the time right to form the Stratemeyer Syndicate. Under the syndicate, Edward would not merely buy stories on speculation and hope he could sell them to publishers. Instead, he would enter into an agreement with a publisher first to buy a series and select the initial titles from a list he provided.

With this contract in hand, he would then define characters and create outlines for the stories. These brief outlines were turned over to ghostwriters who expanded them into book-length manuscripts in three to six weeks. For their work, the writers were paid between $75 and $250, depending on the length of the piece and the writer's skill. Upon payment, the writers signed a release certifying that the work was original and based on Stratemeyer's outlines. It also transferred all rights for the story to Stratemeyer, and required the writer to promise not to use the pen name for his or her own work.

In the early years, the publishers he worked with did not have extensive editing and proofreading departments. Stratemeyer copy-edited the manuscript himself and provided it to the publisher along with typed lists of suggestions for illustrations and advertising text to be used on the book and jackets. In many cases, he contacted the artists directly to inform them what was wanted for the illustrations. For a number of years he even paid for typesetting and leased the printing plates he owned to the publishers to receive an additional royalty payment per copy sold.

The first two books issued under this syndicate system were the initial volumes in the Ralph series, *Ralph of the Roundhouse* (Mershon, 1906) and *The Motor Boys* (Cupples and Leon, 1906). They were ghostwritten by Weldon J. Cobb of Chicago and Howard R. Garis of Newark, respectively.

Between 1905 and 1985, the Stratemeyer Syndicate produced more than 1,400 volumes using this method. This number comprised many popular series, including the well-known Bobbsey Twins, Tom Swift, Hardy Boys, and, of course, Nancy Drew. As descriptions of the syndicate began to appear in publications, the complex operations had to be simplified for the public. This led to a number of syndicate myths and other statements that were taken out of context.

For several of the most popular series, three volumes were published at the same time in what collectors call a "breeder set." The notion was that readers would be more easily "hooked" with several stories to read at once. Many articles have assumed, incorrectly, that all series began with three volumes. However, some had a single volume in the initial year and some series, such as the Alger-like stories published under the "Frank V. Webster" name, had up to ten in the first year. The Tom Swift series began with five new volumes each year from 1910 through 1912; fifteen volumes in three years gave it a very good start, as it proved to be the syndicate's best seller for many years.

Another notion, partially formed because Edward's daughter, Harriet Stratemeyer Adams, was not fully informed about the early years of the syndicate, was that Edward personally wrote the initial volumes of all of the series before bringing in ghostwriters to work on them. Edward did write the first volume in the Bobbsey Twins series (Mershon, 1904) and he wrote the serial "The Rival Ocean Divers" (Rockwood), which became the first volume in the Deep Sea series (Stitt, 1905). Both series were continued by other writers from his outlines. However, these are the exceptions. Most syndicate series were produced completely under the outline system.

A famous article about series books and Edward Stratemeyer appeared in the April 1934 issue of *Fortune* magazine. This anonymous article was the source of many myths about series books and the syndicate. Edward's daughters partially cooperated with the author, Ayres Brinser, by answering some of his questions in letters, attempting to correct errors in the manuscript, and loaning the magazine books and photos of their father. The latter were damaged by the magazine.

One of the myths established in the *Fortune* article was that Stratemeyer persuaded his publishers to sell the syndicate books at 50 cents and that this was responsible for the successful sales for these books (88). In 1934, series books did sell for 50 cents. However, in the period described in the article, syndicate series books sold for almost any price other than 50 cents. For example, the Rover Boys sold for 60 cents, while Tom Swift sold for 40 cents. Often these could be purchased for even less in department stores. Series for Cupples and Leon ranged from $1 for the Musket Boys down to 35 cents for the Webster series.

Another important issue concerns the contracts signed by the ghostwriters. It is often said that the writers were forced to sign contracts and were "legally sworn to secrecy" (Lapin 20). However, the releases (the only contracts for most writers) did not state this. Instead, they included a promise that the writers would not use Stratemeyer's business property. This referred to the pen names. In fact, Stratemeyer told some writers that they could tell publishers they were working for him or even name series on which they worked to help them land additional writing assignments. Some writers, like St. George Rathborne, were a little too free with this information. Rathborne provided long lists of the series on which he worked, including syndicate series, to publishers. Stratemeyer tried to rein these writers in, though the only thing he could do was withhold future assignments from the writers. However, in later years, the contracts became multi-page legal documents and the writers were more specifically admonished to refrain from revealing their specific work for the syndicate. Below is an example of a typically long release signed by a ghostwriter for the first volume in the Hardy Boys series:

> Newark, N. J., Jan. 6, 1927.
> For and in consideration of the sum of One Hundred Twenty-five Dollars, ($125.00) the receipt of which is hereby acknowledged, I hereby

sell, transfer and set aside to Edward Stratemeyer, Literary Agent, his heirs
and assigns, all my right, title and interest in a certain story written by me
on a title and outline furnished by said Edward Stratemeyer and named
The Hardy Boys: The Tower Treasure.

In making this transfer I hereby affirm that my work on the story is
absolutely new, and I hereby grant to Edward Stratemeyer full permission
to print the story under any trade-mark pen name that may be his business property, and I further agree that I will not use such pen name in any
manner whatsoever.

[signed] Leslie McFarlane

Edward Stratemeyer died on May 10, 1930. Most of the more modern articles claim that he paid the writers little and died a rich man. Some
say that he made millions: "He paid ghostwriters $75 for each book and
made millions" (Winship). However, this oversimplification misses many
details of importance. Edward's estate upon his death was worth about
$500,000 — a sizeable sum in 1930, though hardly millions. This came
partly from the books, but also from real estate and other investments he
had made ("Will"). Some writers seem to confuse the sale of millions of
copies with the income they generated.

A typical book like the first volume in the Hardy Boys or Nancy
Drew series earned the writer $125 for the manuscript. The book itself
sold for 50 cents and generated 2 cents royalty per copy sold for the first
10,000 and 2.5 cents per copy thereafter. The $125 was roughly equiva-
lent to two month's wages for a typical newspaper reporter, the primary
day job of the syndicate ghosts. The work done by the writers was often
moonlighting, done in their spare time, and typically lasted about a month
between the time the outline was received and the manuscript turned in.
Hence, writers would invest their spare time for a month and earn a sum
equivalent to two month's wages in their day job.

Although Stratemeyer had agreements with publishers to take a series,
he normally did not earn money until the books sold, though occasionally in the early years he secured advances on the royalties. He paid for the
manuscripts in full upon submission, something writers could not expect
from publishers at that time. The amounts he paid for all rights were comparable to the amounts a publisher would pay for all rights to a story. Few
of the mass-market publishers cared to issue books on royalty, especially
to unknown writers.

With a 2 cents per copy royalty, the publisher would have to sell
6,250 copies to earn back the $125 Stratemeyer paid the ghostwriters. This
was still less than the number that would cause the royalty rate to rise to

2.5 cents per copy. Many series achieved this level of sales because Stratemeyer was very good at sensing the readers' and publishers' wants and in selecting good ghostwriters to do the work. However, many other series failed to reach this sales mark and were a loss. Effectively, Stratemeyer took the risks, minimized them where he could, and reaped the rewards.

Many of the ghostwriters also wrote books on their own, often at the same time they were writing for the syndicate, and yet they continued to write for Stratemeyer. In many cases, these relationships with the syndicate spanned decades. If the writers truly felt abused by the business relationship, they always had the option to decline an assignment or all future work. Although claims to the contrary are plentiful in print and on the Internet, there is substantial evidence to illustrate that the ghostwriters were not treated unfairly.

Nancy Drew

One of the last series planned by Edward Stratemeyer was the Nancy Drew series. There are a number of myths associated with the origin and early history of this important and popular series. Nancy Drew surprised people in the industry when a series for girls outsold the most popular series for boys. Stratemeyer said a few times in interviews that girls often moved on to the "best seller" novels at a younger age than the boys. The boys stayed with books like the series books for a longer period of time (Lawrence). This meant that series for boys were more profitable due to larger numbers of readers.

One of the myths associated with the origin of Nancy Drew is that Edward began it because he wanted to replicate the phenomenal success of the Hardy Boys. However, the royalty records show that the sales of the Hardy Boys were solid but less than half of the other "Franklin W. Dixon" series, Ted Scott. If Stratemeyer wanted to duplicate a success, he would have created a girls' aviation series replicating the Ted Scott stories and following the patterns established by earlier series such as the Motor Girls, Moving Picture Girls, Radio Girls, and the Outdoor Girls, all named and modeled after earlier male counterparts.

With Nancy Drew, Stratemeyer knew that he wanted a new series with a single heroine rather than a group, which was typical for his past series for girls (30 September 1929). He offered such a series to Barse but it was not picked up. This was not specifically a mystery series. He proposed the

"Stella Strong" series, suggesting a new pen name "Clara May Rosemont." One of the stories was "Stella Strong at Mystery Towers." In the proposal he stated: "I have called this line the 'Stella Strong Stories,' but they might also be called the 'Diana Dare Stories,' 'Nan Nelson Stories' or 'Helen Hale Stories'" (1 April 1929).

When Barse did not pick up the series, he made a similar proposal to Grosset and Dunlap (30 September 1929), this time adding the pen name "Louise Keene" and stating: "Stella Strong, a girl of sixteen, is the daughter of a District Attorney of many years standing. He a widower and often talks over his affairs with Stella and the girl was present during many interviews her father had with noted detectives and at the solving of many intricate mysteries. Then, quite unexpectedly, Stella plunged into some mysteries of her own and found herself wound up in a series of exciting situations. An up-to-date American girl at her best, bright, clever, resourceful, and full of energy."

One of the titles on this proposal was called "The Secret of the Old Clock" which relates how "a large estate remains unsettled because of a missing will." Although many names were offered for the main characters and pen name on these proposals, "Carolyn Keene" and "Nancy Drew" were not.

Today it is almost unthinkable for any names other than Nancy Drew by Carolyn Keene to be associated with this series. However, Stratemeyer referred to a proposed series called "Nellie Fay" in a letter to Grosset and Dunlap (19 July 1929). The series was not named in letters to Mildred Wirt (8 April 1929, 27 September 1929). The series was next referred to as "Stella Strong" in one letter (30 September 1929) but was called "Nancy Drew" by "Carolyn Keene" the following day (1 October 1929). The outline was created and sent to Wirt a couple days later (3 October 1929).

It is possible that the publishers suggested the name in a personal meeting. In a similar situation, Laura Harris, a Grosset and Dunlap editor, suggested the "Dana Girls" instead of the proposed name, the "Manley Girls," by picking a name from the Manhattan phone book (17 December 1932). Although it is not yet known whether the name "Nancy Drew" came from the publisher or Stratemeyer, the name was established early in the planning phase, as was the mystery theme for the series.

Stratemeyer wrote to his publisher that he had two young women writers on his syndicate staff who might work on the new series, referring to Mildred A. Wirt and Elizabeth M. Duffield Ward. After writing the four-page detailed outline for the first volume, he sent it to Wirt, who was living in Ohio at the time. Wirt began writing for Stratemeyer in 1926 and was then working on Ruth Fielding, a series for girls that had been begun by W. Bert Foster in 1913 and was continued by Ward. After several Ruth Fielding volumes, Stratemeyer felt that Wirt could provide him the stories he wanted for this new series. As with previous assignments, Wirt returned the completed manuscript in about four weeks, working from Edward's brief outline.

Writing more than four decades later, in 1973, Wirt (then Mildred Wirt Benson) states that Stratemeyer's reaction was crushing. She claims he was "bitterly disappointed" and that she had failed to follow his outlines (something that would bring quick censure from Stratemeyer if true, based on his reactions to other writers who wrote outside his guidelines):

> Mr. Stratemeyer expressed bitter disappointment when he received the first manuscript, *The Secret of the Old Clock,* saying the heroine was much too flip and would never be well received. On the contrary, when the first three volumes hit the market they were an immediate cash-register success for the syndicate. Over a thirty-eight-year period, the series was printed in seventeen languages and, according to published report, achieved sales of more than 30,000,000 copies. As "ghost" I received $125 to $250 a story, all rights released [Benson].

A writer who interviewed Wirt some fifteen years later added an extra element to this story: after Edward's expressed disappointment, the publishers read the story and insisted that the same writer continue the series. In effect, in this version the publisher was granted more control than Stratemeyer. After capitulating to the publisher's request, Stratemeyer sent on the next outline, and the rest was history:

> Mildred Benson finished the manuscript of *The Secret of the Old Clock* and mailed it off to Edward Stratemeyer. She recalls his response: "I remember it very vividly because I was crushed. He wrote that he thought I had departed too much from the pattern of the old series books and made the character of Nancy too flip. He thought I had missed the market and the publishers would not be interested."
>
> For once Edward Stratemeyer was wrong. Publishers Grosset and Dunlap were interested in Nancy Drew. Stratemeyer wrote back to Mildred Benson asking her to write two more volumes to launch the series.... The three volumes were published on April 28, 1930, exactly as Benson wrote them [Martin 17].

This description of events does not match the evidence contemporary with the events. The correspondence files for the Stratemeyer Syndicate are extensive. While it is certain that not all letters were retained, there is a continuous set of letters for this period of time indicating when Edward asked if Wirt could write stories in a new series (8 April 1929, 27 September 1929), sent the outline (3 October 1929), and received the manuscript (8 November 1929). Upon receipt of the manuscript, he immediately sent back some comments on the story and the outline for the next volume:

> I have received the manuscript of "The Secret of the Old Clock" and have given it a first reading.
>
> I thought the first half of the story was a bit slow and that the characters were not sufficiently introduced and also that the various incidents were rather loosely connected. But as soon as Nancy gets to New Moon Lake the story picks up very well indeed and the last eight chapters are particularly well done. We will go over the first part of the story carefully, and if we can intensify a few of the situations we will do so.
>
> But please, Mrs. Wirt, in the future use a thicker and more substantial typewriter paper as the present paper hardly admits of any alterations and corrections.
>
> With this I am enclosing a check for the story with the usual receipt to be signed and returned.
>
> I am also enclosing with this the complete outline for the next story to be called "*The Hidden Staircase*" and with this I am sending the outline for the first story also so that you will have this to refer to [8 Nov 1929].

As is evident, there was no indicated period of time when a Grosset and Dunlap editor would even see the story. He stated that the first part of the story was "a bit slow" but that could be improved by some editing in the office. His harshest criticism was that the paper she used was so thin that it did not afford editorial changes.

Stratemeyer conducted most of his business by correspondence. He retained a carbon copy of these letters. When he had a personal meeting at his home, office, a publisher's office, or over the telephone, he would follow up the contact with a letter for later reference.

The phrase "too flip" was not used in any letters in the correspondence file by Stratemeyer or later on by his daughters. However, as his daughters later managed the business, they did advise changes in Nancy's character that would afford more respect to the police and other authority figures (10 June 1938). Similar changes were made in the Hardy Boys where the early volumes had particularly unflattering portrayals of the Bayport police force. Stratemeyer admonished Leslie McFarlane: "Be careful not to make a characature [*sic*] of the chief and his head detective" (10 April 1928). Harriet offered similar advice to McFarlane when he was writing the first Dana Girls volume (3 April 1933). For a writer who had a certain vision for a character, this sort of change could be seen as criticism. Wirt may have transferred these feelings to Edward over the decades between the events and writing and talking about them in the 1970s and 1980s.

There are varying references to the length of the outlines ghostwriters received, sometimes stating that long or brief outlines were a problem. Unfortunately, the outlines for the early Nancy Drew volumes are not part of the Stratemeyer Syndicate records collection at New York Public Library (NYPL). However, some collector-researchers have obtained photocopies of the outlines for the first three volumes in the Nancy Drew series from a private source, and they report the lengths to be between one and one half to four pages. This length is consistent with or slightly longer than other Stratemeyer outlines of the period.

The Nancy Drew outlines for these first three volumes are very detailed, including quotations of dialogue to begin the story; a detailed plot, including "holding points" for the chapter cliffhangers; and even indications of when to reprise the previous volumes. Key elements of the series, such as the "blue roadster," the "small city of River Heights in the Middle West where the Drews lived," secondary character names such as Helen Corning, and even the detailed description of the ending of the story, such as Nancy asking for the clock as a souvenir for her help in clearing up the mystery, are all described by Stratemeyer, in the outlines he supplied to Wirt.

In one letter, Mildred wrote that she thought she could handle the story better if the outline were longer (11 May 1931). After Harriet and Edna took over the business, they began to produce longer and longer outlines. In some cases, these sketched out the major scenes and even the chapters of the story. They left less room for a writer's creativity and judgment about which scenes and subplot details to include. Later, Wirt found these longer outlines to be too limiting (Grosset). The sisters thought the long outlines, sometimes with chapter-by-chapter details, made the stories easier to write when, in reality, they had the opposite effect. In time they realized this and suggested making the outlines considerably shorter in the last few years that Wirt, then Benson, was associated with the syndicate.

The length and detail of the outlines is important because it determines how much room there was for a writer to include scenes similar to ones with which they were familiar and select names for the secondary characters. When editing one of the early volumes after his death, Edward's assistant, Harriet Otis Smith, wrote that the name Wirt used for a character in *Shadow Ranch* was different from the one indicated in the outline, but since it was not a name used in the series or another syndicate series, Mildred's selection of the name could be retained (12 August 1930).

A popular pastime among Nancy Drew fans is to associate descriptions in the early books with Mildred's experiences, including the states where she was born and lived. When he was still alive, Edward wrote that the next story, referring to *Shadow Ranch,* would be set on a ranch and he wanted to know if Mildred had a preference if it was in the far or middle west (28 April 1930). Although she selected the far west for this story, it is possible that some scenes in other volumes resemble Iowa or Ohio in details, but the ultimate choice of location, along with all other content, was always the syndicate's.

While writing Nancy Drew, Mildred Wirt was also writing her own stories. This was not hidden from the syndicate, and in some letters they congratulated her on her success. The routine when inviting her to write a story was to ask if she had time to do so. Most of the time, she assented. However, for a period in 1932 and 1933, spanning three volumes, she declined, and the syndicate hired Walter Karig to write stories for this series and others.

There is a common notion that the specific reason Mildred Wirt stopped writing the stories during this period was that the payment per volume had dropped because of the Great Depression. This is true to a certain extent, and she chaffed at the lower price offered by the Stratemeyer sisters. However, during this period, she did write other syndicate volumes for low sums, including as a Ruth Fielding volume published in 1934, for which she was paid $75. Plus, when Wirt resumed working on the Nancy Drew series, the prices had not yet risen to their pre–Depression values. Wirt was paid $85 for her next few syndicate volumes, including two Kay Tracey volumes and *The Message in the Hollow Oak* (1935). She was paid $100 for *The Mystery of the Ivory Charm* (1936). Possibly she was in greater need for income if her own books were not selling as well. Another theory is that price wasn't the problem; it was simply a lack of time.

By 1934 Nancy Drew was outselling all other series books. Perhaps this was due to the Depression reducing sales for all books. However, most fans will agree that a big part of this was that they are very good stories to read, particularly in the original-text editions. The revision process for the Nancy Drew series spanned the first thirty-four volumes in a process which began in 1959 and continued through 1977.

The reasons for cutting the stories down and rewriting many of the early volumes are sometimes misunderstood. The most common reason given was that the stories were rewritten to remove racial stereotypes after complaints were received. In fact, the Tom Swift series received a complaint from the Anti-Defamation League (Bogen) about *Tom Swift and His Talking Pictures* (1928) for potentially unflattering references to Jews in one scene at the end (180). The text was changed on that page for the next printing.

However, a larger factor influencing the change of the book length was manufacturing costs. Early books were printed from copper printing plates, which were expensive to make and store and were seldom changed. The plates could also be damaged during use and through improper storage. Both the cost of the metal and demand for it during World War II caused some plates for other series to be melted down for the war effort (Svenson). New methods were available in the 1950s that used photo-offset printing. The masters were now plastic sheets, which were much cheaper to make and store and could be changed cheaply as well. However, to move the old stories to the new method would cost the same as writing a completely new story that might be even more relevant to the modern readers. Thus, the stories were evaluated for content that was racially insensitive or outdated. Tabulations were also made for the number of copies sold, the number of lines per page and total number of pages, and the quality of the printing plates. This enabled the syndicate to prioritize the revisions.

The Bobbsey Twins volumes were revised well before Nancy Drew and the Hardy Boys, in an effort to keep the published versions of the early titles protected even though the first three were passing into the public domain. Many unauthorized publishers seized on this opportunity by publishing these volumes when the copyrights expired. The syndicate considered issuing revised versions of the Rover Boys to maintain the copyright protection. Although the Hardy Boys and Nancy Drew books were not facing imminent copyright expiration, new stories with new copyrights would have a much longer lifespan on the shelf. Between 1909 and 1978 the copyright law afforded a first term for "works for hire" of 28 years with a second 28 years available if the holder cared to renew it. This made for a total protection term of 56 years, more than two generations. The copyright act of 1976 (1 January 1978) extended terms to 75 years and the Sonny Bono memorial extension took these up to 95 years. Hence, it will be a very long time before any Nancy Drews are available in the public domain.

Some of the revised stories are simply abridged from the originals. Others are complete rewrites. A good example of a Nancy Drew volume with a vastly different plot is *The Mystery at the Moss-Covered Mansion* (Grosset and Dunlap, 1941), which was originally a story about stolen heirlooms and became a 1971 story about stolen missile parts at Cape Canaveral and includes an infamous scene with exploding oranges. Most of the stories were not quite so radically altered, but it was deemed appropriate to make the books as modern as possible in every respect. Ultimately, the stories gained more educational content, subplots, and, yes, the racial stereotypes were removed.

The Stratemeyer Syndicate was responsible for so many popular series books that there is a natural curiosity about the people behind them and how the stories were created. In some ways, this was heightened by the secrecy they maintained. When the syndicate revealed anything about the writers' work, it was often simplified into carefully-crafted anecdotes or misinterpreted by reporters. When ghostwriters like Mildred Wirt Benson and Leslie McFarlane finally began to tell their stories to the public, the events they described had occurred decades earlier. Fading memories may have caused some details to be reported inaccurately. Thankfully, there exists much primary evidence to help set the record straight on many of the "myth-teries" that still surround the Stratemeyer Syndicate and Nancy Drew.

Works Cited

1850 United States Census. State of California, El Dorado County. M432, roll 34: 381.
1850 United States Census. State of California, El Dorado County, p. 760. Surname misspelled as "Stratmore."
Abel, Trudi Johanna. *A Man of Letters, A Man of Business: Edward Stratemeyer and the Adolescent Reader, 1890–1930.* Diss. Rutgers, State University of New Jersey, October 1993. Ann Arbor: UMI, 1993.
Adams, Harriet Stratemeyer. Letter to Leslie McFarlane. 3 April 1933. Stratemeyer Syndicate Records Collection, New York Public Library, Rare Books and Manuscripts Division (hereafter NYPL).
"Adams-Stratemeyer." Unidentified Newark newspaper following 20 October 1915 wedding of Russell Vroom Adams and Harriet Stratemeyer.
Alger, Horatio, Jr. Letter to Edward Stratemeyer. 26 October 1897. NYPL.
Appleton, Victor. *Tom Swift and His Talking Pictures.* New York: Grosset and Dunlap, 1928.
Benson, Mildred Wirt. "The Ghost of Ladora." *Books at Iowa* (November 1973): 24–29.
Bogen, Boris D., Anti-Defamation League. Letter to Grosset and Dunlap. 13 February 1929. NYPL.
Bonehill, Capt. Ralph. *When Santiago Fell.* Rahway, N.J.: Mershon, 1899.
[Brinser, Ayres]. "'For it Was Indeed He': The Fifty-Cent Juvenile, Which Anthony Com-

stock Included His 'Traps for the Young.' The Publishers (Principally Three), the Authors (One in Particular), and the Profits (Fabulous) of Literature for Adolescents." *Fortune* (April 1934): 86+.

Burke, W. J., and Will D. Howe. *American Authors and Books*. Revised by Irving Weiss. New York: Crown, 1962 .

Chapman, Allen. *Ralph of the Roundhouse*. Rahway, N.J.: Mershon, 1906.

Commire, Anne, ed. *Something About the Author, Vol. 1*. Detroit: Gale Research, 1971.

"Gallery of Golden Hours Authors, No. 3: Horatio Alger, Jr." *Golden Hours Junior* (October 1901).

Grosset and Dunlap v. Gulf and Western and Stratemeyer Syndicate. United States District Court, Southern District of New York. 27 May 1980. 79 Civ. 2242. 79 Civ 3745.

Harris, Laura. Letter to Edward Stratemeyer. 17 December 1932. NYPL.

"Henry J. Stratemeyer Sr. Another Old and Well-Known Citizen Passes Away." *Elizabeth Daily Journal* (23 December 1891).

Hope, Laura Lee. *The Bobbsey Twins*. Rahway, N.J.: Mershon, 1904.

Keene, Carolyn. *The Mystery at the Moss-Covered Mansion*. New York: Grosset and Dunlap, 1941.

_____. *The Mystery of the Moss-Covered Mansion*. New York: Grosset and Dunlap, 1971.

_____. *The Password to Larkspur Lane*. New York: Grosset and Dunlap, 1933.

"Lapin, Geoffrey S. "The Ghost of Nancy Drew." *Books at Iowa* (April 1989): 8–27.

[Lawrence, Josephine]. "The Newarker Whose Name is Best Known. Edward Stratemeyer, Creator of 'Dave Porter' and the 'Rover Boy,' Admired by Boys Wherever English is Read—Nearly Six Million Copies of His Books Sold—Story of the Author's Early Trials and His Later Success." *Newark Sunday Call* (9 December 1917).

"Life of Elizabeth Author Recalled." *Elizabeth Daily Journal* (25 April 1946).

Martin, Linnea. "The Ghost in the Attic." *Hiram Magazine* (Summer 1988): 14–18.

Masterson, Linda, and Julie Masterson Child. "Edward Stratemeyer and Those Fabulous Fifty-Centers: The One-man Book Machine Who Used Scores of Names and Produced a Bewildering Blizzard of Books." *American Collector* (September 1974).

McFarlane, Leslie. Release for *The Tower Treasure*. 6 January 1927. NYPL.

Optic, Oliver. Completed by Arthur M. Winfield. *An Undivided Union*. Boston: Lee and Shepard, 1899.

Our American Boys. Elizabeth, N.J.: Edward Stratemeyer. Three issues, January 1883, February 1883, March 1883.

Reed, F.L., Grosset and Dunlap. Letter to Edward Stratemeyer. 29 February 1929. NYPL.

"Revenge! Or, The Newsboy's Adventure." *Our Friend* August 1876. NYPL.

Rockwood, Roy. "The Rival Ocean Divers." *Golden Hours* (5 January 1901 to 23 February 1901).

Secretary to Carolyn Keene. Letter to Mrs. Jane Gavere, Secretary, Public Information Bureau, University of Arkansas, Fayetteville, Arkansas. 17 January 1936. NYPL.

Smith, Harriet Otis. Letter to Mildred A. Wirt. 12 August 1930. NYPL.

Stratemeyer, Edward. Letter to Grosset and Dunlap. 19 April 1912. NYPL.

_____. Letter to Leslie McFarlane. 10 April 1928. NYPL.

_____. Letter to Barse and Co. 1 April 1929. Outline for Stella Strong series. NYPL.

_____. Letter to Grosset and Dunlap. 19 July 1929. NYPL.

_____. Letter to Grosset and Dunlap. 30 September 1929. NYPL.

_____. Letter to Grosset and Dunlap. 1 October 1929. NYPL.

_____. Letter to Mildred A. Wirt. 8 April 1929. NYPL.

_____. Letter to Mildred A. Wirt. 27 September 1929. NYPL.

_____. Letter to Mildred A. Wirt. 3 October 1929. NYPL.

_____. Letter to Mildred A. Wirt. 8 November 1929. NYPL.

_____. Letter to Mildred A. Wirt. 28 April 1930. NYPL.

_____. Letter to Olive Augusta Cheney. 22 November 1900. Cited in Abel, pp. 249–250.

_____. "Literary Account Book." NYPL.

_____. *The Minute Boys of Lexington*. Boston: Estes and Lauriat, 1898.

_____. *Oliver Bright's Search*. New York: Merriam, 1895; Boston: Lee and Shepard, 1899.

_____. "One Boy in a Thousand." *Argosy* (12 November 1892 to 4 February 1893).

_____. "The Origin of the Rover Boys." *Life* (9 July 1925).

_____. *To Alaska for Gold*. Boston: Lee and Shepard, 1898.

_____. *Under Dewey at Manila*. Boston: Lee and Shepard, 1898.

_____. "Victor Horton's Idea." *Golden Days,* 2 November 1889 to 30 November 1889.

Svenson, Andrew E. Memo Regarding Old Book Plates. 24 June 1957. NYPL.

The Tale of a Lumberman: As Told by Himself. Elizabeth, N.J.: E. Stratemeyer, 1878. NYPL.

"Will of Edward Stratemeyer." *New York Times* (6 June 1930): 48.

Winfield, Arthur M. "Crele." Unpublished holograph manuscript. NYPL.

_____. "He Will Remember Me." *Illustrated Christian Weekly* (6 April 1889).

_____. "Victor Horton's Idea." Unpublished holograph manuscript. NYPL.

Winship, Kihm. "The Ghost of Nancy Drew." *The Syracuse New Times* (3–10 March 1993). Available online at http://home.earthlink.net/~ggghostie/drew.html 2004. 20 March 2007.

Wirt, Mildred A. Letter to Stratemeyer Syndicate. 11 May 1931. NYPL.

Young, Clarence. *The Motor Boys.* New York: Cupples and Leon, 1906.

Originator, Writer, Editor, Hack: Carolyn Keene and Changing Definitions of Authorship

Linda K. Karell

> *Modern literary criticism ... still defines the author the same way: the author provides the basis for explaining not only the presence of certain events in a work, but also their transformations, distortions, and diverse modifications (through his biography, the determination of his individual perspective, the analysis of his social position, and the revelation of his basic design).*
>
> Foucault 895

> *She [Benson] wrote some of the books, but not all. She wrote some of the prose we see on the page, but not all. She was the "real" Carolyn Keene, and she was not. Her Nancy is the "real" Nancy, and it is not. The essence of the girl sleuth — if the essence of a fictional character is somehow located in authorship or textual sanctity — remains an unsolvable mystery.*
>
> Jenkins 3

By any measure, Carolyn Keene is one of the world's most recognized and beloved "authors." Her authorial signature is instantly recognizable across generations and, nearly eighty years after her debut, still evokes the defining images of her fictional creation, the enormously popular Nancy Drew: "Carolyn Keene. Her name sounded young and fresh and blonde" (Jenkins 2). As the Stratemeyer Syndicate's most famous pseudonym, "Carolyn Keene" simultaneously invokes a romantic image of unitary, individual authorship and its postmodern counter-image of collective, collaborative textual production. Authorship is an insistently contradictory concept and a vexed practice; it is pulled between a (surprisingly recent) cultural definition that posits an individual genius behind the text and the functional reality of multiple, collaborative production. This is especially evident with the Stratemeyer Syndicate's most popular series, Nancy Drew, where differing and often opposing versions of authorship are in play simultaneously and, I will argue, contribute to the lasting popularity and pleasure of the series. In this essay, I examine the Stratemeyer Syndicate's various deployments of authorship and argue that the pseudonym Carolyn Keene both hides and makes visible the tensions that underlie the reality of multiple, collaborative authorship practiced by the two women most regularly associated with the pseudonym, the many ghostwriters and editors who followed them, and the syndicate that deployed and employed them all. In other words, and as Emily Jenkins suggests in the second epigraph above, I argue that the desire for a "real" Nancy who can be located in the text or its author, or a yearning to locate the "real" author of that character or text, is impossible to satisfy. What's more, it is precisely the impossibility of ever locating the origin (of author or character) that gives the text its pleasure and its mystery.

In "What Is an Author?," Foucault's influential 1969 deconstruction of "the solid and fundamental unit of the author and the work," he argues that, rather than signifying infinite possibilities of interpretation, "the author is ... the ideological figure by which one marks the manner in which we fear the proliferation of meaning" (899). By the time of Foucault's writing in 1969, the Stratemeyer Syndicate's iconic girl sleuth Nancy Drew was revised and updated from her 1930 debut, and over the next (nearly) four decades she became the focus of both praise and criticism: was she a crucial role model of female independence and self-confidence or was she a sexless daddy's girl who successfully maintained white privilege and the economic status quo? Even in the midst of criticism, Nancy Drew remained extraordinarily successful, and Nancy Pickard has noted that "the real Nancy Drew mystery may be the Mystery of the Appeal of Nancy Drew herself, and of her phenomenal attraction for successive generations of American girls" (211). What then of her "author," the phenomenally prolific Carolyn Keene? If we could fix her identity, could we perhaps solve the interpretative riddles posed by Nancy Drew and why she remains so popular?

Two women — Harriet Stratemeyer Adams and Mildred Wirt Benson — are regularly trotted out as the "real" Carolyn Keene and are often pitted against one another for the coveted title of "Author." During the last years before her death, Adams breached long-standing Syndicate policy ensuring the anonymity of the identity behind pseudonym by presenting herself in interviews and correspondence as the author — and sometimes even the mother — of Nancy Drew. Adams' efforts were so successful that her obituaries routinely mourned the passing of this literary giant of girls' mysteries. Yet in 1980, Mildred Wirt Benson, the series' first hired ghostwriter, also laid claim to the identity of Carolyn Keene and to Nancy Drew's authorship during a public trial concerning the Syndicate's new publisher, and she was the guest of honor at the University of Iowa's 1993 Nancy Drew Conference put on, in part, to publicize her contribution to the early mysteries' popularity. After Benson's death in 2002, her obituaries mourned not just the death of Carolyn Keene, but of "the original Carolyn Keene — the first, and best, of the ghostwriters, the one who gave Nancy her personality and her keenness, her independence and her spunk" (Frey). Melanie Rehak's deft biographical study *Girl Sleuth: Nancy Drew and the Women Who Created Her* (2005) argues for the ways in which the famous girl detective's two "creators" necessarily share the creative spotlight, but Rehak also redeploys the romantic definition of traditional authorship she works against elsewhere when she locates the various meanings of Nancy Drew in the categories of meaning Foucault challenges: the biographies, perspectives, social positions, and designs of its two most famous writers, Harriet Stratemeyer Adams and Mildred Wirt Benson.

As it is traditionally understood in the humanities, authorship assumes mastery: one individual, endowed with particular genius, creates an original text; that individual is the text's author and, for many readers, the authority on the text's meaning. Such a traditional understanding of authorship emphasizes both the individuality of the writer (there must be only one, not several, and certainly not a syndicate-full), and the writing itself must be original, or is it derivative (bad) or plagiaristic (worse). Originality is key: to be an author, one must possess specific and non-replicable talents for creating; such talents create oeuvres and ensure the signature of the author stands for a specific, reliable set of stylistic traits that in turn vouch for the authenticity of the author. This definition of authorship — with its fidelity to origin, unified meaning, and the knowable identity of an individual author — persists despite a host of challenges that aim to dismantle it. Roland Barthes, for example, points out that insisting on an author for a text arbitrarily limits the meanings of that text, and he argues instead that the pleasure — and multiplicity — of a text is always located in the reader and his or her performance of reading the text. Foucault likewise argues for the demise of the author, resituating the author as a system of constraint on meaning. In contemporary writing practice, a host of researchers in composition studies argue for collaborative textual production, and an increasing variety of postmodern writing practices flourishing on the Internet eschew originality and skirt traditional copyright protections.[1]

When writing practice deviates substantially from traditionally understood definitions of authorship, we question not the possibility of individual authorship, but the authenticity of the differing writing practice; therefore, let's turn first to the Stratemeyer Syndicate's various deployments of authorship. With juvenile literature, literary expectations for original, individual authorship can fall low enough to allow the kind of corporate writing practiced by the Stratemeyer Syndicate to "pass" as literature, so long as some attempt is made to obscure the model of multiple authorship actually practiced.

From the first volume in 1930, Nancy Drew's authorship was always a corporate collaboration, always the product of numerous individuals and the "fiction factory" syndicate that employed them. The contradiction between the fantasy of locating Nancy Drew's "real" author that developed after Carolyn Keene became widely known outside the industry as a pseudonym and the reality of her multiple, overlapping writers gives some indication of the depth of our unconscious convictions regarding individual authorship. It also reveals that, despite juvenile literature's increasing focus on adventure and entertainment at the turn of the twentieth century, it still faced pressures to appear traditionally "literary," which is to say appearing both traditionally original and the product of a single masterful author. But the corporate manner in which the Stratemeyer Syndicate created series books meant that those pressures could never be met. The best the syndicate could do — and over the years it tried very hard — was to deploy various pseudonyms in order to maintain the illusion of an individual author's unique creation of and mastery over a particular character — a character that was, ironically, endlessly and formulaically rehearsed in each successive series volume. With Carolyn Keene, the syndicate struck gold.

A pseudonym masquerades as a signature of the author, appearing to represent the self-identical, individual author of romantic tradition. Yet its very function as simultaneously author and not author, as authority and signifier of the absence of authority, reveals the fluidity and constant negotiation inherent in all writing practices. Since multiple books appearing in the marketplace with a single authorial signature risk signaling mediocre work, using pseudonyms can give writers an economic advantage (we have difficulty believing an author could produce several works in a short time without sacrificing "quality").[2] In this way a pseudonym can multiply the seemingly fixed identity of the traditional individual author into many identities, a postmodern dispersal of identity. But pseudonyms also upend the romantic definition of authorship by condensing identity, taking those many seemingly individual authors and fusing them indistinctly under one signature.

For the Stratemeyer Syndicate, pseudonyms were also used precisely to indicate the absence of originality: a Dixon or a Keene promised a reliably pat formula, a single general story in which only the details of the mystery differed from book to book. Ironically, Stratemeyer pseudonyms promised the most stable of authorial identities, and quality had to do with building suspense and executing action, rather than with more formal aesthetic pleasures. Even then, however, there were constant rips in the fabric of that illusion. Ghostwriters let slip their alternate identities, revealing that, with the support of editors and outlines, many people could write under one pseudonym without concern for originality, and wholesale rewriting of selected series titles created jarringly different texts with the same title, interrupting the experience of seamless repetition with minor variation in detail.

Perhaps because Edward Stratemeyer had written stories under pseudonyms for other firms, he never considered authorship of juvenilia an individual, privileged activity. From the outset, Stratemeyer books were marketed as entertainment. The Stratemeyer Syndicate threw traditional understandings of individual, inspired authorship into question, and historically the most furious objections to its deployments of corporate, collaborative authorship came from professionals, particularly librarians and teachers whose careers turned on what children were reading. Peter A. Soderbergh has delineated three distinct features on which those early twentieth-century objections centered: the "poor quality of prose" in children's series, "their tendency toward exaggeration and sensationalism," and "the assembly-manner in which series books were being produced" (865). Although these objections were aimed at children's series books in general, because his affordable children's books were literally "inundating the marketplace," "Stratemeyer was the main offender" (865).

On the first two points, objections grew out of nineteenth-century ideals reflecting beliefs about the character-building nature of literature. Cultural definitions of children's literature in America changed between the seventeenth and nineteenth centuries. Caucasian children from Puritan New England were reared in a society that valued a formal education that included reading, and literature written for them was intended specifically for instruction in religious doctrine (MacLeod 103). But by the eighteenth century, writing for children, while still focusing on instruction, gradually shifted "toward a more generalized moralism" (MacLeod 106). Entertainment in children's writing became more acceptable, although it was still expected to contain moral instruction. The mid–nineteenth century saw the first series books for children, Jacob Abbott's Rollo stories, a series of twenty-eight different stories that constitute "a handbook of advanced American thinking on child nurture, educational method, and moral teaching in the early nineteenth century" (MacLeod 107).

Because children's literature in the nineteenth century was seen as an important contributor to a child's developing character and moral attitude, there was the potential for dire individual and social consequences in the heavily plotted, suspense-filled entertainment now being demanded by children and supplied by Stratemeyer at the turn of the twentieth century. "The despised books were pronounced 'vulgar,' 'pernicious,' 'trashy,' and 'injurious.' Series book authors were characterized as crass materialists, men of 'no moral purposes,' and managers of fiction factories. Some of Stratemeyer's products (Tom Swift, Motor Girls, Moving Picture Girls, e.g.) were castigated publicly as examples of the current cancer" (Soderbergh 866). Stratemeyer himself was characterized as an "arch fiend" (White 113). Series books were strong sellers, however, and even when banned from public libraries, they steadily made their way into children's personal libraries.

However, it was on the third point, the anti-literary way in which the books were conceived, written, and delivered, that most vehemence was heaped. As Nancy Tillman Romalov notes, attacks on series books were common, largely because they put at risk traditional definitions of literature. Romalov notes that Franklin K. Mathiews, chief librarian for the Boy Scouts of America, "was also annoyed at the way in which the books were produced: 'Not written but manufactured'—that is, they were not 'art' but 'commodity.' This particular objection has remained constant throughout the history of the series books controversy. If a book is mass-produced, or ghostwritten, it is not bona fide literature, and consequently reading such books is an unworthy activity" (117). Deborah L. Siegel also points out that "mass-produced fiction betrayed a Victorian ideal held dear to the children's librarian. The librarian's role was to mediate the sacred connection between author and child. The very concept of the modern fiction factory undercut the romantic notion of authorship" (168). Stratemeyer's goals were neither lofty nor educational:

> Ultimately, Edward Stratemeyer was a conventional-minded businessman with a radical idea that would not have been radical in any other industry. It was to give his customers, who happened to be children, what they wanted, not what he thought they should want — and to make a product that was better than his competitors'. He understood, as George Orwell later wrote, that there was such a thing as the "good bad book" — one that "has no literary pretensions but remains readable when more serious productions have perished" [O'Rourke 8–9].

The syndicate's method of book production foiled conceptions of individual authorship at every turn, and in the process revealed that literary production for juveniles was both about money — lots of it — and at a deeper psychological level, about the pleasure of repetition rather than the aesthetics of originality. Writing to potential ghostwriters, Stratemeyer was clear about his expectations: "We do not ask for what is commonly called 'fine writing,' (usually another name for what is tedious and cumbersome) but want something full of 'ginger' and action" (qtd. in Rehak 93). Stratemeyer explicitly avoids the kind of writing ("fine writing") associated with literature in favor of the plot-filled, action-packed world that he already knew captivated young readers. Mildred Wirt Benson wrote the first volume, *The Secret of the Old Clock* (1930), according to Stratemeyer's outline, paying careful attention to Stratemeyer's expectations: "He only gave me one direction at the time that I was hired. He said you can snap your fingers at literary content but keep the suspense" (qtd. in Johnson, "Paragraphs," 33).

Most often emerging from school and public libraries where budget cuts and parental protests reveal literary fault lines, debates over the meaning and consequences of authorship in children's literature, and particularly in series books, continue today. While a 1934 review essay on series books urged children's librarians to play the role of reformer and therefore "rout" the thrillers from the library (White 113, 116), even by 1993 Nancy was still having a hard time garnering respect. In an editorial that ultimately praised the usefulness of texts such as Nancy Drew, Lillian N. Gerhardt somewhat bizarrely admits, "It's easy to poke fun at Nancy's sterilized world. Like most other librarians, I never thought the Nancy Drew series was worth (in literary terms) the powder and shot it would take to blow it to hell" (4). Nonetheless, Gerhardt, like many of her peers, has come to see value in "less than perfect" books because "for all their faults, these non-prize winners provide role models ... these less-than-stellar titles are consciously purchased for the comfort they may offer their readers, to support their hunger to find somebody like themselves in print, to bolster their sense of security" (4).

In an extensive study of readership published in 1995, Catherine Sheldrick Ross explicitly argues for the value of series books such as Nancy Drew because of the role they may play in producing avid readers: "In [librarians'] cultural battle they have identified the wrong enemy. Rhetoric to the contrary, series books do *not* enfeeble readers or render them unfit for reading anything else.... Series books can be seen as allies in the goal of making readers" (233). Ross's study demonstrates that "free voluntary reading" has a powerful and lasting impact on the development of readers. Ross emphasizes that, rather than reject series books as the enemy, "librarians need to create easy access to all kinds of books at all different levels of difficulty and literary value. And then they need to let the readers choose" (234).

Although the perceived value of reading children's series books has gradually increased over the years, the underlying contradictions that comprise our understanding of authorship reassert themselves in discussions of Nancy Drew's authorship. The desire to position Adams, Benson, or both women as the long-hidden but ultimately authentic Carolyn Keene shows us how deeply engrained our commitment to a concept of idealized, individual authorship continues to be, even in the face of the syndicate's unconventional collaborative approach. That many others — including men — have outlined, drafted, revised, and edited the Nancy Drew mysteries is no longer a secret; nonetheless, readers and critics alike persist in the desire to locate the "real" Carolyn Keene. Ironically, for the majority of their career years, neither Adams nor Benson had a romantic view of authorship as individual, inspired or original. By all accounts, Adams, like her father, saw her writing obligations as part of a business endeavor. Her administrative duties, which included negotiating with ghostwriters and editing their compositions for conformity to character profiles, so clearly and unavoidably positioned writing as an act of multiple creation that myths of individual authorship were impossible to sustain. While the Stratemeyer Syndicate books incorporated somewhat more educational material under her leadership, the chief goal was still to entertain children and therefore sell books. And Benson, in a variety of interviews, dismisses ideas of inspiration or genius and flatly describes writing as work that needed to be done: "I didn't analyze it. It was just a job to do. Some things I like and some things I did not like. It was a day's work. I did it just like I did my newspaper work. I wrote from early morning to late night for a good many years. One year I wrote 13 full-length books and held down a job besides. That takes a good deal of work" (Benfer).

Correspondence between Benson and Adams shows that Benson vacillated in her attitude about the syndicate's style of authorship and its workability for hired writers. Her concerns, however, are uniformly pragmatic: at times, Benson is grateful to have the direction the syndicate provided her in more lengthy outlines; at other times, she chafes against its constraints, particularly when the syndicate was critical of her final product. For example, regarding the plot outline for *The Secret of Red Gate Farm*, Benson writes, "I venture to call your attention to the length of the plot which, you will note, is a full page shorter than usual. In writing the story it was difficult to find chapter endings with sufficient suspense, and the book ran some chapters short. To lengthen them out I added a few incidents but even so it was necessary to dwell upon the 'cave' scenes a bit too long. I believe that I would be able to handle the denouement with a better technique if the plots were somewhat longer" (qtd. in Rehak 148).

However, by 1936, Benson protested the longer plots now being sent by the syndicate as a way to justify their smaller, depression-era paychecks to ghostwriters, and as late as 1947 she complained:

> In recent years, the amount of rewriting on these books has vastly increased, not only for me, but apparently for your office. One of the reasons, I feel, is that the outline is too full, with many big scenes in each chapter. The mere mechanics of transporting the heroine from one place to another thus takes up much space and detracts from the action.... If, in outlining the plot, you could eliminate some of the incidental scenes, or allow me to eliminate them when the chapter is running long, it would not only simplify my work, but I believe, make a better story.[3]

The fundamental contradiction between the syndicate's functional corporate definition of authorship and its attribution of more conventional forms of individual authorship to the pseudonym Carolyn Keene did not appear to trouble Benson until Adams publicly began claiming authorship of the series exclusively for herself. Although writing held no romantic spell for Benson, she was puzzled when other syndicate ghostwriters began revealing their connection to syndicate series. In 1950, she wrote to Adams to complain that Walter Karig, who ghosted three of the early Nancy Drew volumes, was able to claim authorship while she was not: "Persons acquainted with me, publishers I have known have been aware that I wrote the stories for your Syndicate. Now, however, Capt. Karig's broad claim has caused many to say to me, 'How Come?' I'm wondering the same thing. If he wrote some of the books and you have granted him permission to announce such fact publicly, I feel I should have the same privilege."[4]

Adams had of course given no such permission, although her response to Benson acknowledged the complex workings of syndicate authorship: "If it were permissible to make any claim to the pseudonym of Carolyn Keene, you naturally would have more right than Karig. But since all plots and outlines for these stories are supplied to the ghostwriters, it could hardly be truthfully claimed by any one of them that they were the author."[5] Although Adams had long argued that Benson and the other ghostwriters could not consider themselves the sole authors of the books they wrote on the grounds that so many people contributed substantive ideas and revisions, as she aged and took on more fully the writing responsibilities for Nancy Drew, she eventually denied the very fluidity and anonymity of multiple authorship that benefited her as a businesswoman. Ernie Kelly notes, "As we know, she claimed authorship for many titles in syndicate series that she did not solely write, particularly from 1930 to 1960. Clearly she did create outlines (very often detailed) and did alot [sic] of the background work and research herself. She personally edited everything that came in. Whether this qualifies her as having 'written' the book is certainly an open question" (11).

Countering Adams' claims for Nancy Drew's authorship are equally strong claims for Benson as, if not the sole author, at least the most significant author. Because Benson drafted the initial breeder set of three books from syndicate outlines, is she responsible for the essential elements of Nancy's character — her independence, her assuredness, her kindness — that continue to inspire young readers? Geoffrey Lapin argues "yes": "Mildred Wirt has come up with a way to write these books that has sustained Nancy Drew for all these years. None of the other series that Stratemeyer outlined — the Motor Boys, the Outdoor Girls, the Motion Picture Boys, Ruth Fielding, and many others — are with us today. There must be an explanation, and I think a good part of it is found in Mildred Wirt's writing style and characterizations" [54].

Lapin's argument, which is an excellent summary of attempts to solve the mystery of Nancy's ongoing popularity by locating her "real" author, is convincing for devotees of the earliest versions. But perhaps there needn't be an explanation — at least not a single explanation — any more than there is a single interpretation or characterization of Nancy Drew or a single writer behind the pseudonym of Carolyn Keene.

Benson understood that there were multiple authors and multiple Nancys from the start. During the 1980 trial between the syndicate, their long-time publisher, Grosset and Dunlap, and their new publisher, Simon and Schuster, Benson's contributions to the original Nancy Drew characterization were widely revealed. Benson was called to testify about the question of multiple authorship: "Mrs. Adams's style of writing Nancy is not the style I had, and I imagine that things I wrote in there did not hit her as Nancy. I mean, the Nancy that I created is a different Nancy from what Mrs. Adams has carried on.... There was a beginning conflict in what is Nancy. My Nancy would not be Mrs. Adams' Nancy."[6]

With both Harriet Stratemeyer Adams and Mildred Wirt Benson now dead, it may seem like the obituaries were right: Nancy Drew's authors are gone, taking with them the debate about original authorship. Nothing is further from the truth, however. Nancy's adventures continue into the twenty-first century precisely because she is a series book character that has multiple authors, past and present, as we can see in the ongoing process of character revision. Although Nancy Drew has been repeatedly revised and updated — by editors, ghostwriters, and even the publishing companies that have profited most from her enduring popularity — those revisions are calculated surface changes, aimed at revising details while preserving an essential, unchanging core identity. As Arthur Prager noted in 1971, "strictly speaking, Nancy is terribly square" (75). As a character, she remains remarkably the same, always in control, blindingly talented at endless activities, from piloting boats to discerning Morse code, and she is never in any actual danger of true injury. Although she is regularly kidnapped, bound, or knocked unconscious by various blunt instruments, "she always bounces back, bright as a button, to foil the caitiff responsible" (Prager 80). In 2004, Simon and Schuster introduced the most recently revised Nancy: "The titian-haired sleuth is now a strawberry blonde and she volunteers at an animal shelter. She's traded in her blue Mustang convertible for a hybrid car. She's Internet savvy and carries a cell phone. The books are now narrated in the first person" (Connors 12). Nancy Drew's continuing popularity remains one of juvenile literature's best arguments for the psychological comforts of an essential identity, while the inside story of her creation argues for an identity that is constantly reconstructed and negotiated.

Various characterizations of Nancy Drew continue to proliferate, beyond the publisher-sanctioned revisions, in the form of parody. Nancy Drew's status as a cultural icon — as an image onto which multiple and sometimes competing cultural meanings are projected — is demonstrated by the various parodies that now exist of her. Mabel Maney's lesbian rewritings of the girl sleuth, Nancy Clue, and her counterparts, Cherry Aimless and the Hardly Boys, are excellent examples of the ways in which new characters are created from the prior versions, and each new version is no less — or more — "real" than the others. The newly revised characters also prompt revised readings: "Contemporary readers tend to want to read the Drew/ Ames books as artifacts of a nostalgia-filled era ... and Maney pushes us to read the early 1900s in a different way, to understand the Drew/Ames books less as artifacts and more as deliberate revisions of history designed to promote specifically conservative values and to train women to be bold and adventurous, but traditionally feminine nonetheless" (Gibson and Meem 30). Because Nancy Drew's mysteries were invariably and thoroughly solved though the telling of a formulaic story, most young readers spend a season or two on Nancy, bask in the pleasures of formulaic repetition, and then move on to other reading. For adult readers, the pleasures are more complex and the mysteries are irresolvable: there is no "real" Nancy, just as there is no "real" author lurking behind the signature of Carolyn Keene.

Notes

1. See Foucault, "What Is an Author?," Barthes, "The Death of the Author," and composition studies researchers Andrea Lunsford and Lisa Ede. For more detailed discussions about the historical construction of authorship as an individual act of genius, see Buranen and Roy, Hirschfeld, Masten, Stillinger, and Woodmansee and Jaszi.

2. This was the case with L. Frank Baum, for instance. Baum published the Oz series under his name, but he also published under pseudonyms in an effort to sell more books without alerting his audience to the fact that he was, literally, cranking them out.

3. Wirt to Adams, May 6, 1947. Box 44, Stratemeyer Syndicate Records, Mss and Archives Section, New York Public Library, Astor, Lenox and Tilden Foundations.

4. Wirt to Adams, May 4, 1950. Box 33, Stratemeyer Syndicate Records, Mss and Archives Section, New York Public Library, Astor, Lenox and Tilden Foundations.

5. Adams to Wirt, May 23, 1950. Box 33, Stratemeyer Syndicate Records, Mss and Archives Section, New York Public Library, Astor, Lenox and Tilden Foundations.

6. Grosset and Dunlap v. Gulf and Western Corporation and Stratemeyer Syndicate trial transcripts, 1980 (225, 232). Qtd. in Rehak 297.

Works Cited

Barthes, Roland. "The Death of the Author." *Image-Music-Text*. Trans. Stephen Heath. New York: Hill, 1977, p. 142–48.

Benfer, Amy. "Who Was Carolyn Keene? An Interview with Mildred Wirt Benson, the Original Ghostwriter for the Nancy Drew Mystery Novels." *Salon* (October 8, 1999), http://www.salon.com/mwt/feature/1999/10/08/keene_q_a/index.html.

Buranen, Lise, and Alice M. Roy, eds. *Perspectives on Plagiarism and Intellectual Property in a Postmodern World*. Albany: State University of New York Press, 1999.

Connors, Lisa Leigh. "Gee, Nancy, You're So Smart!" *Christian Science Monitor* 96.66 (March 2, 2004): 12.

Foucault, Michel. "What Is an Author?" Trans. by Josué Harari. *The Critical Tradition: Classic Texts and Contemporary Trends*. Ed. David H. Richter. 2nd ed. Boston: Bedford, 1998, p. 890–900.

Frey, Jennifer. "A True Woman of Mystery." *Washington Post* (May 30, 2002): C1.

Gerhardt, Lillian N. "Editorial: Nancy's New Social Security." *School Library Journal* (May 1993): 4.

Gibson, Michelle, and Deborah T. Meem. "The Case of the Lovely Lesbian: Mabel Maney's Queering of Nancy Drew." *Studies in Popular Culture* 19.3 (April 1997): 23–26.

Hirschfeld, Heather. "Early Modern Collaboration and Theories of Authorship." *PMLA* 116.3 (2001): 609–22.

Jenkins, Emily. "The Case of the Girl Detective." *Salon* (June 10, 2002), http://dir.salon.com/story/books/feature/2002/06/10/drew/index.html.

Johnson, Deidre. *Edward Stratemeyer and the Stratemeyer Syndicate*. New York: Twayne Publishers, 1993.

_____. "From Paragraphs to Pages: The Writing and Development of the Stratemeyer Syndicate Series." *Rediscovering Nancy Drew*. Ed. Carolyn Stewart Dyer and Nancy Tillman Romalov. Iowa City: University of Iowa Press, 1995, pp. 29–40.

Kelly, Ernie. "Inside the Stratemeyer Syndicate, Part I." *Yellowback Library* 54 (October 1988): 5–11.

Lapin, Geoffrey S. "Searching for Carolyn Keene." *Rediscovering Nancy Drew*. Ed. Carolyn Stewart Dyer and Nancy Tillman Romalov. Iowa City: University of Iowa Press, 1995, pp. 52–58.

Lunsford, Andrea, and Lisa Ede. *Singular Texts/Plural Authors: Perspectives on Collaborative Writing*. Carbondale: Southern Illinois University Press, 1990.

MacLeod, Anne Scott. "Children's Literature in America, from the Puritan Beginnings to 1870." *Children's Literature: An Illustrated History*. Ed. Peter Hunt. Oxford and New York: Oxford University Press, 1995, pp. 102–129.

Masten, Jeffrey. *Textual Intercourse: Collaboration, Authorship, and Sexualities in Renaissance Drama*. Cambridge: Cambridge University Press, 1997.

O'Rourke, Meghan. "Nancy Drew's Father: The Fiction of Edward Stratemeyer." *New Yorker*, http://www.newyorker.com/printables/critics/041108crat_atlarge.

Pickard, Nancy. "I Owe It All to Nancy Drew." *Rediscovering Nancy Drew*. Ed. Carolyn Steward Dyer and Nancy Tillman Romalov. Iowa City: University of Iowa Press, 1995, pp. 208–211.

Prager, Arthur. *Rascals at Large; or, The Clue in the Old Nostalgia*. Garden City, N.Y.: Doubleday, 1971.

Rehak, Melanie. *Girl Sleuth: Nancy Drew and the Women Who Created Her*. Orlando: Harcourt, 2005.

Romalov, Nancy Tillman. "Children's Series Books and the Rhetoric of Guidance: A Historical Overview. *Rediscovering Nancy Drew*. Ed. Carolyn Steward Dyer and Nancy Tillman Romalov. Iowa City: University of Iowa Press, 1995, pp. 113–120.

Ross, Catherine Sheldrick. "'If They Read Nancy Drew, So What?': Series Book Readers Talk Back." *Library and Information Science Research* 17.3 (1995): 201–236.

Siegel, Deborah L. "Nancy Drew as New Girl Wonder: Solving It All for the 1930s." *Nancy Drew and Company: Culture, Gender, and Girls' Series.* Ed. Sherrie A. Inness. Bowling Green: Bowling Green State University Popular Press, 1997, pp. 159–182.
Soderbergh, Peter A. "The Stratemeyer Strain: Educators and the Juvenile Series Book, 1900–1973." *Journal of Popular Culture* 7 (1973): 864–872.
Stillinger, Jack. *Multiple Authorship and the Myth of Solitary Genius.* New York: Oxford University Press, 1991.
White, Hope. "'For It Was Indeed He' (50 cents Thrillers Exposed)." *Illinois Libraries* (October 1934): 113–116.
Woodmansee, Martha, and Peter Jaszi, eds. *The Construction of Authorship: Textual Appropriation in Law and Literature.* Durham: Duke University Press, 1994.

Alice Roy, Détective: Nancy Drew in French Translation

Melanie E. Gregg

When I read Nancy Drew as a child, there were certain words I grew to expect each time I cracked open a volume in the series, atmospheric words like "spooky" and "spine-tingling," and a host of detective- and mystery-related terms like "sleuth," "snoop," "hoax," and "hunch." I relished the repeated use of unusual words like "titian," "retort" and "scowl" as much as I enjoyed the efficient and familiar three-word character descriptions that invariably included some form of the modifiers "tomboyish" and "plump." Yet many of my favorite words, so specific to the series and the genre, do not have direct equivalents in French. Certainly, these terms can be conveyed in French, but the sounds of the words and shades of their meaning are very particular, and it is, in many cases, impossible to pin down an exact translation for them.

Often unable to render words literally, translators of the Nancy Drew series were forced to start from plainer, less-nuanced synonyms in English for which there are more direct translations in French: "sleuth," for example, is translated as *détective*, and "hunch" is rendered as *intuition*. A word like "spooky," however, is trickier, and translators varied their word-choices in French, opting for adjectives that range from *inquiétant* (worrying, disturbing) and *lugubre* (gloomy, dismal) (*Dame du Lac* [*Mirror Bay*] 7, 34) to *sinistre* (sinister) and *hanté* (haunted) (*Fusée Spatiale* [*Moss-Covered Mansion*] 35, 83). None of these translations quite captures the full meaning of "spooky," which, for me, connotes something unnervingly eerie and supernatural at the same time it implies and provokes, by the very sound of the word, a suspenseful jumpiness. To avoid the risks imposed by words like "spooky"—words that appear to be fairly simple but are in fact packed with cultural significance—the translators of the series occasionally omitted them altogether. This small sampling of words—and the linguistic conundrums they entail—invites a closer look at the French editions. If the very building blocks for the setting and ambiance the authors of Nancy Drew had created were impossible to convey directly into French, then what other impact did translation have on the series?

Addressing the question first in global terms, I should mention that I anticipated several of the changes seen in the translated editions: adjustments to book titles, the re-creation of word play or code words (which simply do not work if translated literally), and changes in cultural and historical references that might not make sense to young French readers without some explanation. Translators also had to deal with the sparseness and fast pace of the prose—the "rapid, no-frills story-telling," as Carol Billman describes the stylistic compression of the originals (113). To foster the more fluid and expansive expression often associated with French narrative style, the translators lengthened descriptions, smoothed out transitions, and, in some cases, shifted narrative descriptions to monologues.

In addition to the stylistic revisions they made the translators, working in the beginning from the original, unrevised editions, modernized the stories by excising the bigoted and racist portrayals of minority characters, far in advance of efforts to do so in the United States. They also avoided slang or any other language that would date the texts (an attention to detail that would have certainly pleased Harriet Stratemeyer Adams).

Revisions of this nature were mostly fairly predictable. Other changes I encountered, however, such as chapter title changes and modifications to the formulaic structure (the removal of the standard reference at the end of each volume to the next title in the series, for example), did take me by surprise. One of the most peculiar changes I found across the volumes I compared was the consistent elimination of any mention of the main characters attending church services (even though religion plays no significant role in the lives of the characters). Alterations such as these are striking because they seem entirely unnecessary. Without direct communication with the translators themselves, we may never be able to determine the reasons behind some of the decisions that were made.

The task for translators of Nancy Drew is to take a profoundly American heroine from the Middle West and reconstruct her in another language for an audience entirely different from the one for which she was originally created. The French translators were certainly successful in this endeavor; the popularity of the series in France, bolstered by its remarkable array of formats (on display at Lea Shangraw Fox's marvelously informative Web site), has been phenomenal. Peter Soderbergh claims that in the seventies, Nancy Drew was "the most popular juvenile book in France" (870). In a 1996 newspaper article announcing that Nancy Drew had been adapted for a thirteen-episode television series on France 2, the journalist states that more than 200,000 copies had sold each year since 1955, totaling more than 21 million copies since the début of the series ("Alice Aujourd'hui").

As these numbers show, the success of the series in France is indisputable, but is the French Nancy Drew the same Nancy Drew that has captivated generations of American readers? Are Mr. Drew, Hannah Gruen, Ned Nickerson, Bess Marvin, and George Fayne the same characters Anglophone enthusiasts know and love? The act of translation inherently involves and necessitates changes to a text, sometimes on barely discernible levels, but, often, in more significant ways, if the retelling is to be as effective and captivating as the original. To achieve a faithful rendering of a story in another language, however, assuming that is the goal, a translator should go to great lengths to protect and maintain the essence of a story's characters, even when intentionally altering the style of the original narrative. It occurred to me, as I began comparing the characters of the Nancy Drew series in English and in French that certain characteristics and qualities — the hearts of the series' characters — are non-negotiable, at least for me, and must be preserved in translation for the characters to remain authentically themselves. The validity of a translation comes down in part to the translator's ability to perceive, respect, and reproduce the fundamental qualities of the main characters. Stable characters like those of the Nancy Drew series, reliable in their consistency, even if stunted in their development, can withstand some fluctuation, but they possess certain basic qualities that cannot be tampered with. What those essential qualities are, and how they are defined, may be different for different readers, but one quickly becomes aware, by comparing the translations with their originals, of just how much change is tolerable.

Fans have been conditioned over the decades to abide some changes to the series and have witnessed changes in Nancy Drew herself. As Diana

Beeson and Bonnie Brennen have argued, "Nancy, as a fictional character, is anything but static, enduring, and unchanging" (193). Beeson and Brennen lay bare the transformation the heroine undergoes not only from print to film, but also from one version of a volume to another, as a result of editorial revisions required over time to accommodate and reflect the changing mores and politics of American society. In light of Nancy's various incarnations in English, it is logical to assume that translation of the series from one language to another would result in further, and perhaps more substantive, transformation. The likelihood for changes to the series was greater still since multiple translators worked on the texts, and the authors themselves, as Mildred Wirt Benson once pointed out, were not at all involved with the translated editions (Rehak 253).

One of the immediately noticeable changes made to the series concerns the names of the characters. Nancy Drew is not Nancy Drew in the French editions: her name is Alice Roy. Her father, Carson Drew, becomes James Roy. Hannah Gruen's name is changed to Sarah Berny, George Fayne becomes Marion Webb, and Bess Marvin's name is changed to Bess Taylor. Although many fans have conjectured that these name changes were made for reasons of pronunciation (the idea being that the original names are too difficult to pronounce in French), I am convinced that pronunciation is not the reason for the name changes, because even names easily pronounced in French, and names that are already French, are changed. *The Mystery of the 99 Steps* holds one of the most obvious examples: the young French women Marie et [and] Monique Bardot are given the names Catherine et Monique Tardy in the translation (*Alice à Paris* 5). Moreover, in cases where the names may appear difficult to pronounce in French, the substitutions are equally or even more difficult to pronounce in French. For instance, to select randomly from among countless examples, Mr. Bowen in *Moonstone Castle* becomes Monsieur Frazer in *Pierre d'Onyx*, and Mrs. Sheets in *Nancy's Mysterious Letter* becomes Madame Trick in *Quand Alice Rencontre Alice*, names that are not any more French-sounding than their originals. So, there must be some other reason for these name changes, one that unfortunately is not revealed in the official correspondence between editors and translators housed at the New York Public Library.

The name changes, however, mark only the beginning of the modifications the translators brought to the characters in the Nancy Drew series. Alice Roy's ancestral history differs significantly from that of Nancy Drew, whose Scottish heritage, revealed in *The Clue of the Whistling Bagpipes*, can be traced back, as Karen Plunkett-Powell has done, to her maternal great-great-grandmother (*The Nancy Drew Scrapbook* 74–75). Alice Roy is descended on her mother's side from an old French family living in Louisiana. Hélène Commin, the translator of the first few volumes of the series, invents details about Alice's lineage that conflict with the genealogical history Nancy's authors provide in later volumes. In the English-language originals, it is not until the thirty-fourth volume, *The Hidden Window Mystery*, that we learn Nancy's mother's maiden name, which is Austin. Commin, on the other hand, establishes Alice's history from the opening pages of the first volume, giving Alice's mother, Elise Roy (a name somewhat similar to Nancy's aunt Eloise Drew), the unmistakably French maiden name Beauchamp.

In *Alice Détective*, the French edition of *The Secret of the Old Clock*, originally published by Librairie Hachette in 1955, Commin elaborates on the young sleuth's background, specifying one detail that Mildred Wirt Benson had avoided: While Nancy is a "true daughter of the Middle West" (26), Alice is from Missouri (28). The translator inserts a long paragraph about Nancy's love for her home state (a quality that would be particularly appealing to the French), adding some details about visits she had made since her youngest childhood to Louisiana, to see her maternal grandparents. The translator also includes mention of a three-month stay Alice had made in France the year before, in Touraine, a region in Central Western France to which Alice feels a strong connection and where she still enjoys family ties:

> Elle aimait profondément ce pays où elle était née et où elle avait toujours vécu, à l'exception des vacances qu'elle passait depuis son enfance en Louisiane, chez ses grands-parents maternels, et d'un séjour de trois mois qu'elle avait fait en France l'année précédente.
>
> La famille Beauchamp avait en effet conservé des attaches dans sa patrie d'origine: en Touraine, vivaient encore les descendants d'une branche cadette. Ceux-ci avait accueilli Alice à bras ouverts, et la jeune fille ne pouvait songer sans émotion à ces parents lointains qui avaient voulu lui faire connaître le pays de sa mère sous les plus beaux aspects. Elle avait vu Paris, Versailles, visité la Bretagne, la Provence et, plus belle encore peut-être que celles-ci, cette chère Touraine, avec ses douces eaux, ses horizons nacrés et ses châteaux de contes de fées. Alice en avait gardé la nostalgie. "Je retournerai là-bas un jour...," se disait-elle [28].

> [She deeply loved the region where she had been born and where she had always lived, except for the vacations she had spent in Louisiana at her maternal grandparents' house since her childhood and her three-month stay in France the year before.

The Beauchamp family had indeed preserved ties to their native land: descendants of a younger branch of the family still lived in Touraine. Alice thought fondly of these relatives, who had welcomed her with open arms and introduced her to all of the beauty that her mother's country had to offer. She had seen Paris and Versailles, visited Bretagne and Provence, and perhaps most beautiful of all, the beloved town of Touraine, with its gentle waters, glowing horizons, and fairytale castles. Alice felt nostalgic for the time she had spent in France. "I will return there one day...," she told herself.]

The decision to make this French connection was surely a strategic move to create a link between young French readers and the series' quintessentially American heroine.

Commin fills in other gaps in Nancy's history to build a character with whom Francophone readers could identify. In the opening volume she clarifies why Alice is not in school, for example, since the notion of a girl her age not attending classes would be an entirely foreign concept for French readers. Commin deals with this anomaly by explaining that Alice, greatly admired by her friends and her teachers, is very advanced for her age, and had left school at the age of fifteen-and-a-half in possession of a high school diploma, a detail we are not given in the original: "Très en avance sur les jeunes filles de son âge, Alice avait quitté le collège à quinze ans et demi, en possession de son diplôme de fin d'études secondaires. Excellente élève, elle était estimée de ses professeurs tout autant qu'adorée de ses compagnes" (17).

Commin is forced, as well, to justify Alice's driving privileges, and does so by explaining that there is no age-minimum for a driver's license in America: "Heureusement pour la jeune fille ... la loi américaine n'imposait pas d'âge minimum à l'octroi du permis de conduire" (18). The translator adds other minor informational details here and there to explain various cultural differences for her French audience. She also fleshes out certain descriptions, such as with Nancy's "shiny new blue roadster" (13), which Commin captures as "un joli cabriolet décapotable, tout pimpant avec sa carrosserie bleu vif et ses chromes étincelants" (18) (a pretty open-topped convertible, all decked out in bright blue bodywork and gleaming chrome) — a wordier, and perhaps more vibrant, description illustrative of the stylistic modifications the translators brought to the series.

Explanations and descriptions such as these merely represent technical and stylistic changes and serve to provide a background for the protagonist that may indeed make her more attractive to a French audience. The heroine's altered history does not in actuality generate any notable change to her character. The only change in Nancy's personality that can be confirmed by textual evidence is that she is slightly more affectionate with her father in French versions of the stories, both verbally and physically, an adjustment that may simply reflect a cultural difference in the way parents and children interact in France. The formality of the language Nancy uses with her father, which may have been typical in the Midwest at the time of her creation, is not preserved in the French. Where she refers to him as "Father" in the early, unrevised versions, she calls him "Papa" in French, which sounds more endearing (and certainly less stuffy) than "Père" (Father). The greater physical affection between Alice and her father, however, is where the change becomes more noticeable, but only as a result of a side-by-side reading of the original and translated editions (c.f. *Secret of the Old Clock* 180, 183, 191; *Alice Détective* 156, 160, 166).

Beyond this barely perceptible change, there is no jarring difference in the French version of the young American sleuth: Alice Roy is, for the most part, a true and proper reincarnation of Nancy Drew. Nancy's kindness, optimism, resourcefulness, and poise all come through in translation. In fact, in some cases, the translators accentuate a quality the heroine is already known to possess. In *Alice et la Pierre d'Onyx* (*The Moonstone Castle Mystery*), for instance, translator Claude Voilier modifies a confrontation between Alice and a police officer in a way that allows him to emphasize Alice's sense of integrity. In one of the formulaic scenes where a local policeman discovers the young sleuth's identity and her relationship to one of River Heights' most distinguished attorneys, the conversation takes a familiar turn: "Carson Drew? Everybody knows him. So you're his daughter? Why didn't you tell the River police that in the first place?" Nancy doesn't answer him, but just smiles and the officer winks, saying, "Case dismissed" (113). In the translation, Alice replies: "Je n'ai pas besoin de me recommander d'un père honnête pour l'être moi-même!"(121) (I don't need the backing of an honest father to be an honest person myself!). The police officer reddens with embarrassment at her fiery retort, recognizing that he had unintentionally suggested that Alice might not be honorable in her own right.

Emphasis on a character's most attractive and admirable traits is not limited to Alice; her father receives similar treatment from the translators. While we are often limited to a physical description in the English original of Nancy's "tall handsome father" (*Moonstone Castle* 10), along with the prescribed mention of his stellar reputation as a lawyer, the French translators place emphasis on his respectability, underscoring above all his close

relationship with Nancy. For example, in *The Secret of Mirror Bay*, Mr.
Drew is introduced as "tall, handsome Carson Drew ... a well-known attorney in River Heights" (4). In the French translation, Anne Joba adds two
sentences to this description that highlight Monsieur Roy's adoration of
his daughter and his high regard for her skills as a detective. "James Roy
était un avocat dont la réputation s'étendait bien au-delà de sa ville, River
City. Très tôt, il avait initié sa fille qu'il adorait — et elle le lui rendait
bien —, aux secrets de son métier. Étonné des dispositions qu'elle révélait,
il lui avait peu à peu confié des affaires qui exigeaient de réelles qualités
de détective" [10]. (James Roy was a lawyer whose reputation was known
far beyond River City. Very early, he had initiated his daughter, whom he
adored and who adored him in return, to the secrets of his job. Aston-
ished by her natural gifts, he had, little by little, entrusted her with affairs
that required true detective qualities.)

Joba injects even the briefest of physical descriptions of James Roy
with modifiers that reflect his decency and moral uprightness. In *The Mystery of 99 Steps*, the author describes Nancy's father with the usual adjectives: "The tall handsome man beamed in delight at seeing the girls" (40).
Joba matches this description, but again adds two short phrases that round
out the portrait, infusing his features with honesty and goodness: "C'était
un grand et bel homme, au regard droit, au visage empreint de bonté" (46).
(He was a tall and handsome man with an honest gaze and a face that
exuded goodness). The French translators capitalize on well-chosen
descriptors to enhance Mr. Drew's two-dimensional existence, as Joba has
done here, but beyond this they make no notable modification to his character.

Hannah Gruen, on the other hand, does enjoy a new identity in the
French translation of the series. We know from the English original of *The
Quest of the Missing Map* that Mrs. Gruen had previously been employed
by the Smiths (a well-to-do family in River Heights) before coming to work
for the Drews. Commin invents an entirely different background for her
Mrs. Gruen (Mrs. Berny). The narrator explains in the first volume that
Sarah Berny had accompanied her mistress Elise (Alice's mother) from
Louisiana at the time of her marriage to James Roy (*Alice Détective* 17).

Just as they had slightly expanded their portrayals of Nancy's father,
the translators allow certain moral qualities to surface in their descriptions
of Mrs. Berny that do not appear in the English. Or rather, they accentuate qualities different from those highlighted in the originals. In *The Sign
of the Twisted Candles*, for example, Hannah is described as "the warm-

hearted, efficient housekeeper of the Drew household" (18). In the translated version, Sarah is "la brave et fidèle domestique de la famille Roy" (*Alice et le Chandelier* 23). The translator stresses the housekeeper's honesty (*brave*) and good nature as well her loyalty to the Roys.

Further along in the same text, Hannah appears as the "sweet, motherly-looking housekeeper [who] had helped rear Nancy since she was three, when Mrs. Drew had died" (29). Commin slightly modifies this passage in her translation and adds a detail that appears only in later volumes of the English originals. She mentions that Sarah loved Alice as if she were her own child, establishing right away a more familial and tender relationship between Alice and Mrs. Berny than exists between Nancy and Mrs. Gruen in the earlier volumes of the series: "Sarah s'était occupée de la fillette et elle l'aimait comme s'il s'agissait de son propre enfant" (35). Joba similarly handles her portrayal of Sarah Berny in her translation of *The Secret of Mirror Bay*, emphasizing the esteem in which Sarah is held by the family and her status as an equal in their household — notions that are not overtly mentioned in the original:

> Mrs. Gruen had been with the family since the death of Mrs. Drew when Nancy was only three years old. The tenderhearted woman was like a mother to her and was very proud of Nancy's accomplishments as a young amateur detective. Nevertheless, she was always a little fearful when Nancy set off on one of her sleuthing expeditions [3].
>
> La jeune fille avait à peine trois ans quand sa mère était morte. C'était Sarah qui avait veillé sur elle avec une inlassable tendresse et tenu le ménage de M. Roy. Respectée de tous, elle faisait partie de la famille. Elle était très fière de la beauté d'Alice, de ses magnifiques cheveux blonds et, surtout, des qualités qui la rendaient chère à ses amis et connaissances, fière aussi de ses dons de détective. Cela dit, elle tremblait chaque fois que la jeune fille se lançait dans une nouvelle enquête, car elle était d'une intrépidité à faire frémir [9].

In addition to the comments Joba inserts about Sarah's respected position in the family, Joba expands what in the original is expressed simply as Hannah's pride for Nancy's accomplishments. Her French counterpart, Sarah, is proud more specifically of Alice's beauty, her magnificent blonde hair, her skills as a detective, and especially the qualities she possessed that endeared her to her friends and acquaintances. In the final sentence, Joba explains that Sarah fears for Alice because the young girl herself was "frighteningly fearless." While some of these added details may be intended to round out the characters, they also cast an even brighter light on Alice, since the additions usually relate to the admiration and affection those around her feel for her. Occasionally, in scenes where the presence or mention in the original of Hannah, and sometimes even Nancy's friends, does not serve to spotlight Nancy, the passages or references are eliminated or trimmed to a bare minimum from the translation (cf. *Moonstone Castle* 16, 18, 21 [*Alice et la Pierre d'Onyx* 25,]; *Moss-Covered Mansion* 6, 61 [*Alice et la Fusée Spatiale* 11–13, 69]. The omissions appear inconsequential, but are nonetheless notable, since the translators deliberately modify the original versions.

A look at the translators' treatment of Nancy's friends, who are more centrally involved in the action of the stories than Mr. Drew or Mrs. Gruen, yields other noteworthy findings. Somewhat underdeveloped characters in the original stories, Nancy's friends Ned, Bess, and George undergo a few changes in translation, some of which result in marked revisions to their characters, especially in the case of George Fayne. Yet before considering the specifics of George's case, I will point out some of the less problematic (but equally intriguing) changes I observed in Nancy's friends.

Ned Nickerson, for example, plays rugby in most of the French editions, instead of football, although in *Quand Alice Rencontre Alice* (*Nancy's Mysterious Letter*) the translator keeps "football" and offers an explanatory footnote to distinguish the sport from soccer (44). While this change is inconsequential, it is paired with a more significant adjustment to Ned's character or, more specifically, to his role in Nancy's life. With the exception of *The Clue in the Diary*, where the translation faithfully renders their initial meeting and nascent attraction to one another, Ned's status as Nancy's "special friend" or Nancy's "favorite date" changes in subsequent translated volumes to simply her "friend" or to her "best friend from childhood." Any allusion to romantic interest or intimacy that may be present in the originals is stripped from the texts in translation. In *The Sign of the Twisted Candles*, Ned Nickerson is described as Nancy's "favorite date" (31). In translation he becomes her "childhood friend" ("son camarade d'enfance") (*Chandelier* 37) or "long-time friend" (135). In his translation of *The Moonstone Castle Mystery*, Claude Voilier leaves out mention of their frequent dating (*Moonstone Castle* 2), and refers to Ned as Nancy's "best friend" (*Alice et la Pierre d'Onyx* 9). Joba adds to the characterization in her translation of *Nancy's Mysterious Letter* that Ned was an old schoolmate at the co-ed high school of "River City" ["Ned Nickerson, camarade d'enfance et ancien condisciple d'Alice au lycée mixte de River City, était le meilleur ami de la jeune fille"] (*Quand Alice Rencontre Alice* 43). The fact that all three translators omit allusions to any sort of relationship beyond friendship suggests that there must have been directives from the French editors about character portrayals in the translated version of the series.

Interestingly, the primary characteristics used to identify Bess and George from volume to volume — Bess's love of food and George's tomboyish ways — are the very traits that the translators tend to adjust and revise. Occasionally, lines referring to these most prominent of their qualities are not included in the French editions (cf. *The Moonstone Castle Mystery* 92, 149; *Mirror Bay* 2). Moreover, the bickering and banter that goes on between the two cousins is attenuated, as in one scene in *The Moonstone Castle Mystery* when Bess becomes exasperated with George's teasing about her latest tennis date. She cries, "George Fayne, there are times when I could pull your hair right out by the roots!" (54). In the French version, targeting both Nancy and George, who have been poking fun at her, Bess exclaims: "Vous êtes insupportables! C'est la jalousie qui vous fait parler!" (62). ("You two are unbearable! You're just jealous!")

In another scene in the same volume when Bess worries about what could have happened to George, she says, "George takes such wild chances. Goodness only knows what she may have gotten into" (30). Sentences such as these that supplement the generally restricted descriptions of Nancy's companions are eliminated from the French. Bess continues to fret: "She and George had many little misunderstandings and sometimes found fault with each other, but the two girls were very close. The thought that George might be a prisoner was almost too much for Bess" (32). Such revelations, although handled cursorily, are expected by readers of the original series and may even be the reason we remember what do about the characters (when we do not remember the stories themselves). There are countless other omissions of this sort in the French editions and while, individually, they may appear trivial, the exchanges between the two cousins reveal a great deal about the dynamics of their relationship. French readers, excluded from some of the cousins' interactions, may have a slightly different understanding of George and Bess than Anglophone readers do.

In spite of the omissions and attenuations, there are, paradoxically, a number of examples in the French editions that illustrate the close attention the translators brought to these two characters, and more specifically to Bess, whose femininity and epicurean appetite must have appealed to their Gallic sensibilities. Indeed, there are instances when the translators flesh out scenes where Bess is raving about food. In the translation of *Nancy's Mysterious Letter*, an entire paragraph is added to a scene where

Bess is indulging in cocoa and sweet cakes. The narrator goes on about Bess's *"péché mignon"* ("partiality") for *"la gourmandise"* (fondness for food), and describes her charming face with her laughing eyes, and her plump but delightful "silhouette," which provoked the envy of other girls: "La gourmandise était le péché mignon de Bess qui se trouvait trop grosse. Elle était pourtant charmante avec ses joues roses creusée de fossettes, ses yeux rieurs, et malgré un léger embonpoint, sa silhouette faisait bien des envieuses" (12).

The translators play up Bess's femininity and accentuate her vulnerability in passages where it is not even suggested in the original. In *The Mystery of the 99 Steps* for example, when Nancy is about to venture down the steps alluded to in the title, the original reads simply: "Bess and George followed her to the steps" (145). Joba writes: "Marion la suivit, Bess, tremblante, fit de même. Tout, se disait-elle, plutôt que de rester seule!" (*Alice à Paris* 157). (Marion followed her [Alice], and Bess, trembling, did the same. "Anything," she said to herself, "is better than staying here alone!")

In some cases, the translators give Bess lines of dialogue, and even thoughts, that are originally uttered by other characters. For example, in *Alice à Paris* (*99 Steps*), Bess ponders an attractive man the three young women have just met at a ball, expressing a thought that had been accorded to Nancy in the original version (69). Joba even grants Bess greater sophistication than American readers might associate with her character. In the translation of *The Mystery of the 99 Steps*, she distinguishes Bess's attitude from Marion's silly joking-around about the Venus de Milo (Marion asks where the statue lost her arms) by endowing her with an artistic appreciation that is only obliquely suggested in the original. In the English version, Mr. Drew answers George first, joking that if he knew where the statue had lost her arms, he might go look for them (54). Bess replies simply that one thing she would like to see is Da Vinci's *Mona Lisa*. In the French, Alice is the one who answers Marion, and Bess "qui avait un sens artistique plus développé que sa cousine" (who had a more developed artistic sense than her cousin) chides: "Oh! Marion tes plaisanteries ne sont pas drôles! ... [J]e m'étonne qu'Alice ait relevé ta remarque stupide..." (61). ("Oh! Marion, your jokes are not funny! I'm surprised that Alice even acknowledged your stupid remark.")

A comparison of the description of Bess and George in *The Mystery of the 99 Steps* and in *Alice à Paris* reveals the special interest the translators have in Bess's appearance. The original reads: "Blond Bess's warm smile revealed two dimples. George, with close-cropped dark hair, was slim and athletic — the exact opposite of her slightly plump cousin" (2). In the translation, Joba adds a few details to Bess's description, noting her pink complexion, round cheeks, and "very feminine" appearance. ("Bess était blonde, rose, très feminine, un peu trop replète à son gré et, quand elle souriait, deux fossettes creusaient ses joues pleines. Marion, elle, était brune, mince et musclée; elle portait les cheveux coupés très court et affectait des allures garconnières" (4).)

In this passage, George is given equal time, and Joba even emphasizes what she calls Marion's "allures garçonières" (her boyish look). But frequently, the translators do not accord George the same respect they offer Bess. Sometimes, descriptions of George are removed entirely from the translation or, on one occasion, in *The Mystery of the 99 Steps*, she is cut from a scene altogether (43; *Alice à Paris* 49). When the translator does preserve George's look, it is more in a critical way, and as a means to contrast her with Bess. In *The Moonstone Castle Mystery*, George is described as: "dark brunette, very slender, and tomboyish" (1). Voilier translates this fairly literally, but adds, unnecessarily it seems, that George in no way resembles her cousin Bess: "[Marion], brune, mince, et élancée, ne ressemblait guère à Bess qui était sa cousine: on eût dit un garçon manqué!" (*Alice et la Pierre d'Onyx* 8).

Of all the main characters in the series, George Fayne is the one who is most drastically altered by the translators. There almost appears to be a collective intent to subdue her character. Many of George's lines of dialogue are omitted, and some of her lines are even given to Bess, further suggesting a preference for George's cousin (cf. *Moss-Covered Mansion* 35, 78 [*Alice et la Fusée Spatiale* 43, 86]; *Mysterious Letter* 4 [*Quand Alice* 9]; *99 Steps* 109 [*Alice à Paris* 120]). All three translators strive to tone down her personality. Some passages or phrases that bring to light George's gusto and keen spirit of adventure are cut entirely from the translations (*Moss-Covered Mansion* 142, *99 Steps* 96, and *Mirror Bay* 17). One of the distinctive marks of George's character is her unshakable fighting spirit, and when Bess fears, in *The Moonstone Castle Mystery*, that she and the others will not stand a chance if the owners of the Moonstone come back to claim it, George disdainfully replies: "Why not? We're not weaklings!" (160). In the French version, the men Bess imagines are "armed," and George's reply is edited out.

The most incomprehensible and unfortunate change the translators bring to Marion is in their failure to infuse her fully with George's boyishness and, perhaps more specifically, George's own enjoyment of her boyishness. One particularly good example of the translators' unfaithful rendering of her character is in *Quand Alice Rencontre Alice*. In the original (*Nancy's Mysterious Letter*), the ghostwriter is unabashed in his portrayal: "George, her cheeks rosy and her eyes sparking from the keen November air, strode into the hallway and doffed her boyish ulster.... She was proud of her masculine name, and dressed the part" (95). Joba betrays George's character in her translation, insisting that underneath her "affectations," George is actually quite feminine: 'Marion, très sportive, s'habillait avec goût mais simplement et affectait une allure garçonnière, ce qui ne l'empêchait pas d'être excellente ménagère et, dans le fond, très féminine" (91). (Marion, very athletic, dressed tastefully but simply, and affected a boyish look, which did not prevent her from being an excellent housekeeper and deep down, very feminine.") Marion is clearly not George in French disguise; she takes on an identity of her own, one that would surely leave readers of the original series feeling cheated.

To make matters worse, some of George's best and most humorous lines are excluded from the French editions. Jokes and comebacks that bring her character to life are conspicuously absent from the French editions, such as the one in *The Moonstone Castle Mystery* where she shouts: "I knew being a tomboy would come in handy someday!" (148) or when she learns in *The Mystery of the 99 Steps* that she and Nancy and Bess are to be exchange guests in France and she inquires: "Will I be in exchange for a boy?" (3). Deletions of passages like these add up over the course of the series, and in effect result in a different character.

Unfortunately for George, her original character does not fit in to the stories as they have been reproduced in French, for a French audience. Giggly Bess Marvin, the darling of the translators, on the other hand, comes through in French perhaps even more blonde and plump than she is in the original. And despite the name changes and a few modifications in Nancy's and Hannah's backgrounds, and in Nancy's relationships with her father and with Ned, the changes brought to these characters and to the heroine herself do not, in the end, significantly alter their identities or personalities. Thus, for the most part, with the very regrettable exception of George, the main characters of the Nancy Drew series do come out "intact" on the other side of translation. We are left to wonder, however, whether Alice really can be Nancy and Bess be Bess, if Marion is not an accurate replica of George.

Although extremely disappointing, the translators' consistent, and therefore intentional, downplaying of George's boyishness and her humor exemplifies what translation actually is and the hazards it can entail. Translation does not just involve linguistic conveyance of words from one language into another. Translation is interpretation and adaptation, driven by culture, psychology, politics, and countless other factors. Understanding why the translators made the choices that they did, in terms of the changes they brought to the Nancy Drew series, would require a much broader and deeper cultural and socio-linguistic investigation than my comparative readings of the stories can allow. Yet what I have demonstrated here is that translators, in their reproduction of a text, assume an authorial role (a role for which they often go unrecognized); the creative work that goes into the translation of a novel results in a new piece of fiction. Accordingly, one might even assert that the translators of Nancy Drew have a certain claim on the authorship of the series. Whether they render the originals as literally as possible or they modify, incorporate, and revise along the way, as they have done in the case of Nancy Drew, the translators play an integral role in the identity of Carolyn Keene (or Caroline Quine as the name is spelled in French). When Melanie Rehak asks, as she does in the title of her book chapter devoted to the 1980 lawsuit filed by Grosset and Dunlap over breach of contract and copyright infringement, "Will the Real Carolyn Keene Please Stand Up?," translators have every legitimate reason to jump to their feet, right alongside Mildred, Harriet, Walter, and the rest of the ghost writers who continue to produce the series to this day. While unsuspecting fans of the original series might be surprised, and even outraged, to discover some of the changes that surface in the translations, it is thanks to translators that the series has flourished and touched the lives of millions of young readers across the globe. In some ways, Nancy Drew herself, so assured and solid in her heroism, defies the risks of translation: no matter what the language, the core of her character will stride right through with confidence.

Works Cited

"Alice Aujourd'hui dans les Villes." *Humanité*. July 22 1996. http://www.humanite.fr/jour nal/1996-07-22/1996-07-22-757013.

Beeson, Diana, and Bonnie Brennen. "Translating Nancy Drew from Print to Film." In *Rediscovering Nancy Drew*. Eds. Carolyn Stewart Dyer and Nancy Tillman Romalov. Iowa City: University of Iowa Press, 1995, pp. 193–207.

Billman, Carol. *The Secret of the Stratemeyer Syndicate: Nancy Drew, The Hardy Boys and the Million Dollar Fiction Factory*. New York: Ungar Publishing, 1986.

Deane, Paul. *Mirrors of American Culture: Children's Fiction Series in the Twentieth Century*. Metuchen, N.J.: Scarecrow, 1991.

Keene, Carolyn. *The Clue in the Diary.* New York: Grosset and Dunlap, 1962.

_____. *The Clue of the Whistling Bagpipes.* New York: Grosset and Dunlap, 1964.

_____. *The Moonstone Castle Mystery.* New York: Grosset and Dunlap, 1963.

_____. *Mystery of the Moss-Covered Mansion.* New York: Grosset and Dunlap, 1971.

_____. *The Mystery of the 99 Steps.* New York: Grosset and Dunlap, 1966.

_____. *The Mystery of the Tolling Bell.* New York: Grosset and Dunlap, 1976.

_____. *Nancy's Mysterious Letter.* New York: Grosset and Dunlap, 1932.

_____. *The Quest of the Missing Map.* New York: Grosset and Dunlap, 1942.

_____. *The Secret of Mirror Bay.* New York: Grosset and Dunlap, 1972.

_____. *The Secret of the Old Clock.* New York: Grosset and Dunlap, 1930.

_____. *The Sign of the Twisted Candles.* New York: Grosset and Dunlap, 1968.

Plunkett-Powell, Karen. *The Nancy Drew Scrapbook: 60 Years of America's Favorite Teenage Sleuth.* New York: St. Martin's Press, 1993.

Quine, Caroline. *Alice à Paris.* Trans. Anne Joba. Bibliothèque Verte. Paris: Librairie Hachette, 1973.

_____. *Alice Détective.* Trans. Hélène Commin. Bibliothèque Verte. Paris: Librairie Hachette, 1973.

_____. *Alice en Écosse.* Trans. Anne Joba. Bibliothèque Verte. Paris: Librairie Hachette, 1966.

_____. *Alice et la Dame du Lac.* Trans. Anne Joba. Bibliothèque Verte. Paris: Librairie Hachette, 1975.

_____. *Alice et la Fusée Spatiale.* Trans. Anne Joba. Bibliothèque Verte. Paris: Librairie Hachette, 1977.

_____. *Alice et la Pierre d'Onyx.* Trans. Claude Voilier. Bibliothèque Verte. Paris: Librairie Hachette, 1976.

_____. *Alice et le Carnet Vert.* Trans. Anne Joba. Biliothèque Verte. Paris: Hachette, 1964.

_____. *Alice et le Chandelier.* Trans. Hélène Commin. Idéal-Bibliothèque. Paris: Librairie Hachette, 1971.

_____. *Quand Alice Rencontre Alice.* Trans. Anne Joba. Bibliothèque Verte. Paris: Librairie Hachette, 1975.

Rehak, Melanie. *Girl Sleuth: Nancy Drew and the Women Who Created Her.* Orlando, Fla.: Harcourt, 2005.

Shangraw Fox, Lea. "Nancy Drew World," http://www.nancydrewworld.com/Frenchframe.html.

Soderbergh, Peter. "The Stratemeyer Strain: Educators and the Juvenile Series Books, 1900–1973." *Journal of Popular Culture* 7 (Spring 1974): 864–72.

Race and Xenophobia in the Nancy Drew Novels: "What kind of society...?"

Leona W. Fisher

Tracking racial and ethnic attitudes — implicit as well as explicit — through the seventy-seven years of Nancy Drew's existence demonstrates that, even when attempts have been made to revise in the direction of increased "tolerance" (itself a problematic concept), the texts assume a white implied reader whose sense of default privilege, "colorblindness," and xenophobia can be counted upon to remain unexamined. In Catharine Stimpson's words about the absence of women in history, "omissions, distortions, and trivializations" (55) of racial and ethnic "others" continue to mar the books that contain so many women's favorite cultural icons. The question that Donnarae MacCann asked twenty years ago in "Nancy Drew and the Myth of White Supremacy" (in reference particularly to the 1930s Nancys) continues to be relevant today: "What kind of society is it that entertains one group of children at the expense of another?" (135). Because the books span three-quarters of a century of our history, it is possible to begin to answer that question.

I too would prefer the discourse of "white supremacy" rather than that of "racism" to explain the series' persistent ideology. Like bell hooks in her 1994 *Killing Rage: Ending Racism*, I am persuaded that "many changes in social policy and social attitudes that were once seen as ways to end racial domination have served to reinforce and perpetuate white supremacy" (186). Seeing white supremacy, even among enlightened academic whites, as "all-pervasive ... both as ideology and as behavior," hooks points out that "when liberal whites fail to understand how they can and/or do embody white supremacist values and beliefs even though they may not embrace racism as prejudice or domination (especially domination that involves coercive control), they cannot recognize the ways their actions support and affirm the very structure of racist domination and oppression that they profess to wish to see eradicated" [185].

This attitude parallels the implicit imperialism that characterized the Stratemeyer Syndicate books from the beginning — not surprisingly, since Edward Stratemeyer belonged to the same world that produced the following 1910 statement (by white Frenchman Jules Harmand) justifying turn-of-the-twentieth-century colonialism:

> It is necessary ... to accept as a principle and point of departure the fact that there is a hierarchy of races and civilizations, and that we [white Frenchmen] belong to the superior race and civilization, still recognizing that, while superiority confers rights, it imposes strict obligation in return. The basic legitimation of conquest over native peoples is the conviction of our superiority, not merely our mechanical, economic, and military superiority, but our moral superiority. Our dignity rests on that quality, and it underlies our right to direct the rest of humanity [qtd. in Said 17].

It is an easy leap from this statement to a justification for the moral "colonizing" of boys and girls (and persons of color) using a similar discursive model — based on race, class, age, and moral superiority. It is not a paradigm that can withstand much self-scrutiny, but the Stratemeyer Syndicate was, after all, the company that produced the enormously popular series Bomba the Jungle Boy from 1923 to 1938 — and confidently revived it in 1953, even as awareness of oppressive colonial policies had begun in the United States and as African nations were initiating their struggles for independence.

Almost from the beginning, the archetypal girl sleuth and her creators — ghostly and real — have had to contend with American history and its discontents around issues of race and immigration. Conceived by Edward Stratemeyer and perpetuated by his daughters (particularly Harriet Stratemeyer Adams), Nancy Drew was born into Jim Crow America in 1930 and would need repeatedly to face what W.E.B. Du Bois called the central "problem of the twentieth century," that of the "color-line" (9). As early as 1935, Harriet Adams was writing (with a characteristic tone of *noblesse oblige* and evasive euphemism) to the editors at the Stratemeyer Syndicate's publisher Grosset and Dunlap, about their other popular series, the Hardy Boys: "We think it best, owing to the fact that there is some feeling in this country between whites and blacks, that the jacket for this volume should not picture anyone of the dark-skinned race" (SSR/NYPL, box 37).

Objections to the series' race and ethnic politics continued to be leveled by the books' readers and their parents, however, and in 1948 Mrs. Adams responded more defensively to charges of anti–Semitism and "race prejudice" in the Hardys' *The Hidden Harbor Mystery*: "The word 'Jew' is not mentioned ... anywhere ... in the book," and "On the subject of Negroes, the woman [who complained] has more of a case, but the whole idea revolves around 'Can't a Negro be an evil-doer in a story?'" She does admit that no persons of color are heroes in the tale, either, but she insists that the book makes a "missionary" (in other words, imperialist?) statement: "Unfortunately, there is no fine, kindly Negro character portrayed as a contrast, but certainly there is nothing in the book either said or implied which should give any child reader the idea all colored folks are bad.... Furthermore, there is one very good bit of missionary work in the story. In several places it denounces lynching. What could be more timely!" (SSR/NYPL, box 37).

As Melanie Rehak has recently written about Adams, "Harriet's genteel manners failed to cover the racism so typical of her generation and class ... the 'soft racism' that passed for tolerance in her circles" (244). Or, as James P. Jones wrote over thirty years ago in "Nancy Drew, WASP Super Girl of the 1930s," "The treatment of national groups [in the Stratemeyer books] read like a quota chart of the 1920s immigration law" (711–12). In an unpublished internal "History of [the] Stratemeyer Syndicate" in the Nancy Axelrad papers at Yale University, the anonymous writer (probably Axelrad herself, who had become a partner in the syndicate by the 1970s) seeks to justify and explain what s/he calls the "nativism" of the syndicate's policies in the 1920s and 1930s: "In her [Adams's] defense, stereotypes are not created in vacuums. As with *clichés*, stereotypes have a measure of truth in them. Many blacks did speak in dialect and many Orientals did sound like Charlie Chan" (76–77). S/he admits: "Blacks were friendly and harmless [in the books], but they always spoke in dialect and were not very ambitious or intelligent. Foreigners and others who acted 'different' were sinister and always subject to suspicion" (82). These admissions certainly do not exonerate Adams or the syndicate; rather, they validate the parents' objections and demonstrate that the Stratemeyers uncritically accepted the white "consensus about the character of African Americans" (and others) that MacCann interrogates in her essay.

Numerous critics (see, for example, Deane, Jones, MacCann, and Nash) analyze egregious examples of racism from *The Secret in the Old Clock* (#1) and *The Hidden Staircase* (#2), the first two "breeders" published in 1930, because they make the case so vividly with their appalling insensitivity to difference. The comic alcoholic caretaker in *The Secret of the Old Clock* speaks in an embarrassing dialect and "points to blacks as unruly, untrustworthy, dissipated, and mentally deficient" (MacCann 133). The black maid and accomplice to the villain of *Staircase* is described as "vicious," even as she is represented as a mammy figure *manquée*, with what MacCann calls "a kind of mock-dialect, since the emphasis is not on the oral qualities but on suggesting a lack of intelligence" (134). She is usually referred to as "the colored woman" or "the fat [or old] colored woman" and speaks in the Stratemeyer's peculiar version of black dialect: "How you talk! Crime? What you mean crime? I's just an old culled woman who makes her victuals workin'! You can't bluff me with yo' scary talk" (*Hidden Staircase* 191).

Ilana Nash, in her recent *American Sweethearts: Teenage Girls in Twentieth-Century Popular Culture*, has discovered perhaps the most crucial structural function of these early black (and other subordinate) characters, in relation to her larger point about Nancy's attractiveness as an inspiring role model for girls. She writes that while the early series' "messages about gender are .... mixed, ... those regarding class and race are more consistently negative." As a result,

> the series' fundamentally retrograde social politics camouflage its more progressive elements, allowing Nancy's image of powerful personhood to pass unchecked. At the same time, however, the radical notion of girls' personhood also becomes less radical when we realize how heavily it depends upon her [Nancy's] negative interactions with the oppressed. These reviled characters in fact help to constitute Nancy's freedoms: she achieves her status as a full person partly through scenes that juxtapose her with characters who are less than persons. The ego strength Nancy models for readers, then, necessarily carries a toxic link to bigotry [53].

In Nash's analysis, Nancy's compelling characterization depends largely on her conquest of (and moral superiority to) inferior or suspect persons of color and low social class — repeatedly reinvoking the colonialist project as theorized in the nineteenth and twentieth centuries ("the basic legitimation of conquest over native peoples").

As both Adams's and the "History's" defenses suggest, the racism and xenophobia were probably an inadvertent "default" position (what linguists would call the "unmarked case"); except when challenged, the consensus about white privilege was unconscious and largely unexamined by any member of the syndicate or its publishers. Written near the beginning of the Great Depression, *Nancy's Mysterious Letter* (#8 1932) includes some of the series' most egregious unremarked classism as well as portrays Nancy's insensitive exchange with a Polish woman who works as a maid at a "venerable mansion" across the street from the Drews. The narrative tells us without irony — and focalizing through Nancy — that the maid is "a brawny woman redolent of yellow soap and with bubbles from the wash-tub's suds fresh on her arms." When Nancy demanded to know if anyone is home and reports a crime, the maid does not understand her: "'Not speak Engulsh, me,' she smiled. 'You speak maybe Polish?'" Nancy's reply would be comical if it were not so appalling, lapsing as it does into the same pidgin English as the maid's and punctuated to suggest a rise in volume: "Please try to understand. Mailman — letters — somebody steal them.... Lots of letters. In a bag! Bad man steal!" (12). The book is also dotted with obsequious "colored porters" who all sound and act like Step 'n' Fetchit (for example: "'Scuze me, sah, but de bank am closin'.... Ah just natcherly got to shet de do" [78]). While the 1968 revision omits the Polish maid and the black porters, if anything it accentuates the classlessness of the villain (who prefers "kind of flashy" cuff links) and the shabbiness of other characters (46). Trappings of privilege remain as well: Bess has a mink-collared suit, for example, and the girls fly off to New York at a moment's notice. The plot's non sequiturs and flagrant coincidences have been smoothed over and made more logical, and the offensive dialects eliminated, but the basic premises and implicit sense of white privilege are unchanged.

The 1937 *The Whispering Statue* (#14) further illustrates the casualness of the attitude toward "non–Americans" in its depiction of a "swarthy, heavy-set foreigner" of unnamed ethnicity who happens to own a monkey and sounds like this: "'You own-a da place?' he questioned Nancy.... 'I do-a good work....' 'I no cheat. I honest man. When I make-a da promise, my word fine'" (71). Ironically, the Italian stereotype is re-evoked by the 1970 revision, which retains nothing of the original plot except the statue itself and the following reference to an Italian woman who "never got over a feeling of homesickness" after emigrating and "passed away while still in her twenties" (15). The gratuitous empathetic reference seems unconsciously compensatory.

In 1940 a Grosset and Dunlap editor explicitly advised omitting "the very touchy race question" from a Nancy Drew novel (SSR/NYPL, box

37), probably in reference to the about-to-be-published *The Mystery at the Moss-Covered Mansion* (#18 1941). Yet, the finished product reveals that neither the syndicate nor the publisher actually understood what that omission might mean. In fact, the story contains the usual smiling "colored" maid (17) who speaks in awkwardly-spelled dialect ("He say to tell yo' dat so far nothing done develop from de Karter clue" and "He say yo' is not to look for him befo' noon" [174]), as well as a "swarthy" (48) villain with the foreign-sounding name of Ramo ("a gypsy-like looking man ... who wore large dangling earrings and a bandana on the back of his head" [47]) whose sister works as a "psychic reader" and exerts criminal control over her helpless daughter (214). A peripheral character, a servant named Bongo whose origin is the "jungle," is referred to as a "savage" who would not notice that Nancy needed medical attention (211), and the setting is populated by lions, snakes, parrots, monkeys, and leopards (in case the reader has missed the connection to primitivism). It is impossible to see how this book avoided the "touchy race question." In fact, when the book was revised in 1971, the bizarre plot could not be salvaged and the setting is moved to Florida, where only the exotic animals are retained. But even in this attempt to eliminate racist overtones, there is an awkward mention of "Asiatic tourists" (Is this a term that was ever used in ordinary discourse?) and a gratuitous-sounding anti-imperialist speech on the Aztecs (151), both revealing the syndicate's continuing discomfort with (or misunderstanding of) its own racial politics.

When the publisher asked for sweeping revisions and condensations of the early Nancys and Hardys in April 1957, Harriet stalled (as she had balked at earlier criticisms), and by December 1958 Grosset and Dunlap had begun to lose patience (SSR/NYPL, box 39). While it is not clear exactly what was holding up the syndicate's revisions, Harriet Adams only later admitted that those changes included more than linguistic updates (frocks to dresses, roadsters to convertibles, omission of long natural descriptions, and so on): "All the books are being reread and each interracial [*sic*] reference is being examined and changed if necessary so that it is not offensive. We are removing dialect, and seeing that black people are not depicted in demeaning jobs. It is difficult to know whether to call them black, Negro or colored, but we check with the NAACP for the current preference when making the changes. For a long time it has been company policy never to make the "bad men" members of a racial or religious minority" [SSR/NYPL, box 39].

As Nash notes, Adams's "public comments about the process were more grudging than gracious" (55) and remained so throughout her life, but they also reveal a failure to understand the problem.

The solution to accusations of prejudice was, as many have noted, simply to omit the black and ethnic characters and their stereotyped discourse, thereby erasing the presence of racial and linguistic difference. But, Paul Deane asks: "How .... can healthy ideas be revealed about persons who never appear?" (114). "The result of Adams's efforts," writes Nash, "was less a 'cleaning up' than an ethnic cleansing" (55). The erasure of ethnic and racial stereotypes is somewhat more complex than notions of elimination suggest, however; instead, Nancy Drew books have for the last fifty years represented those of other-than-white race, Anglo-Saxon ethnicity, and "American" origin euphemistically — as, for example, "dark-complexioned" rather than "swarthy," or menacing, or slant-eyed, but often without naming their national identities or ethnic origins. The effects of this second, ostensibly "color blind," strategy are both confusing and insidious.

While many children's books in the 1960s and 1970s decidedly changed in the direction of cultural diversity and ethnic and racial specificity (as a glance at the Newbery Award winners for the decade 1970–1980 immediately reveals), in the Stratemeyer revisions that began in 1959, modernization became less a matter of adding "difference" than a deliberate attempt to render it invisible or implicit. *The Clue in the Old Album* (#24), originally published in 1947 and revised in 1977, provides many examples of this "whitening." In both, an unruly young girl, Rose, is being reared by her grandmother, Mrs. Struthers. Rose's mother, now dead, had been married to a "gypsy violinist" who has gone missing and is believed to be in thrall to a "mad," self-proclaimed gypsy king.

In the 1947 version, the exotic gypsy, Madame Mazorka, invites Nancy, her father, and Mrs. Struthers to tea and fully plays the part: "The charming hostess was known in the community as a patron of the arts, particularly music. Attired in a gown of flowing gray chiffon, she received her guests graciously. "'Eet ees a pleasure to see you, Mrs. Struthers, Mr. Drew and Miss Drew,'" she greeted them. "'You have enjoyed ze recital, yes?'" (7).

In the revised version, "The charming hostess received her guests graciously" (1977 7), period, without any hint of residual linguistic idiosyncrasy — or the chiffon dress.

In conversations with Nancy about Rose, the 1947 Mrs. Struthers minces no words as she describes both her daughter's romantic foolishness at having fallen in love with someone clearly below her in class and her son-in-law's suspect ethnic origins. She explains Rose's transgressive behavior in terms of her parentage: "Perhaps it's because of her heritage on her father's side.... You see, Rose's father was a very talented violinist. Also, he was a gypsy, and gypsies, as you know, do not live as conventionally as we do. My daughter became entranced with him.... [Rose's] gypsy father deserted them." (16–17). In the revision, almost all signs of "suspect" ethnicity (as well as class) are erased and the anti-gypsy comments have been softened: "Perhaps it's because she does not have the strong hand of a father" (14) and the "entrancement" of Mrs. Struthers's daughter is partially explained by the legitimating adjective "Spanish" and the addition of one sentence: "Rose's father was a Spanish gipsy and a talented violinist. He gave many concerts in this country. My daughter became entranced with him..." (15). The sentence about desertion is omitted.

Later in the earlier text, when Nancy and her "escort," Ned, are in the gypsy camp, one of the gypsies is accordingly described in this tone of exoticism and xenophobia: "Her fierce, blazing eyes studied Nancy appraisingly.... Turning to a couple of children, she said something in the gypsies' Romany language which neither Ned nor Nancy could understand" (1947 38). Similarly, in answer to a question about Rose's father's origin, the response is the indeterminate "Somewhere out West, I believe" (1947 39). Seeking to "clean up" the obvious ethnocentrism, the 1977 revision sanitizes the scene and preserves the more-respectable "Spanish" origin; he is no longer from "Somewhere out West" but from "'Spain, I believe'" (1977 34). Gone too are the references to "Romany," and the "fierce, blazing" eyes have become merely the clichéd "flashing" (33).

Yet, despite the cultural erasures, in the post–1959 new books the implicit distinction between "us" and "them" remains entrenched. For example, while Nancy travels widely around the world, the books never lose their relentlessly imperialist attitudes (even though Harriet Adams bragged that they never produced a book set in a foreign country unless a syndicate member — usually herself — had been there). For example, in *The Star Sapphire Mystery* (#45 1968), Kenya is referred to only as "East Africa" — an odd gesture at a time when this nation was newly independent from Great Britain, if going through its post-independence struggles in the aftermath of Mau Mau — and Nancy goes on safari. Joking in response to a quip by Ned, she asks, "'And have me become one of the chief's wives?' Then she became serious. She knew [as Nancy always 'knows' everything] that while tribal customs were kept, the men, women and children were becoming more civilized and educated all the time and polygamy was fast becoming a thing of the past" (129). The Kenyan natives (probably Maasai, but not so named) are introduced as carrying "spears," their eating implements are "crude," and their children are gratuitously "handsome"—and this novel was published ten years after the revisions of the early books began.

Even a random survey of books published after the 1959 date reveals either evasion or condescension, both before and after Simon and Schuster's publishing takeover of the series from Grosset and Dunlap in 1979 and Harriet Adams's death in 1982. Although one of the central reasons for the scheduled revisions was the erasure of ethnic and racial slurs from the earlier books, the never-revised *The Haunted Showboat* (Number 35 1957) contains servants and another African-American character, who are all sentimentalized and dehumanized in their coziness: "A moment later an elderly colored couple, wearing a maid's and a butler's uniforms, came from the house. They were introduced as Mammy Matilda and Pappy Cole. The two smiled pleasantly. Then, as Pappy Cole started to unload the car, Mammy Maltilda said to the visitors: 'I sure hope you all have a fine time durin' your visit here'" (41). In *The Hidden Window Mystery* (#34 1956), written just one year before and revised to eliminate these elements in 1975, the Charlottesville, Virginia, setting seems to give the excuse for a similar treatment of a black maid and several references by Bess to "romantic" (116) and "quaint" (143) slave quarters. It also contains a typical depiction of the ethnically-indeterminate female conspirator: "Nancy and Hannah saw a strange woman standing there. Her bleached blond hair, blown by the wind, stuck out straight from her head. She was short and sallow-complexioned. Her dark eyes blazed" (5). In *The Mystery of the Fire Dragon* (#38 1961), set in Hong Kong, the Chinese are described as residing in the "Orient," one of the characters has exotic "Eurasian features," and George is (implausibly) allowed to impersonate her successfully. Chinese persons bow a great deal, begin all their celebrations with firecrackers, and are described as "quaint." The combination of erased difference and condescending tourism may have more to do with anti–Communist sentiments than with overt racism at this point in the Cold War, but it is instructive to see how little difference there is between this text and the earlier (and then not yet revised) *The Clue of the Leaning Chimney* (#26 1949), which also featured Chinese art, and characters whose name was also Soong, as if that were the only possible Chinese-sounding name the syndicate could come up with across twelve years.

Yet Adams was clearly alert to, even nervous about, the criticisms she had received. Notes in Adams's hand for possible revisions of the new novels *The Invisible Intruder* (#46 1969) and *The Phantom of Pine Hill* (#42 1965) and others, even though these suggestions were not accepted by Grosset and Dunlap, suggest changing the word "spook" to "ghost" (and "queer" to "strange," but that's a different story), revealing hypersensitivity to possible misinterpretations of the old-fashioned word (for example, see SSR/NYPL, box 239). Multiculturalism also seems gratuitous and overdone in many of the books, without becoming materialist or concrete: superficial or celebratory references to American natives in Ohio (#42), Arizona (*The Crooked Banister* #48 1971), Nevada (*The Secret of the Forgotten City* #52 1975), and Peru (*The Clue in the Crossword Cipher* #44 1967) abound. *The Secret of the Forgotten City*, for example, contains many stereotyped Indian references. The suspected thief of a buried gold treasure is "five feet ten, rather large-boned, had tanned, tightly drawn skin, black eyes, and shiny black hair. 'Part Indian,' Nancy told herself" (4), as if that explains everything. There are also references to "garbled" Spanish (99), which of course Nancy can translate: "I've traveled in Mexico a good bit,' she said, 'and picked up some of the dialects.' ... Nancy spoke to the men in the vernacular of the Spanish-speaking province from which she thought they had come" (98); the group's leader has "a long black mustache twisted at the ends" and wears a sombrero (100). Similarly, in *The Clue in the Crossword Cipher*, Nancy meets a "pleasant-looking man, definitely a descendant of the Incas.... His head was broad, and he had high cheekbones and an aquiline nose. The man's eyes were somewhat almond-shaped, like an Oriental's, and his expression kindly and humorous" (100). Predictably, Nancy is able to speak to him in his native Quechuan. Then, when she and Bess encounter some children, "'They're adorable children,' said Bess, 'and they look happy, but certainly poor.' 'Yes,' Nancy agreed. 'Don't you long to do something for them?'" (115). Considering that Bess uses almost the same language when she meets her first alpaca ("Aren't they darling?" [118–19]), it is difficult to take either her or Nancy's tourist response to the children as sincere or committed.

Many later texts present a range of minor characters whose names constitute a United Nations–like taxonomy of racial and ethnic varieties, usually for no apparent narrative purpose. But occasionally the books use ethnic difference to preach a point, as in *The Music Festival Mystery* (#157 2000), in which Bess comes across as an ignorant xenophobe, asking the Australian Cyril, "Why don't you have more of an accent?" and an Asian girl, "Joann? Is that an Asian name?" while George "nudged her again" (7); and George states clumsily: "Life's a lot simpler when you're a detective.... You get to suspect *everyone*, regardless of race, creed, or national origin" (66; emphasis in original). George's comment seems superficially liberated, but in fact can be read as an implicit attack on so-called "PC" defenders of fairness, particularly in light of Stratemeyer history (including Adams's earlier comment about anti-lynching "missionary work").

The new Nancy Drew: Girl Detective series that began in 2004 may succeed in further "whitening" the River Heights world, insofar as that is possible, if only because the clumsy first-person narrative voice makes it nearly impossible to interlace external authorial attitudes into the discourse. It would be awkward for Nancy to spend much time describing or commenting on racial or ethnic issues when she is stretched enough simply trying to tell the story in a plausible way. (After all, she has to keep commenting on her own wardrobe choices and propensity for running out of gas.)

Yet, Nancy Drew: Girl Detective, *Stop the Clock* (#12 2005) certainly continues the implicitly xenophobic cultural representations of racial, ethnic, and linguistic others, if only through adherence to the (revised) discursive frame in place since the late 1950s, which includes silence, innuendo, and mystery surrounding issues of "foreignness." Thus, when Nancy encounters her "friend Lucia Gonsalvo," "our own River Heights fortuneteller," she states, irrelevantly: "She has an accent, but I've never been able to place it — and Lucia has never talked about where she lived before she moved to River Heights" (7). There is nothing in the plot that requires this detail — but it of course reminds the reader of the Romany gypsies from sixty years before. When Lucia appears again one hundred pages later, she is mentioned by a suspect in the theft of a library clock as "Lucy Gonsolvo" (with a nickname and the replacing of the "a" with an "o") (108); "Lucy" may be the character's substitution but the misspelling is almost certainly the editor's, revealing editorial disrespect, not the character's. Attempting to cast blame on Lucia and deflect attention from himself, the suspect, Mr. Franklin, remarks, "She kept saying it reminded her of a clock she used to have back in the old country.... That's what she called it, the *old country*— but she never did say where that was." And Nancy comments, again with no overt relevance to the plot, "I don't think anyone really knows where she's from" (108). As a red herring, this detail seems at best gratuitous (and these books are very short — only approximately 140–150 pages each) and at worst ethnocentric and anti-immigrationist, casting de facto doubt on Lucia's legitimacy as an "American." She has been allowed to assimilate (by no longer having a nationality of origin) but is denied both an ethnicity and a specific language.

It will be interesting to see if the Stratemeyer Syndicate's patrician and imperialistic attitude — as well as its view of American exceptionalism — will continue to follow Nancy into the second decade of the twenty-first century. Certainly the "foreign" names and racial descriptions continue in the series: in *Framed* (#15), the central suspect is an Italian, Prince Carlo; in *Dangerous Plays* (#16), "a tall man with dreadlocks" named Duncan Smithson sings reggae but is never called black or African British (86–87); in *Dressed to Steal* (#22), two of the (false) suspects are a French man named Jean-Georges de Vouvray and a possible Asian-American named "Michael Tsao, Esq.," neither of whom is ever referred to in culturally or ethnically specific terms. Even the Asian "model minority" is given an implicit nod in the brief characterization of the "workaholic" Melissa Wong, "the ritziest florist in River Heights ... who was oblivious to everything but flowers, flowers, flowers" (#11 72).

Given the importance of polarizing discursive frames in the current national debate on immigration — including conceptual and descriptive words and phrases such as "illegal alien," "real American," and "NIMBY" (Not In My Back Yard) — we can only hope that even formulaic wish-fulfillment children's books will not be able to continue to suppress or trivialize the enriching varieties of American and transnational experience. In defense of the syndicate's early years, both the archival materials and the revised texts reveal a willingness to grow and change, albeit reluctantly. As in the past, perhaps the responses of children and their parents to the new books will force the publishers (and their ghost writers) to re-examine their "colorblindness" and sense of white privilege, and substitute "a color conscience, a meta-color consciousness" (Wu 151); for, as Frank H. Wu writes in *Yellow: Race in America Beyond Black and White,*

> People who truly would like to be color blind must be willful to the point of perversity. Imagine what their lives would be like if they censored race fastidiously. They must assume that it is equally likely that a white, black, and Asian person whom they encounter is foreign-born, speaks Chinese, or is named "Wu." They could only deduce, without directly asking, that it was the Asian person who was foreign-born, spoke Chinese, and was named "Wu" if they impermissibly relied on race. They could not decide that the Chinese restaurant with many Asian diners is "authentic." They would have to refrain from telling two friends who were meeting one another for the first time beneath the clock tower at Grand Central Sta-

tion that one should look for a white woman and the other should look for a black woman [150].

It is difficult to imagine that such illogic could persist in an era of globalization, transnational movement of peoples (both voluntary and involuntary), and the Internet — girl readers are simply too knowledgeable and aware to tolerate such perversity.

Works Cited

Deane, Paul. *Mirrors of American Culture: Children's Fiction Series in the Twentieth Century.* Metucheon, N.J., and London: Scarecrow, 1991.

Du Bois, W.E.B. *The Souls of Black Folk.* 1903. New York: Dover, 1994.

"History of Stratemeyer Syndicate." Stratemeyer Syndicate Records, SSR/Beinecke.

hooks, bell. *Killing Rage: Ending Racism.* New York: Henry Holt, 1995.

Jones, James P. "Nancy Drew, WASP Super Girl of the 1930s." *Journal of Popular Culture* 6 (1973): 707–17.

Keene, Carolyn. *The Clue in the Crossword Cipher* (#44). New York: Grosset and Dunlap, 1967.

_____. *The Clue in the Old Album* (#24). New York: Grosset and Dunlap, 1947.

_____. *The Clue in the Old Album* (#24 revised). New York: Grosset and Dunlap, 1977.

_____. *The Clue of the Leaning Chimney* (#26). New York: Grosset and Dunlap, 1949.

_____. *The Crooked Banister* (#48). New York: Grosset and Dunlap, 1971.

_____. *Dangerous Plays.* Nancy Drew: Girl Detective #16. New York: Simon and Schuster, 2006.

_____. *Dressed to Steal.* Nancy Drew: Girl Detective #22. New York: Simon and Schuster, 2007.

_____. *Framed.* Nancy Drew: Girl Detective #15. New York: Simon and Schuster, 2006.

_____. *The Haunted Showboat* (#35). New York: Grosset and Dunlap, 1957.

_____. *The Hidden Staircase* (#2). New York: Grosset and Dunlap, 1930.

_____. *The Hidden Window Mystery* (#34). New York: Grosset and Dunlap, 1956.

_____. *The Hidden Window Mystery* (#34 revised). New York: Grosset and Dunlap, 1975.

_____. *The Invisible Intruder* (#46). New York: Grosset and Dunlap, 1969.

_____. *The Music Festival Mystery* (#157). New York: Simon and Schuster, 2000.

_____. *The Mystery at the Moss-Covered Mansion* (#18). New York: Grosset and Dunlap, 1941.

_____. *The Mystery of the Fire Dragon* (#38). New York: Grosset and Dunlap, 1961.

_____. *The Mystery of the Moss-Covered Mansion* (#38 revised). New York: Grosset and Dunlap, 1971.

_____. *Nancy's Mysterious Letter* (#8). New York: Grosset and Dunlap, 1932.

_____. *Nancy's Mysterious Letter* (#8 revised). New York: Grosset and Dunlap, 1968.

_____. *The Phantom of Pine Hill* (#42). New York: Grosset and Dunlap, 1965.

_____. *Riverboat Ruse.* Nancy Drew: Girl Detective #11. New York: Simon and Schuster, 2005.

_____. *The Secret in the Old Clock* (#1). New York: Grosset and Dunlap, 1930.

_____. *The Secret of the Forgotten City* (#52). New York: Grosset and Dunlap, 1975.

_____. *The Star Sapphire Mystery* (#45). New York: Grosset and Dunlap, 1968.

_____. *Stop the Clock.* Nancy Drew: Girl Detective #12. New York: Simon and Schuster, 2005.

_____. *The Whispering Statue* (#14). New York: Grosset and Dunlap, 1937.

_____. *The Whispering Statue* (#14 revised). New York: Grosset and Dunlap, 1970.

MacCann, Donnarae. "Nancy Drew and the Myth of White Supremacy." Eds. Carolyn Stewart Dyer and Nancy Tillman Romalov. *Rediscovering Nancy Drew.* Iowa City: University of Iowa Press, 1995, 129–135.

Nash, Ilana. *American Sweethearts: Teenage Girls in Twentieth-Century Popular Culture.* Bloomington and Indianapolis: Indiana University Press, 2006.

Rehak, Melanie. *Girl Sleuth: Nancy Drew and the Women Who Created Her.* New York: Harcourt, 2005.

Said, Edward W. *Culture and Imperialism.* New York: Vintage, 1993.

Stimpson, Catharine. "The Future of Women's Studies." *Women's Studies in the University Structure: A Report to the Ford Foundation.* New York: Ford Foundation, 1986.

Stratemeyer Syndicate Records (SSR/Beinecke). Yale Collection of American Literature, Beinecke Rare Book and Manuscript Library.

Stratemeyer Syndicate Records, 1832–1984 (SSR/NYPL). Manuscripts and Archives Division, New York Public Library.

Wu, Frank H. *Yellow: Race in America Beyond Black and White.* New York: Basic Books, 2002.

"They blinded
her with science":
Science Fiction and
Technology in Nancy Drew

Michael G. Cornelius

Former Harvard University President Lawrence H. Summers noted at the National Bureau of Economic Research Conference in January 2005, "It does appear that on many, many different human attributes — height, weight, propensity for criminality, overall IQ, mathematical ability, scientific ability — there is relatively clear evidence that whatever the difference in means — which can be debated — there is a difference in the standard deviation, variability of a male and female population" (Summers). Though Summers denied his remarks were meant to suggest that women enjoined less of an innate ability for science than men, one observer noted, "It is so upsetting that all these brilliant young women [at Harvard] are being led by a man who views them this way" (Bombardieri). When Summers states that "there is reasonably strong evidence of taste differences between little girls and little boys that are not easy to attribute to socialization" (Summers), he does seem to imply that there is something inborn within women — whether distaste, disinterest, or lack of aptitude — that prevents them from establishing equal access in the world of the hard sciences.

Women have also been denied equal access in the world of science fiction, both as progenitors and protagonists. Robin Roberts writes, "Sci-

ence fiction is customarily thought of as a masculine genre" (3). Although
the status quo is slowly changing for both science and science fiction, these
changes are coming very slowly. Women continually struggle for acceptance and equality in these traditionally masculine spheres.

Nancy Drew is a woman who has never struggled in any traditional
masculine realm. As a girl sleuth, she has had relatively unfettered access
to the influential spheres of the patriarchy few women in fiction have ever
possessed. The result of this access is a panoply of freedom that belies both
Nancy's gender and her age. As Anne Scott MacLeod observes: "The point
about Nancy Drew's freedom is not just ... its completeness; it is its dig-
nity. Nancy's independence is not a gift coaxed from dim or fond adults.
Autonomy is her *right* ... and is never seriously questioned. The enviable
ease with which she exercises her total independence of adult authority is
as impressive as the independence itself" (427). Nancy's independence is
not, strictly speaking, a freedom from the world of adults; indeed, who is
more adult than Nancy, whose unselfish desire to exert authority and seek
justice is a quality not traditionally associated with youth. Rather than freedom from adults, Nancy's autonomy is quite literally a freedom from men;
she exists in a feminine/feminist sphere largely because she has constructed
that space, her space, a veritable "no man's land." Her boyfriend Ned
Nickerson is no more than an effectual eunuch, useful for manual labor
or punching out a bad guy, but never threatening her career or her control over him. Nancy realized early on in her career that the roles within
a traditional male-female romance in her day would result in a reconstruc-
tion of her feminine sphere, creating a space around her over which she
no longer exerted ultimate autonomy.

Nancy's feminist ontology cannot be overstated here. Carolyn Heilbrun calls Nancy a "moment in the history of feminism;" Sally Parry suggests Nancy is a "good feminist hero;" while Joanne Furtak writes that
Nancy "was a feminist's dream before the dream became fashionable, a Glo-
ria Steinem without an air of defiance" (Heilbrun 11, Parry 150, Furtak 90).
Despite this, though, Parry considers Nancy "more likely to uphold the
ideological status quo," an avenging arm that works for and not against
the patriarchy, a trait that Parry considers not "expressive of the tension
that exists when a woman tries to succeed in a nexus of systems — political, economic, ethnic, and gender — that define society" (Parry 145, 156).
Examining this nexus as a typeset of relational units, however, demonstrates Nancy's ability to not only navigate these systems but to thoroughly
dominate or reject them altogether, whichever she so chooses. Nancy's

feminism is a direct result of her ability to construct a feminine space that allows her to create a "nontraditional" (to use Parry's word) but utterly feminine identity. As Julia Kristeva writes, "[B]y demanding recognition of an irreducible identity, without equal in the opposite sex, and, as such, exploded, plural, fluid, in a certain way nonidentical, this feminism situates itself outside the linear time of identities which communicate through projection and revindication" (37). As Deborah Siegel notes, Nancy Drew "arrived on the heels of an era that witnessed the rise of the revolutionary demographic and political phenomenon known as the New Woman" (160).

The essence of Nancy's "New Woman" freedom is hegemony. By exerting an unyielding control over her environment, her friends, and her mysteries, Nancy assures her ability to do what she most wants — solve crimes — without the interference of the (masculinized) police, her father, her boyfriend, or any other patristic figure who may happen to inhabit her space. Nancy's utter refusal to allow any male to occupy her feminine space creates an aura of authority around her, an aura that has often been misinterpreted as masculinity. Patricia Craig and Mary Cadogan note that "Nancy has never had to waste time wishing she were a boy; for all practical purposes she *is*.... She drives a blue roadster, knows how to handle a speed-boat and an aeroplane, round up steers, keep control of an unruly mount and can stun a would-be kidnapper with a single blow" (150). Sally Parry adds, "Some of Nancy's attributes can be seen as traditionally masculine" (149). In another description of Nancy's abilities, Peggy Herz writes, "Nancy Drew personifies all the best qualities of every girl. She can do everything. She can swim, sew, paint. She travels, she solves mysteries. You name it, she can do it! She is almost Wonder Woman" (9). In their descriptions of Nancy Drew, these critics have focused on Nancy's abilities, those actions that she can do, and list them as those they believe to be wholly masculinized (Craig and Cadogan) or feminized (Herz.) Yet all are limited by an anti-feminist perspective; almost all of the activities named require finesse, skill, and a cool head, qualities Nancy possesses in droves. Even rounding up steers, as thoroughly masculine as it may sound, is done from horseback and involves ability and skill, not brute force or raw, masculine muscle. The proliferation of women's self-defense courses would suggest that more women are capable of defending themselves from an attacker with "a single blow" than men, because they (like Nancy) have the proper training and knowledge to do it. In fact, Nancy's amazing "physical" abilities reflect consistently her cool, well-developed intellect, a construct that requires no actionable strength at all on the individual's part.

Intellect, however, has consistently failed Nancy in one particular realm — that of the hard sciences. When confronted by technology she cannot understand, Nancy, rather than seeking to understand this new component in her tightly-constructed and ultimately-controlled world, retreats. Lee Zacharias writes that, for Nancy, solving mysteries "is an act of power. The solution confirms her theories" (1035). When the case moves into the realm of the technological, however, Nancy must look to the male characters in the book to solve at least that portion of the crime for her. Thus a series of professors, experts, electricians, and even Ned Nickerson take center stage in proposing hypotheses and ultimately solving the technological riddles before Nancy herself steps in and, generally speaking, oversees the solution to the mystery, while never directly solving it herself. By requiring the aid of men to solve even a portion of her mystery, Nancy is forced to allow them in to invade her feminine space. The end result of this is devastating. Sarah LeFanu suggests that science fiction "offers language ... for the dissolution of the self" (23). This is precisely what happens to Nancy Drew in the few mysteries that feature a science fiction theme, but in Nancy's case, the reduction of identity results in a deconstruction of the feminist detective. In this essay, I plan to examine the role of science fiction technology in three Nancy Drew Mysteries — *The Invisible Intruder* (1969), *The Crooked Banister* (1971), and *Mystery of the Glowing Eye* (1974) — in order to demonstrate the catastrophic impact of technology on Nancy's identity as both feminist and detective. Each time the girl sleuth is confronted by technology, a crisis of confidence results, and only the male with the solution to the technological mystery can restore order, a role that had previously always been Nancy's. Usurped and overshadowed, Nancy thus becomes a simulacrum and stereotype of the dependent female rather than the independent woman she has long represented.

As a genre, science fiction has been difficult to define, perhaps because it is limited only by the orthographic imagination of its varied authors. Without anything as limiting as reality intervening, science fiction is a perfect medium for exploration. As so many of its most famous tomes have explored alien realms and outer (or inner) spaces, thematically and socially speaking, science fiction has long been a genre used for the investigation and reinterpretation of societal ideas and ideals. As Kingsley Amis notes, "science fiction's most important use ... is a means of dramatizing social enquiry, as providing a fictional mode in which cultural tendencies can be isolated and judged" (99). This statement seems at odds with Lucie

Armitt's assertion that "science fiction has traditionally been a genre obsessed with nostalgia and conservatism" (2).

These two constructs, however, are not as paradoxical as they may first appear. Science fiction is very much about the creation of worlds; Betty King labels these worlds a "projected (future or alternative) universe" (King v). These "projected universes" may very strongly resemble our own or may critique it savagely. What is essential is the creation and maintenance of this world. This new world represents a status quo, one that the work may seek to challenge, but a status quo that is ultimately preserved. Sometimes the status quo represents very much our own ideals. For example, Roland Emmerich's 1996 film *Independence Day*, through its tale of a united world fighting off a vicious alien invasion on the Fourth of July, very much reinforces not only American patriotic and militaristic ideals but imposes these ideals on a larger world order, as the United States not only "saves the day" but preserves independence for the entire globe. The result is a ratification of American ideals and their imposition on a larger global community. Emmerich's "projected universe" is ultimately a global version of the United States, a utopia of democracy through military might, patriarchal rule, and American family values.

Conversely, a text like Suzy McKee Charnas' *Motherlines*, part of her Holdfast Chronicles, creates a "projected universe" whose values represent a continuum different than our own traditional social mores. Charnas's fantasia on the hertopia presents a world of feminist empowerment that focuses on the matriarchal and the essence of the female. Charnas' characters inhabit a world not unlike River Heights, where women have the opportunity to do as they wish and to impose their will on others, something that was long denied women in traditional patriarchal society. Charnas, however, used her work to project a universe that not only differed from our own reality but also proffered a vision of where a wholly different set of societal values may have or may still someday take us.

Similarly, Nancy Drew's River Heights is a world that exists only in the realm of fantasy. Nancy's authority and independence may be the stuff of legends, largely because they could only exist in such a tall-tale. Most series books inhabit such realms. Franklin K. Mathiews, former chief librarian of the Boy Scouts of America, complained of this very improbability in a 1914 essay on boys' series literature: "Boys move about in aeroplanes as easily as though on bicycles; criminals are captured by them with a facility that rivals the ability of Sherlock Holmes; and when it comes to getting on in the world, the cleverness of the hustling boys is comparable only to those captains of industry and Napoleons of finance who have made millions in a minute. Insuperable difficulties and crushing circumstances are as easily overcome and conquered as in fairy tales" (652–53). Betsy Caprio has also commented on the *un*reality of Nancy's world: "Her adventures take place outside of space as well as time. In fairy tales, one easily journeys to 'the next kingdom,' or travels 'east of the sun and west of the moon' ... and the same is true in River Heights" (132).

This unreal world is the heart of the science fiction genre. Maintaining (or destroying) this world, and whatever values it represents, is generally the crux of the science fiction story. In River Heights, Nancy's world causes her to become the primary source of justice and order in her own feminist domain. If her world is not a utopia — could a land inhabited by so many criminal elements be considered ideal? — it is perfect for her, a personalized hertopia, because it allows Nancy to engage in the one pastime that brings her immense satisfaction: detective work. Everything else pales in Nancy's world; she has no other facet to her identity other than that of girl sleuth.

Technology, however, disrupts Nancy's identity, eliciting internal crises that cause Nancy to doubt her abilities, doubts that, in significant ways, shake the core of Nancy's foundational identity as sleuth. This seems at odds with the purpose of technology in the series world. After all, science and technology have played an important role in boys' series books. Tom Swift, Rick Brant, Christopher Cool, Ted Scott, the Three Investigators, and even the venerable Hardy Boys have oft utilized and confronted technology when solving their mysteries. According to Fred Erisman, technology in boys' series literature is designed to proffer "the picture of American youth as mechanically competent" (14). Erisman notes that technology and a technical education was a way to become "universally acknowledged and respected" (15). Russel B. Nye, writing about the Tom Swift, Boy Inventor, series, suggests that what made the series so popular is that "Tom Swift grasped the technology of the machine age and brought it under control" (83). Erisman echoes this when he suggests that in these books, "technology is something that *can* be, and *must* be, mastered" (24).

By not mastering technology, Nancy demonstrates an area where her hegemony is threatened and, indeed, subjugated. Nancy relinquishes control of the technology to males, mirroring the manifestations of technology in series books as a whole. While most of the boys' series confront and master technology at some point or another, most of the girls' series books do not. Judy Bolton, the Dana Girls, Connie Blair, and Penny Parker, for example, lack significant confrontation with technology. Those few girls' series that do allow for the female sleuth to master some form of technology do so in only a limited sphere: Cherry Ames, detective nurse, has a limited knowledge of medicine; Vicki Barr and Shirley Flight, both flight attendants, possess technical knowledge related to aeronautics. John Axe classifies the information presented in the Vicki Barr series as being "surprisingly technological," which ratifies that, with a few very minor exceptions, technology is something that has long been relegated to the boys' series world (143).

Thus when Nancy confronts science fiction and technology, she is staking out new feminine, and possibly feminist, territory. This seems very much in hand with feminist science fiction narratives. As Betty King notes: "Science fiction has become an increasingly popular genre for fiction by and/or about women. Perhaps this is due, in part, to the fact that our present world cultures allow women so limited an opportunity for courage, bravery, strength, and command. Those qualities are still, for the most part, forbidden to women — except within the realm of a projected universe: a remote future or galaxy where equality, even superiority, is possible for women! In science fiction these whole women can be safely allowed full powers" (v). This is especially true of the 1960s, since "with the New Wave writers also came a new wave of speculation about women (rather than men) in positions of power and control" (King 107). The 1960s also proved a heady time for Nancy Drew, whom Melanie Rehak labels "the rising 'it' girl of the 1960s women's lib movement" (262). Thus if both science fiction and the 1960s allowed for such advances with women and science fiction, why is it that Nancy's own confrontations with technology result in the most significant crises of confidence and indeed, failures, in her entire series?

A careful examination of three works in which Nancy is confronted by her technological nemesis should offer some light on this question. The first of these works is *The Invisible Intruder* (1969). In the text, Nancy is invited to attend a "ghost-hunting" expedition with several other couples. The first "ghost" the group intends to chase down is a haunted canoe at Sevanee Lake: "'You won't believe this,'" he [Jim Archer] replied, 'but the canoe propels itself.' Burt shook his head. 'Sounds impossible to me. Something must make it go.' 'Spooks,' Helen replied" (Keene 7). This initial discussion of the "otherworldly" phenomenon paints a telling portrait of the differences between men and women and their relationship to technology in the Nancy Drew series; Burt, a student at Emerson University, expresses his disbelief that the phenomenon is supernatural; Helen, a married friend of Nancy's, states just the opposite.

When the group first spots the canoe, it is the men who attempt to solve the riddle of why it propels itself:

> Ned: [upon first spotting the canoe] "I'll bet there are a couple of spoofers under that canoe!" he called. [After seeing no one, Ned remarks,] "That's strange" [Keene 10].

As the detective, Nancy should be the one to chase the canoe and proffer the first — and in her case, usually accurate — suggestion as to how the mechanism works. Instead, once Ned's initial hypothesis that the canoe is propelled by human beings underneath the craft is proven wrong, Nancy is reluctant to share her views: "George went on, 'Anybody have an idea as to what made the canoe propel itself? There has to be a reason.' No one answered, but an idea was forming in Nancy's mind. She did not express it aloud because at the moment it seemed too far-fetched. 'But it just might work,' she said to herself" (Keene 11).

Nancy's hesitation belies her uncertainty; while she has formed an idea about the locomotion of the canoe, she refuses to share her hypothesis. This is very unlike Nancy, who has always used her friends as a sounding board for her theories of the crime, and whose ideas are almost always proven correct. Nancy's reluctance here seems to imply a crisis of confidence regarding the possible technological origins of the canoe; lacking, perhaps, the expertise to correctly describe what she believes to the underlying cause of the "ghost canoe," she remains silent.

Ultimately, Nancy never shares her assumptions with the group. Instead, it is Ned who doggedly pursues the answer to this mystery. After he and Nancy find themselves in another canoe that also moves on its own accord, Ned begins his investigation: "Ned pulled the aluminum craft up on the beach and began to inspect it. He said, 'Something was keeping Nancy and me from making any progress in the water. Maybe there's a hidden gadget'" (Keene 40–41). Though Ned finds nothing on that particular canoe, he does uncover technological devices on other camp canoes: "Ned pointed out a complicated set of gadgets under both the front and rear seats. One motor worked the front paddle, another the stern. Both were attached by permanent swiveling fixtures. Still another motor was used to receive remote-control signals. 'Actually it's very ingenious,' said Don" (Keene 49).

This same pattern is repeated when Ned is attacked by a mysterious octopus in the lake. Nancy, believing that a man is hiding in an octopus costume, dives down to rescue Ned, and is shocked to discover that there is no person operating the threatening animal. Later, Burt and Dave uncover the true solution to this technological mystery: "Burt said that he and Dave found the fake octopus lying on the beach. While examining it, they had discovered how to start the mechanism which made it wriggle through the water" (Keene 40).

In both cases, Nancy's ability to solve the overall crime is hampered by her reaction to the technology that is instrumental in committing it. Writing of detective fiction, Ellen O'Gorman notes: "The detective seeks a solution to a mystery of mysteries. The solution is arrived at through the scrutiny of material evidence and the careful questioning of witnesses: in short, through a process of retracing, recovering the past. The detective is bound by an obligation beyond that to any human individual: an obligation to Truth" (O'Gorman 20). Yet rather than confront these technological "truths" head-on, Nancy retreats, a puzzling reaction for the sleuth. Sarah LeFanu suggests that science fiction technology may "defamiliarise the familiar, and make familiar the new and strange" (LeFanu 21). The detective functions to make the unfamiliar known, but Nancy has not proven capable of doing this as it relates to technology.

Conversely, Susan Thomas writes that "where woman and machine meet provides the catalyst for change" (110). Change is largely anathematic in the Drew series; the static nature of the character, who changes little over time (though her mysteries, hometown, and hemlines do), is highly suggestive of exactly what it is that makes Nancy Drew so popular. Thus, it is technology, something that itself changed so dramatically in the years since Nancy Drew was first introduced in 1930, that causes "change" in Nancy's character, a change not deemed for the best. Perhaps Robin Roberts unwittingly puts it best when she notes, "In science fiction, 'hard' refers to fiction that focuses on technology" (5). Indeed, for Nancy, technology has proven too "hard" for her to master. Perhaps this is why Thomas ultimately suggests that technology still exists as a male "rite of passage" (110). In *Invisible Intruder*, Ned, Burt, and Dave must solve the technological aspects of the crime in order for the mystery to be resolved.

The Invisible Intruder features another female character whose interaction with the "ghostly" technology is highly illustrative of the book's redaction of women and science fiction. Rita Rodriguez is a strong believer in the supernatural and the member of the group who generally leaps to the conclusion that the ghostly events the group witnesses are all, in fact, caused by otherworldly forces. After listening to Ned and the other males dissect possible explanations for the canoe, for example, Rita shares her opinion of the phenomenon: "Rita Rodriguez spoke up. 'We have no proof of that. I'm sure the canoe incident was supernatural.' Her husband laughed. 'Honey, this moonlight has got you.' He turned to the others. 'Forgive me, but I can't go along with Rita and her belief in ghosts.' To make amends for his remark, Rod put an arm around his wife" (Keene 16). The implication that Rita's husband Rod needs to make "amends" for his remark suggests that he is well aware of his patronizing, patriarchal manner. Nevertheless, the male characters in the book all adopt this aggrandizing attitude towards Rita and any woman who believes in the supernatural. Later, when a local medium's hut has been burned, and neighbors report seeing her spirit rise out of the flames, Rita is horrified: "Rita caught her breath. 'Oh dear! That means Madame Tarantella is dead.' George smiled. 'Or wants people to think she is. The whole thing is probably a hoax.' The officers looked at her amused. Then Watson said, 'I'm glad you don't believe such nonsense'" (Keene 148).

Rita's reaction is telling to the police officers who have just informed the group of the hut's destruction. To these males, belief in the supernatural is "nonsense." They are clearly amused by her response. George's rejoinder almost seems intended more for the police than for Rita; George seems concerned that the police may view her to be as flighty and ill-informed as Rita.

Characters like Rita, who seems to exist solely to be derided by the males she encounters in the book, including her own husband, had never previously existed in the Nancy Drew universe. Her inclusion counterbalances the rational, educated perspective of the men who embrace, accept, and understand technology, but it also underscores Nancy's own reluctance to engage this new and mysterious marvel. In her book *Feminism and Science Fiction*, Sarah LeFanu writes of the "extraordinary relationship between feminism and science fiction that flowered in the 1970s" (7). Writing on the same topic, Jeanne Gomoll notes, "huge numbers of us [women] rejected the traditional role of anonymous, self-sacrificing helpmate that has so long trapped women" (Gomoll 8). Nancy Drew has never been described as anyone's "helpmate;" in *The Invisible Intruder*, however, science fiction technology has reduced Nancy from an active detective into a passive bystander who assists Ned, Burt, and Dave as they solve the mystery. As LeFanu noted, science fiction can result in the dissolution of the self; for a feminist icon like Nancy Drew, this dissolution results in an inability to both solve crimes and exude the independence, confidence, and leadership that has marked her own identity for so long.

The Crooked Banister (1971) features an even larger crisis of confidence and an even more severe dissolution of identity thanks to Nancy's interaction with science fiction technology. In this case, the technology is Robby, a robot, that Nancy first encounters with her father and her father's client, Mrs. Melody: "'Oh! What's that?' Mrs. Melody cried out, pulling back. All of them heard a strange whirring sound. The next instant a weird metal figure whizzed across the hall, then went out of sight. But in a couple of moments it returned and shot past the callers. 'It's a robot!' Nancy exclaimed. 'He must be guarding the place'" (Keene 16).

In *The Crooked Banister*, Nancy suffers not one but two distinct crises of confidence. The first occurs shortly after Nancy's initial encounter with the "mysterious" robot, when Carson Drew informs Nancy that he must leave: "'Mrs. Melody and I must leave directly after lunch.' Nancy was disappointed. She had just become involved in a baffling mystery and now she must give it up. To her surprise, Mr. Drew said, 'Nancy, if you are willing to stay here, I'd like you to continue work on the case'" (Keene 25).

Nancy's reaction to Carson's proclamation is shocking for the girl sleuth. She presents no argument to her father about staying on and solving the mystery on her own; had her father not suggested it, she would not have stayed. This does not sound like the same girl sleuth who once confidently told her father, "You let me do anything I like" (Keene *Broken Locket* 53). Karen Plunkett-Powell writes of Carson Drew, "He is her staunchest supporter when she wants to go the extra mile to solve a particularly complex case. That 'extra mile' often turns into hundreds of miles as Nancy routinely asks for permission to scurry off to places like New York, Canada, or Louisiana"— or Turkey, Scotland, Florida, Hawaii, Louisiana, Argentina, Peru, France, or Kenya, all places Nancy traveled to before she encountered Robby (72). If Nancy longs for nothing but a mystery to solve, and has found one in a town only an hour from River Heights, why does she not ask for permission from her father to solve it? It could be that Nancy does not believe she can solve it. Later in the same scene, Nancy experiences strong feelings of self-doubt: "Nancy smiled back, though she did not feel confident about solving this mystery. She had been given the difficult task of learning the whereabouts of a man who had not only disappeared but had left behind a frightening robot!" (Keene 27). When has

Nancy ever admitted to feeling unconfident about solving a mystery? The girl sleuth's unremitting and unyielding belief in her own abilities has always been the strongest asset in her crime-solving arsenal. Yet Nancy's confrontation with the robot has so shaken her confidence, the girl sleuth doubts she will solve the case.

Nancy's crisis of confidence is highlighted by an unpleasant encounter she has in a restaurant. A couple named Aldrin have been swindled by Rawley Banister, the very criminal Nancy is seeking, and stumble across the girl sleuth at lunch:

> (Bess) "Nancy Drew is a detective. Maybe you'd like her to work on your case."
>
> Mr. Aldrin's answer was a loud haw-haw, followed by, "She's only a girl!"
>
> His wife laughed uproariously. "Can you imagine such a thing? I can see a headline now — TEEN-AGE GIRL CAPTURES CON MAN!"
>
> Nancy was embarrassed. Her face flushed with anger as patrons in the restaurant stared [Keene 54–55].

Never before had crime victims expressed such staunch disbelief about Nancy's abilities, and nowhere else in the series is a scene where Nancy ends up so sharply humiliated. After this encounter, she does not speak for two pages, and even refuses to take on the Aldrins' case when Mrs. Aldrin returns to apologize.

The author's inclusion of this scene seems to reflect Nancy's discomfort at having to confront the robot and its sinister maker. Indeed, as in *The Invisible Intruder*, when directly confronted by the science and technologies Rawley Banister has left behind in his strange house, Nancy turns to male characters for the solutions to the technological puzzles. When the robot ceases to function, a local electrician is able to repair him. When the moat repeatedly lights up in flames, a visiting Ned Nickerson provides an explanation: "Ned looked into the moat. 'The fire's out. Probably oil was poured on the water and set ablaze. It didn't last long'" (Keene 67). When Nancy looks for clues in a scientific picture depicting various poisons, she confesses to Ned: "'I don't know much about poisons,' Nancy admitted. 'Are you familiar with them?' Ned said that in one of his courses he had learned about many of them" (Keene 69). In perhaps one of the most telling encounters with technology in all of Nancy Drew, Nancy is even directly confronted by technology when she is physically assaulted by the robot. She proves unable to save herself, and George must rescue her by attacking the robot with a large wrench and disabling it.

Plunkett-Powell writes that this scene was the "only time that neither Nancy's brawn nor her mental abilities did her much good" (64). Actually, though, Nancy's intellect fails her whenever she is confronted by technology. The confrontation between Nancy and Robby only emphasizes this point. It also works to animate one of the main distinctions between the representation of men and women that technology in the series creates. Technology works to emphasize that the men in the series all possess some form of formal education or specialized training, while none of the women in these texts have any higher schooling at all. In both *Invisible Intruder* and *Crooked Banister* the men who are able to puzzle through the technological portions of the mystery can do so because of their education. Ned, Burt, and Dave are all university students who have studied, to some extent, engineering and other hard sciences (indeed, Ned even indicates that his studies have included toxicology, a useful field for the boyfriend of a girl sleuth.)

It is suggested that the men on the ghost hunt in *Intruder* are all gainfully employed, and one of them, Jim Archer, works for the oil industry in an engineering capacity; the question of education and occupation for the women, however, is more or less passed over. While there is no reason to assume that none of the women went to college or work in a field requiring education, there is also no reason to assume the opposite. The impression given by Rita Rodriguez and the other women is that, in fact, they lack the same education and background the men possess. And while it may seem improbable that a small-town electrician can repair a sophisticated piece of science fiction technology like a robot, as happens in *Banister*, in the world of Nancy Drew, any man possessing an iota of education or scientific training is able to work with technology in a manner far beyond any of the women in the text.

The 1970s marked a boom time for women in higher education. Eugenia Proctor Gerdes notes that affirmative action in higher education, the women's movement, state and institutional commissions on women, and the evolution of women's studies all contributed to bringing more women into colleges. In her article, Gerdes cites several studies that suggest "the 1960s to the mid–1970s resulted in legal and institutional changes benefiting women in higher education and society at large" (157). According to United States' Census Bureau Office data, by the end of the 1970s, women represented the majority of students in American colleges and universities ("Census Bureau Facts"). Despite these positive changes, however, Nancy Drew and her chums remain woefully undereducated. At no point in the original Nancy Drew series does the girl sleuth ever learn about or study technology in any official manner or capacity; even here, in the context of a mystery, where Nancy has learned so much in the past, the basic constructs of technology are denied her.

Fred Erisman writes, "The initial message of ... technical books is that science, technology, and the changes that result from them are facts of life. They exist, they are not going to disappear, they are going to have far-reaching consequences, and they must be accepted" (23). Erisman goes on to note that, "technological mastery will open the door to a world of new careers," and that "the final message of the technological series is that only through the acceptance, mastery, and application of technology will a person become a truly up-to-date, truly progressive American citizen" (24, 25). The kind of "technological mastery" that Erisman writes about was readily available in most American institutions of higher learning. However, the kind of technical education needed to master the ever-changing technologies of the twentieth century was often denied to women, and this disparity is reflected in the reactions of the male and female characters to technology in the Drew series.

This connection between career, education, and technology is perhaps most evident in *Mystery of the Glowing Eye* (1974). Set partly on the campus of Emerson University, *Glowing Eye* is about the disappearance of Ned Nickerson, who has been kidnapped by an Emerson graduate student, Zapp Crosson, so that Crosson may learn the secrets behind Ned's engineering project.

Glowing Eye does not begin with Ned's disappearance, however; rather, it begins with the most severe crisis of confidence in Nancy's career. This crisis concerns Marty King, a young female lawyer and new employee of Carson Drew. In an attempt to ingratiate herself with her new boss, Marty King has taken it upon herself to solve the new case he has been saving for Nancy: "[Nancy] 'Marty King is trying to be an amateur detective —' 'And,' George finished, 'take your place'" (Keene 3).

Though Nancy describes her feelings as "a case of just plain jealousy," the possibility that another young, talented, and in this case educated woman could take her place is a palpable threat to the girl sleuth (Keene 2). After a late night incident with an intruder at her house, Nancy frets over another worry: "[Nancy] 'Dad, you never finished telling me about the glowing eye.' [Mr. Drew] 'No, but I will. It's too late now. We must all get to bed.' Nancy went to her room, but she kept thinking, 'Did Dad mean it was too late because Marty is working on the case?'" (Keene 20).

While one would not expect Nancy to be concerned over a break-in at her home (since it is hardly an infrequent occurrence,) one would expect Nancy to show sincere concern when she discovers that Ned has been kidnapped. Yet Nancy's anxiety in the first quarter of *Glowing Eye* stems from Marty King's threat to her identity and hegemony as girl sleuth and not from any concern over Ned's well-being. Though she rushes off to the Anderson Museum in Hager, where she is told there may be a clue to Ned's kidnapping, her thoughts are still on Marty's involvement in her case. The entire trip Nancy is unsurprisingly disconsolate until she coincidentally runs into her father and Marty eating lunch in Martin City, a town on the way to Hager. Cornering her father when Marty leaves the table, Nancy grills him — not about her missing boyfriend, but about the earlier mystery he promised her. When Carson finally relents and informs Nancy about the mystery, her reaction is telling: "Nancy returned to her table in a far better mood than she had left it. Her father was not sidestepping her detective work in favor of Marty's after all!" (Keene 25). Rather than demonstrating concern for her missing beau, Nancy is relieved to learn that Marty has not replaced her in her father's — or the world's — eyes.

Plunkett-Powell labels Nancy's reaction to the Marty King affair as "viciously jealous," a reaction that is wholly uncharacteristic for the girl sleuth (Plunkett-Powell 73). Her focus is on her self and her emotions. Parry considers Nancy Drew a "protector" of the wronged and weak, but in *Glowing Eye*, it is Nancy's own feelings that she seems most interested in protecting, not the kidnapped victim (150). Again, technology has led to the dissolution of the self.

The science fiction technology in *Glowing Eye* appears early on in the form of a remote-controlled helicopter, and later at the Anderson Museum as both a weird, glowing eye and a paralyzing ray. After she first views the glowing eye and discovers that the wood of the wall the eye was projected upon was not hot, Nancy suggests a strong hypothesis: "'There must be a cold light behind this panel,' she said to herself. 'A very bright heatless light.' Her friends had come back. 'Learn anything?' George asked. 'No,' Nancy replied. 'It's a puzzle'" (Keene 29). As with *Invisible Intruder*, Nancy suspects the technological solution to the crime at hand, but is reluctant to share that information with anyone. Here, she even provides a cogent scientific explanation for the phenomenon she has witnessed, but when questioned by George, Nancy lies and suggests she is still puzzled by the event.

Without Ned to explain the technology she encounters, Nancy relies on first Burt and Dave, and then later on Glenn, a helicopter pilot who is also "an expert mechanic and know[s] a lot about electricity and other sources of power," and Professor Titus, Ned's engineering professor at Emerson (Keene 128). Nancy's ability to marshal so many technical minds must be commended, but again, when she herself is confronted with technical aspects of the mystery, she is reluctant to engage them: "[Nancy] pulled open the top drawer and found it filled with books. They were of a technical and specialized nature and Nancy doubted that they would lend a clue. 'I'll look at them later,' she decided, closing the drawer" (Keene 58). Later, when she finally examines Ned's papers, Nancy can only conclude: "They are very technical.... I'm sure, though, that they are not for a computer" (Keene 75). Though she is sure of what the papers are not, Nancy never uncovers what they do, in fact, represent, or how they may help her find her missing friend.

Later, Nancy is again confronted directly by technology when she is injured by a strange device at the museum. Fortunately, Professor Titus is nearby to provide an explanation of the phenomenon:

> The science professor said he believed that under the [wall]paper there was a metal plate on a screen attached to the wall itself. "Nancy must have been standing on some electric conducting material."
> Again Glenn went to peer into the closet. He reported, "There is a rug on the floor."
> Professor Titus nodded. "Most likely it's made of an electric conducting material. The hidden plate in the wall is no doubt positive and Nancy is negative. These unlike charges create a strong electrical force which pulled Nancy's hand to the wall and held it there" [Keene 127].

Later, after experiencing the paralyzing ray, Professor Titus again explains:

> "Have you any explanation for it?" Nancy asked him.
> "Not exactly," he [Prof. Titus] replied, "but it reminds me of something I read about medical students studying the brain waves of a person who had been put to sleep under hypnosis. It was discovered that his wave pattern could be imprinted upon another brain by using a laser beam of a certain wavelength. Of course the original brain waves had to be programmed in order to be modulated. This in turn produced a 'paralyzing' sleep" [Keene 150].

In both instances the professor demonstrates a knowledge that only a serious student of the field could reasonably be expected to know. A careful reader would never expect Nancy to hold the same level of knowledge as a professor. However, all of the men in *Glowing Eye* and these other mysteries seem to hold the same level of technological information. When Ned is finally saved and his invention is revealed, it is as technical and complex as anything Professor Titus has suggested:

> [Ned] "My invention is a new way for a scientist to produce laser light so that even a small source of energy will do great feats. It's done by converting all of the energy into light."
>
> "How wonderful!" Nancy exclaimed, feeling particularly proud of her friend.
>
> George agreed, also Burt and Dave.
>
> Bess made no comment for several seconds, then she said, "Ned, your invention sounds marvelous but it's about as clear as mud to me!" [Keene 178].

Ned's invention, and Bess's remark regarding it, perfectly highlight the difference between men and women in the universe created by the original Nancy Drew series: men master technology, while women remain in awe of it (it bears noting that in subsequent Drew series, such as the current Nancy Drew, Girl Detective series, secondary female characters do master technology; Nancy, however, remains relatively technologically inept). When Nancy hears of Ned's invention, she feels "particularly proud" of him, a feeling that stalwart Ned has never managed to elicit from his girlfriend before. It is only because Ned shines in an area where Nancy herself has faltered so often that she finally sees Ned as something more than a good date, football hero, and oft rescuer. Ned's technical expertise and mastery of science has made him whole, while at the same time, Nancy's lack of expertise and exposed lack of education has caused her own identity as protector and detective to erode. In other words, when he triumphs, she falters.

This view is perfectly expressed by Mr. Schneider, the director of the Anderson Museum's board. When Miss Wilkins, who has been running the museum for some time, leaves abruptly, Nancy, Bess, and George ask to take her place. Mr. Schneider responds: "I wish we could invite a scientist to try finding an explanation to what has been going on" (Keene 134). Fortunately, Professor Titus agrees to accompany Nancy and her chums to the museum, but Mr. Schneider's response is telling about how Nancy's world views her and all women's relationship to technology. Though Miss Wilkins' job as caretaker involved taking admission and tending to the museum as a whole, and not caring for exhibits, once the science fiction mystery has reared its head, Mr. Schneider is reluctant to let three "girls" run the place themselves. His demand for a scientist — and by implication, a man — is indicative of the lack of confidence Nancy herself feels at the venture. Rather than try and talk Mr. Schneider into letting her give it a go on her own — something Nancy had done numerous times in the past — she acquiesces, as she does with her father in *Crooked Banister*, with nary an argument.

In her book *The Mystery of Nancy Drew*, Betsy Caprio records several reader reactions to Nancy Drew. One woman notes: "No matter what anyone said in 'real life,' Nancy gave me proof that, in theory, a girl could be smart, strong, and respected — a revelation in 1956!" (92). In the 1950s, Nancy Drew surely *was* smart, strong, and respected. In the 1970s, however, as science fiction and technology crept their way into the Nancy Drew series, the girl sleuth transformed from an unstoppable crime-solving feminist hero into an unconfident, uneducated, and unintelligent woman, a failure as a detective who relied on men to solve the technological portions of the crime she could not. Lucie Armitt suggests that science fiction "provides a forum for fictionalizing frightening possibilities" (10). For Nancy Drew, the loss of hegemony — the loss of her feminist iconicity, the loss of her ability to solve crimes — must be as frightening a possibility as she can imagine.

Works Cited

Amis, Kingsley. *New Maps of Hell: A Survey of Science Fiction.* New York: Harcourt Brace, 1960.

Armitt, Lucie. "Introduction." *Where No Man Has Gone Before: Women and Science Fiction.* Ed. Lucie Armitt. London: Routledge, 1991.

Axe, John. *All About Collecting Girls' Series Books.* Grantsville, Md.: Hobby HousePress, 2002.

Bombardieri, Marcella. "Summers' Remarks on Women Draw Fire." *The Boston Globe* 17 January 2005, online at www.boton.com/news/local/articles/2005/01/17/summers_remarks.

Caprio, Betsy. *Girl Sleuth on the Couch: The Mystery of Nancy Drew.* Trabuco Canyon, CA: Source Books, 1992.

"Census Bureau Facts for Features." 13 April 2001. U.S. Census Bureau main Web page, 18 May 2007, www.census.gov/Press-Release/www/2001/cb01ff03.html.

Charnas, Suzy McKee. *The Slave and the Free.* New York: Tor Books, 1999.

Craig, Patricia, and Mary Cadogan. *The Lady Investigates: Women Detectives and Spies in Fiction.* New York: St. Martin's, 1981.

Erisman, Fred. *Boys' Books, Boys' Dreams, and the Mystique of Flight.* Fort Worth: Texas Christian University Press, 2006.

Furtak, Joanne. "Of Clues, Kisses, and Childhood Memories: Nancy Drew Revisited." *Seventeen* (May 1984): 90.

Gerdes, Eugenia Proctor. "Women in Higher Education since 1970: The More Things Change, the More They Stay the Same." *Advancing Women in Leadership* 211 (Summer 2006): 155–170.

Gomoll, Jeanne. "An Open Letter to Joanna Russ." *Aurora* 10.1 (Winter 1986): 7–10.

Heilbrun, Carolyn G. "Nancy Drew: A Moment in Feminist History." *Rediscovering Nancy Drew*. Eds. Carolyn Stewart Dyer and Nancy Tillman Romalov. Iowa City: University of Iowa Press, 1995.

Herz, Peggy. *Nancy Drew and the Hardy Boys*. New York: Scholastic Books, 1977.

Independence Day. Dir. Roland Emmerich. Perf. Will Smith, Bill Pullman, Jeff Goldblum. 20th Century–Fox, 1996.

Keene, Carolyn. *The Clue of the Broken Locket*. New York: Grosset and Dunlap, 1934.

_____. *The Crooked Banister*. New York: Grosset and Dunlap, 1971.

_____. *The Invisible Intruder*. New York: Grosset and Dunlap, 1969.

_____. *Mystery of the Glowing Eye*. New York: Grosset and Dunlap, 1974.

King, Betty. *Women of the Future: The Female Main Character in Science Fiction*. Metuchen, N.J.: Scarecrow, 1984.

Kristeva, Julia. "Women's Time." *Feminist Theory: A Critique of Ideology*. Eds. Nannerl O. Keohane, Michelle Z. Rosaldo, and Barbara C. Gelpi. Chicago: University of Chicago Press, 1982.

LeFanu, Sarah. *Feminism and Science Fiction*. Bloomington: Indiana University Press, 1988.

Lundwall, Sam J. *Science Fiction: What It's All About*. New York: Ace Books, 1971.

Macleod, Anne Scott. "Nancy Drew and Her Rivals: No Contest." *Horn Book* 63 (1987): 422–450.

Mathiews, Franklin K. "Blowing Out the Boy's Brains." *The Outlook* 108 (11 November 1914): 652–653.

Nye, Russell B. *The Unembarrassed Muse: The Popular Arts in America*. New York: Dial Press, 1970.

O'Gorman, Ellen. "Detective Fiction and Historical Narrative." *Greece and Rome*. 46.1 (1999): 19–26.

Parry, Sally E. "The Secret of the Feminist Heroine: The Search for Values in Nancy Drew and Judy Bolton." *Nancy Drew and Company: Culture, Gender, and Girls' Series*. Ed. Sherrie A. Inness. Bowling Green: Bowling Green State University Popular Press, 1997.

Plunkett-Powell, Karen. *The Nancy Drew Scrapbook*. New York: St. Martin's Press, 1993.

Rehak, Melanie. *Girl Sleuth: Nancy Drew and the Women Who Created Her*. Orlando: Harcourt, 2005.

Roberts, Robin. *A New Species: Gender and Science in Science Fiction*. Urbana: University of Illinois Press, 1993.

Siegel, Deborah L. "Nancy Drew as New Girl Wonder: Solving It All for the 1930s." *Nancy Drew and Company: Culture, Gender, and Girls' Series*. Ed. Sherrie A. Inness. Bowling Green: Bowling Green State University Popular Press, 1997.

Summers, Lawrence H. "Remarks at NBER Conference on Diversifying the Science and Engineering Workforce." 30 January 2007, www.president.hardvard.edu/speeches/2005/nber.html.

Thomas, Susan. "Between the Boys and their Toys: The Science Fiction Film." *Where No Man Has Gone Before: Women and Science Fiction*. Ed. Lucie Armitt. London: Routledge, 1991.

Linda Carlton: Flying Sleuth/Sleuthing Flier

Fred Erisman

Barely a year after Nancy Drew solved her first case, in April 1930, she had a rival: Linda Carlton, heroine of five books written by Edith Lavell and published between 1931 and 1933. Linda resembles Nancy in numerous ways. Like Nancy, she lives in a small community, Spring City, Ohio, with her widower father, Thomas Carlton, a prosperous land investor and rancher (later an importer). Like Nancy, she is affluent and socially prominent, generally living a life of comfort and privilege. Like Nancy, she is attractive, with blue eyes, curly blonde hair, a trim figure, and a circle of loyal friends, notably best chum Louise Haydock and stead-fast wooer Ralph Clavering, son of the wealthiest family in town. Like Nancy, she is independent and mobile; Linda and her blue roadster are familiar sights in the haunts of the well-to-do. And, like Nancy, she solves crimes with easy-going panache.

There, however, the similarities end, for Linda, moreso even than Nancy, is her own woman. Whereas most of her classmates at Miss Graham's School are thoroughly conventional in their ambitions, aiming at prestigious marriages and lives as the aristocrats of the community, Linda has other plans. Despite the pressures on her to blend into the rituals and routines of Spring City's social elite, Linda is determined to make her way in a traditionally male-dominated profession — that of aviation. She enjoys, certainly, socializing with her peers at clubs and parties, and she tolerantly accepts the attentions of Ralph Clavering and other young men of the city. She takes pride, moreover, in righting the wrongs that crime creates.

Yet, whatever else might come her way, her heart and soul belong to aviation. As Linda juggles the challenges of solving crimes, meeting social expectations, and mastering the intricacies of flight, she becomes a complex and intriguing person whom young female readers can properly admire.

The five volumes of Linda's adventures are classic series-story fare, combining adventure, peril, and a modicum of romance to keep their readers engaged. The first volume, *Linda Carlton, Air Pilot* (1931), introduces eighteen-year-old Linda and her friends, on the brink of graduation from their elite private school, and establishes her yearning to learn to fly. Despite a graduation prophecy that she and Louise Haydock will be the next generation's social leaders, she takes flying lessons, rehabilitates the tarnished reputation of instructor Ted Mackay, and recovers a fifty-thousand-dollar pearl necklace. *Linda Carlton's Ocean Flight* (1931) picks up three months after the events of the first volume, as Linda enters a St. Louis ground school, thwarts a scheme to put her father out of business, and becomes the first woman to fly solo across the Atlantic. Volume three, *Linda Carlton's Island Adventure* (1931), finds Linda newly graduated from ground school and holding commercial and transport pilots' licenses (the highest ratings) plus full mechanic's certification. Flying to Georgia in her autogiro, she is kidnapped by a gang of bank robbers. Skillfully making her escape, she recovers the bank loot and uses the autogiro to help the police round up the gang.

Linda Carlton's Perilous Summer (1932), the fourth in the series, opens with Linda summering with her aunt and assorted chums at the elite Green Falls Resort on the shores of Lake Michigan. After taking an amnesiac girl, Helen Tower, under her wing, she meets Britisher Lord Dudley, gently refuses his proposal of marriage, takes part in a flying treasure hunt with her friends, and discovers that "Lord Dudley" is actually Ed Tower, a scoundrel seeking to swindle Helen out of a substantial legacy. Retrieving the papers that guarantee Helen her inheritance, Linda turns Tower over to the authorities. The final volume, *Linda Carlton's Hollywood Flight* (1933), takes Linda and new chum Dot Crowley on a cross-country flight to Hollywood, in pursuit of an imposter posing as Linda. There they meet secret service agent Bertram Chase, who is on the trail of a counterfeiter. When the imposter and her husband-accomplice flee to Hawaii, Linda and Dot follow by air, and, working with Chase, reveal the husband as the fugitive counterfeiter. At a festive dinner celebrating Linda's flight, Chase proposes marriage and urges her to join the secret service. The series ends with Linda considering both offers.

Three continuing plot elements forge the five books into a coherent, developing series. The first is the mystery component, which grows in prominence and seriousness as the books progress. When flight instructor Ted Mackay is accused of stealing a valuable pearl necklace, Linda, convinced of his innocence, sets out to absolve him. She discovers an unbreakable alibi and uses it to clear his name: "It suddenly occurred to her that she might help Ted in another way. She could establish his alibi for him — by means of his company...! She would take means of proving it. Then, if Ralph's detectives insisted upon throwing him into prison, there would be a way to have him released" (*AP* 116, 130–31, 150). Her father's business crisis, for its part, leads to her action: "'If we could only help Daddy in some way,' mused Linda. 'Find out who the man is who is trying to kill his business'" (*AP* 87, 92). Marshaling evidence with the help of Louise Haydock, she returns in triumph, confident that justice will prevail: "The facts as they saw them were surprisingly clear and simple, and could not fail to convince the police" (*AP* 132). In neither case are the perpetrators hardened criminals; rather, they are weak folk, unable to resist the temptation of easy money or easy fame.

The third and fourth volumes introduce her to overt criminality and awaken her to crime's effect upon the innocent: "I have to do all I can to get that money back. Think of the hundreds of people hurt by that bank robbery — if the bank is forced to close its doors!" (*IA* 121). In much the same spirit, she consigns Ed Tower to prison, even though Helen Tower's inheritance is preserved and Tower begs their forgiveness: "Linda nodded: it was not safe for a man like Ed Tower, who could even pose successfully as an English lord, to be at large. There was no telling what wickedness he might accomplish in the future" (*PS* 246).

Her final adventure, *Linda Carlton's Hollywood Flight*, shows her capturing criminals for the sake of the capture, even temporarily setting aside her flying ambitions to achieve this end. As Linda and Dot Crowley, after a single day's preparation, prepare to fly the Pacific in a borrowed airplane, Linda declares: "It's not an aviation feat this time, like flying the Atlantic. The main object is to catch those two criminals" (*HF* 18, 181). By story's end, her crime-solving skills are apparent even to the professional detective, Bert Chase, prompting him to say: "I want you to go into the secret service, Linda ... you'd be a marvellous detective" (*HF* 254).

A potential detective she may be, but Linda Carlton has other, more pressing concerns. Whereas the Nancy Drew stories were intended from the outset to be mysteries and little else, the Linda Carlton books explicitly take up far more complex issues (Rehak 112–115; MacLeod 314). The commitment to social order and social justice that leads Linda to crime-solving also leads her to consider the entire question of society and its priorities. False accusations, business conspiracies, and outright criminal behavior are evil, without question, and must be scotched as quickly as they appear. Yet what of the other, more conventional attributes of society? Might it not be possible for these, too, to be worthy of questioning, and even challenge? For Linda, the answer is an emphatic "yes," culminating in her mid-series outburst, "I can't be bothered with social codes at a time like this" (*IA* 121). She has no quarrel with society and its mores, but she is not a person to accept its dictates without question. Instead, she considers which actions are appropriate and which are inappropriate *for her*. From that questioning and self-evaluation comes the second of the unifying elements of the series, Linda's response to the pressures of conventionality.

Speaking for the social side is Linda's Aunt Emily, Mr. Carlton's spinster sister, who, though she lives with the Carltons as chaperone and family doyenne, is herself financially secure and a person of stature in the community. For her, there is no other path for her niece to follow. Now a graduate of Miss Graham's prestigious private school, Linda is to be formally introduced into Spring City society, marry into a good family, and take her rightful place among the city's monied elite. In the opening pages of the first volume, when the graduating class prophecy foresees Linda and Louise Haydock "[marrying] wealthy men and [becoming] the society leaders of Spring City," Aunt Emily turns to Louise's mother, saying, "That would suit us, wouldn't it, Mrs. Haydock?" (*AP* 19–20). Her plans appear even more explicitly later in the same work: "She had been so happy about the friendship between Ralph [Clavering] and Linda — it was so eminently right! When her niece did decide to get married ... she couldn't imagine any young man who would suit her so well as Ralph Clavering. Such family! Such social position! And plenty of money!" (*AP* 144). Her goal firmly in hand, Aunt Emily bends every effort to make certain that Linda is seen in all the right places and by all the right people.

Whenever Linda ventures out, Aunt Emily is there to remind her of her social obligations. She plans a three-month stay at an "exclusive" summer resort for the two of them, where Linda "could swim and drive and play tennis and dance to your heart's content...! Why, you'd meet all the right people!" (*AP* 23–24). Prior to a flight, she gives Linda "a pair of white flannel knickers, with a jaunty blue sweater and helmet of knitted silk," saying: "I never could see why girls have to look masculine.... And I want you to look nice the very first minute you arrive at Green Falls. First impressions are always so important and there is sure to be a crowd to meet you" (*AP* 82–83). Later in the series, speaking to a reporter who's interviewing Linda about flying, Aunt Emily interrupts: "'She is to be a bridesmaid at Miss Katherine Clavering's wedding next week.' ... As usual, social events were all-important to her, especially affairs with the Claverings, the richest people in Spring City" (*IA* 10). To her credit, she means well, wanting only the best, as she understands it, for Linda, yet she is blind to the comparable opportunities that an independent life can provide for the girl.

Somewhat more broad-minded is Linda's father, Thomas Carlton. Largely occupied with business matters, he has encouraged Linda to develop her independent side as well as her social side. In the opening volume of the series, readers learn that Linda's father has encouraged her "to shoot a gun, ride a horse, and drive a car"—all activities fostering independence and responsibility (*AP* 22). He reinforces that independence when he gives her an airplane as a graduation present. For all his progressive actions, however, Mr. Carlton is still very much a man of his times. When Linda outlines to him her dreams of winning a pilot's license, then going to ground school to master aircraft construction and maintenance, he praises her ambition, yet remains skeptical: "You don't expect to be one of those independent girls who insist upon earning their own living, do you, dear?" (*AP* 57–58). Still later, he reflects that, while Linda has indeed made a name for herself, "he didn't want her to miss the happiness that marriage would bring her" (*HF* 221). Though he has faith in his daughter's common sense and determination, even he cannot resist measuring her by the prevailing standards of the era.

Facing outright opposition from her aunt and tepid support from her father, Linda must prove to them the rightness of her desire for independence. In this she reaps the benefit of far-reaching social changes taking place in American life—changes that gave the independent woman new prominence in the late 1920s and into the 1930s. Seeing the independence generated by the "New Woman" of the nineteenth century and the autonomy of the free-thinking "flapper" of the 1920s, American women took these models to be "[symbols] of liberated aspirations," and strove to create for themselves equal places in a largely masculine world (Woloch 256; Spencer 49). In this they were aided by the 1930s mass media, which increasingly portrayed women "in assertive roles," ranging from "the ambitious career girl" to "the worldly wise reporter." These role models, for their part, "exuded vitality," acting in ways that seemed to an older set to be "dynamic, aggressive, even flamboyant" (Woloch 318). These are the models that motivate Linda, and she shapes her life as one of individualism, competence, and independence.

From the outset, Linda recognizes that she will be entering a man's world. Early in the first volume, she muses that "her ambition was to fly, to fly so expertly that she could go to strange lands, do a man's work perhaps, carry out missions of importance" (*AP* 21). Having sampled flight, she determines to make it her career, telling her father that she wants to win a transport pilot's license "so that I can earn my living in aviation. I want to go in for it seriously, Daddy. Not just play!" (*OF* 37). And take it seriously she does. She impresses the owner of her ground school with her single-mindedness ("We have 'em all the time here [he says] — society dames, flying as a fad, school-girls, for the excitement of the thing, married women who are tired of housekeeping.... There isn't one in a thousand who takes it seriously, as you do, Miss Carlton."), and she thinks of a woman's flying the Atlantic as "history — great as the moment when the suffrage movement had been won!" (*OF* 216–17, 249; ellipsis in the original).

In establishing herself as an independent person, Linda speaks for the modern American woman, always conscious of the importance of women proving themselves as persons of competence and responsibility. She criticizes a hoaxer's female accomplice as having "brought dishonor on all our sex," and, though she relishes the acclaim that flying the Atlantic brings her, she can say, in all seriousness, "I sincerely hope that more and more girls and women will be doing things in aviation, so that my little stunt will seem trivial. That is progress, you know" (*OF* 259; *IA* 13–14). She even convinces men of this new female role when her having mastered radio-telegraphy leads an airport attendant "to decide that girls could do almost anything now-a-days" (*HF* 127, 211–12). Retaining her femininity and her social ease though she does, Linda thinks of herself as an able, competent, independent person, and expects to be treated as such.

So successful is she in her efforts that even Aunt Emily is at last won over. She has never wavered in her belief that Linda should settle into the roles that society expects of her, yet she is sensible enough to accept the reality of Linda's achievements. Turning to her brother at series' end, she confesses the foolishness of her desires:

> "I've learned my lesson, Tom," she said, "in this year and a half since Linda's been out of school. I had expected her to have a year of parties —

to 'come out,' you know — and then marry some nice young man. But Linda has plans of her own, and I realize now that I might as well save my time as to try to arrange anything for her.... And, as for wealth and social position — well, they simply mean nothing in her life. Besides, she doesn't need them; I can see that. Linda could go anywhere, be accepted at Court, if she wanted to, because of what she has accomplished herself" [*HF* 220; ellipsis in the original].

Spokesperson for the status quo though she may be, Aunt Emily is a sensible individual, recognizing that Linda's competence, responsibility, and serious-minded approach to aviation have won as much prominence and social acceptance as her own more conventional means could have done. The world has indeed changed, and the able, independent woman is taking her place in American society. It is a notable message.

The third, and most prominent, element unifying the books is aviation, the agency that enables Linda to make her way so triumphantly. Linda's era, the decade of the 1930s, was in every respect a Golden Age of aviation for women. Although women had been a presence in aviation from its very start (Harriet Quimby, the first American woman — and second woman worldwide — to earn a flying license, received her license in 1911), they sprang into national prominence in the years immediately following Charles A. Lindbergh's trans–Atlantic flight of 1927. In 1928, Amelia Earhart became the first woman to fly the Atlantic, though she did so as passenger in a male-operated aircraft. Jessie Keith-Miller flew from England to Australia with a companion in the same year, the first woman to do so, and Amy Johnson made the flight solo in 1930. The National Women's Air Derby (the "Powder Puff Derby") of 1929 drew nation-wide attention as twenty women pilots, including Earhart, Keith-Miller, and Ruth Nichols, raced their airplanes from Santa Monica, California, to Cleveland, Ohio. A year later, Nichols, on her own, set three women's records between December 1930 and October 1931: world records in altitude, distance, and speed (Brooks-Pazmany 34–51; Cadogan 110–17; Oakes, 49).

Capping the achievements of women pilots during the decade were Amelia Earhart's solo flight across the Atlantic in 1932, making her the first woman to fly solo across the ocean and only the second person to do so, and her solo flight from Hawaii to the mainland in 1935. Other women fliers, including Ruth Nichols and Laura Ingalls, were planning Atlantic flights, but Earhart accomplished the feat first (Adams; Oakes 24). With the two landmark ocean flights accomplished and their other deeds receiving national publicity in the press, technical journals, and popular magazines, women pilots were in the public eye. As G.K. Spencer wrote in 1930, "there has not been a single step in aviation's development in which the student woman, the woman of action or the woman of derring-do has not played an important role" (Spencer 49). Julie Wosk reinforces this view seventy years later, remarking that aviation by the 1930s had become for women "a way to transcend the boundaries of traditional social roles and assumptions about women's limited capabilities" (Wosk 149). This emerging society of women aviators is the milieu into which Linda Carlton dreams of moving.

Throughout the books, Linda makes clear her awareness of women pilots' achievements. The opening pages of *Linda Carlton, Air Pilot* link her to Earhart and Elinor Smith (another record-setter of the time), and her success at looping-the-loop causes Ralph Clavering to compare her to Laura Ingalls, who at the time held the world record with 980 consecutive loops. When a donor in 1931 establishes a prize for the first woman to fly the Atlantic alone, Earhart is mentioned as a possible competitor, but those in the know consider her "too good a sport to take honors from a younger, less-experienced flyer.... She doesn't have to. She has already won her place." The same volume lauds Ruth Nichols and Mrs. Keith-Miller as being among those "women [who] are working so hard to establish our place in aviation." Finally, in *Linda Carlton's Perilous Summer,* Linda describes Amy Johnson as "the most courageous woman flyer in the whole world to-day!" The women pilots and their achievements are Linda's inspiration, confirming her desire to earn her living in the emerging, exciting world of aviation (*AP* 8, 86; *OF* 206, 259; *PS* 28).

Crucial to Linda's determination to build a flying career are the airplanes themselves. Early craft had been fragile, unreliable machines, built of wood and varnished silk and powered by cranky, often home-built engines. By the late 1920s, however, advances in aviation technology had made airplanes safer, more comfortable, and far more reliable than their predecessors. Metal framing and (often) metal covering gave the craft new durability; new instruments, including the artificial horizon, the radio directional compass, and the Kollsman altimeter, simplified the physical act of flying an airplane, and new engines such as the Wright Whirlwind (the engine that powered Charles Lindbergh's *Spirit of St. Louis*) made long-distance, long-duration flights almost commonplace. With this new reliability came new accessibility. Light aircraft were more affordable than they had been in the past, and flying, as a sport as much as an occupation, quickly became acclaimed as a part of progressive daily life (Bilstein, 87–88, 70–74).

These advances are reflected in the three airplanes most closely associated with Linda's exploits, for all three represent some of the most advanced aviation technology of the time. Linda receives her first ship, an Arrow Sport "Pursuit," as a graduation gift from her father, stimulating her to sign up for flying lessons. Despite its fanciful name, the Arrow Sport is an actual airplane, built by the Arrow Aircraft and Motors Corporation of Havelock, Nebraska. A "side by side, two place, bi-plane" priced at just under $3000, it was certified by the Civil Aeronautics Authority in February 1929 and quickly gained popularity as a sport and training airplane. The "Pursuit" model shared the dual controls and side-by-side seating of the earlier models, but was driven by a more powerful Kinner radial engine, rated at 100 horsepower (Arrow Aircraft and Motors Corp.; "Arrow Sport A2–60").

In this craft, often accompanied by Louise Haydock, Linda makes a number of notable flights. In the first volume alone she flies from Ohio to Colorado to visit friends, from Colorado to Texas to help her injured father, and from Texas to Louisiana and back to bring a noted surgeon to his aid. Her excursions continue in the second volume, as she flies from Spring City to Philadelphia to deliver a strangling baby for emergency surgery, takes part in Kitty Clavering's newly-formed flying club, and flies from Spring City to New York City, and thence to Canada, trailing the competitor who is threatening Mr. Carlton's business. At this point, however, the Arrow is sabotaged and crashes in flames, as Linda and Louise parachute to safety: "Tears came into the young aviatrix's eyes, and she hugged her chum tightly in her grief. It was as if she had lost a very dear friend" (*OF* 138). The advanced technology of her aircraft has given her new freedom and new opportunity, and she grieves over the loss of all three.

Despite her dismay over losing the Arrow, Linda does not long remain airplane-less. To fly the Atlantic, she selects a new aircraft, the Bellanca J-300. "It has everything to make it perfect!" she gushes to her father. "A capacity for carrying one hundred and five additional gallons of gasoline, besides the regular supply in the tanks of one hundred and eighty gallons! And a Wright three-hundred-horsepower engine, and a tachometer, and a magnetic compass —.... You can be sure it will have every modern invention, every safety device there is today" (*OF* 201–02). Priced at twenty-two thousand dollars, its instrumentation makes it "a marvel of modern science, Linda thought, proud to be the possessor" (*OF* 269). The Bellanca proves to be all she thinks it is, and she makes her flight from New

York to Paris without incident, "beating Lindbergh's time by a little more than an hour" (*OF* 274).

In selecting a Bellanca J-300, Linda chooses wisely. The Bellanca Aircraft Company of Delaware had a well-deserved reputation for building sturdy, reliable airplanes suitable for long-distance flights. Charles Lindbergh attempted to buy a Bellanca WB-2 for his Atlantic flight, before turning to the Ryan Airline Company of San Diego. A WB-2 had set a record for non-refueled flight of over fifty-one hours in April 1927, and the same ship, as the *Columbia*, flew non-stop from New York to Germany in June 1927. A Bellanca J flew non-stop from Maine to Spain in July 1929, and a J-300, equipped much as Linda's, flew non-stop from Brooklyn to Istanbul in July 1931 (Abel and Abel 28–32, 42, 55–56). Since the copyright deposit copy of *Linda Carlton's Ocean Flight* was logged by the Library of Congress on 22 May 1931, the books were clearly providing their readers the latest developments in modern aircraft.

No other aircraft, however, was more emblematic of modernity and progress than the machine associated with Linda's last three adventures — the Pitcairn-Cierva PCA-2 autogiro. A three-passenger ship with vestigial wings and a conventionally mounted propeller in the front, the autogiro is distinguished by a large, overhead rotor. This unpowered rotor is activated by the ship's forward motion and acts as a wing, enabling the craft to take off in a remarkably short distance and land almost vertically. Linda first encounters the autogiro in *Linda Carlton's Ocean Flight*, when one lands at the ground school where she is studying. Like her classmates, she is enthralled by the possibilities of the machine, agreeing with her instructor when he says, "I believe it is the plane for the city dweller." Its ability to fly low and slow is also attractive, and one of her classmates proclaims, "Everyone can keep an autogiro in his back yard" (*OF* 214).

Linda buys her autogiro directly from the Pitcairn plant in Pennsylvania, having decided that it is the ship best suited for her purposes: "I want to take a job, and I think an autogiro will be the most convenient plane I can have, to take with me anywhere I want to go. I shan't have to depend on big fields for landing." She pays for her craft with a certified check for fifteen thousand dollars, earnings from her Atlantic flight, and flies away in it, certain in her mind that it "is the plane of the future, or of the present" (*IA* 19, 25). The autogiro, named *Ladybug*, proves to be everything she hopes. Its short-take-off, short-landing capabilities assist her in trapping the bank robbers; she makes a roadside landing to rescue Helen Tower from an attacker, and later lands on the deck of an ocean liner at sea to confront Ed Tower. In *Linda Carlton's Hollywood Flight*, she treks to California in it, landing on the roof of an office building en route. She then heads to Mexico in pursuit of the counterfeiters, where the ship's short take-off seems "nothing short of miraculous to him [Bert Chase], accustomed as he was to the prolonged taxi-ing of a fast plane," and, when they are forced down by a lack of fuel, Linda brings it in for "a dead-stick landing, so much easier with an autogiro than with an ordinary plane" (*HF* 146–47, 151).

In her admiration of the autogiro, Linda reflects the interest commanded by the machine during the early 1930s. Invented by Spaniard Juan de la Cierva in the 1920s, it flew in the United States for the first time in 1928; the following year, Harold Pitcairn began manufacturing the craft under license from Cierva. Pitcairn demonstrated a Mark II version at the Cleveland National Air Races in the summer of 1929, and began production of the PCA-2, the model that Linda buys, in late 1930 (Brooks 304–08). News accounts of autogiro flights hailed it as an "everyman's" machine from its first appearance. Amelia Earhart took a passenger aloft in one in December 1930, saying that "its amazing features of stability and safety will be the most important factors in bringing women into active aviation because of the added ease of control and security," and later set an altitude record of 19,000 feet in one. Cierva himself praised it as a "family" machine, inviting "the general use of the air for business and pleasure, for travel and sport, for pleasure jaunts as well as for speedy communications" ("Miss Earhart;" "Miss Earhart Sets;" "Autogiro Is Hailed").

Earle Ovington, a well-known aviation journalist and pilot, called the autogiro "the 'missing link' that aviation is waiting for; it will get the man-in-the-street off the ground when he would not consider the ordinary type of ship," and, when Harold Pitcairn received the Collier Trophy in 1931 for "the development and demonstration of the autogiro, that remarkable new type aircraft considered by many the most revolutionary development in heavier-than-air craft since the first flight of the Wright brothers," one of the machines landed on the South Lawn of the White House to enhance the award ceremony (Ovington 36; "For the Greatest" 31). Another juxtaposition of dates confirms Linda's awareness of the latest in aviation; the PCA-2 received its certification from the Civil Aeronautics Authority on 2 April 1931, while the copyright deposit volume of *Linda Carlton's Island Adventure* reached the Library of Congress on 22 May 1931 (Brooks 308). In her knowledge of advanced technology as much as in her outlook, Linda is, indeed, an up-to-date, modern young woman.

The five volumes of Linda Carlton's adventures won neither the longevity nor the fame of the contemporaneous Nancy Drew books, but they capture a singular moment in the portrayal of the young American woman. Like her literary kinsperson Nancy Drew, Linda solves crimes; like her real-life contemporary, Amelia Earhart, she masters a challenging new technology and wins national esteem in a predominantly male milieu. Like "Carolyn Keene," author Edith Lavell presents Linda's crime-solving as a conceivable undertaking for an intelligent young woman, but, more clearly than "Keene," she understands that young women will be better served by a life that is reality-based and career-oriented. To this end, she gives Linda a set of modern attributes, more comprehensive even than those given Nancy, allowing her to embrace both the latest advances in technology and the latest advances in progressive social thought.

These attributes place Linda at the forefront of 1930s feminism. She appears as a forward-looking, highly competent young woman who will live in a world in which the men of society will recognize and applaud the achievements of a woman, whatever her field of endeavor. That field, for Linda, is aviation. Acclaimed throughout the nation as "Queen of the Air" and the "WORLD'S MOST FAMOUS AVIATRIX," she accepts her status modestly, desiring only to establish herself as a reliable, capable flier (*IA* 10; *HF* 13; capitals in the original). Her adventures, however, do more. They encourage their young readers to question conventionality. They inform those readers of cutting-edge technology. They demonstrate that women can grasp, and master, that technology. And they show that women, too, can make effective progress in the technological as much as the social world. Detective though she may be, Linda Carlton is a flier first, foremost, and always, and her accomplishments send a singularly empowering message to the young women who read of them.

Works Cited

Abel, Alan, and Drina Welch Abel. *Bellanca's Golden Age.* Golden Age of Aviation Series 4. Brawley, CA: Wind Canyon Books, 2004.

Adams, Mildred. "Woman Makes Good Her Claim for a Place in the Skies." *New York Times* (7 June 1931): SM 4.

Arrow Aircraft and Motors Corporation. Common Stock Notification. *New York Times* (15 April 1929): 43.

"Arrow Sport A2–60," National Air and Space Museum, Smithsonian Institution, http://www.nasm.si.edu/research/aero/aircraft/arrowsport.htm.

"Autogiro is Hailed as Family Machine." *New York Times* (6 June 1931): 14.

Bilstein, Roger E. *Flight in America: from the Wrights to the Astronauts*. Rev. ed. Baltimore: Johns Hopkins University Press, 1994.

Brooks, Peter W. *Cierva Autogiros: The Development of Rotary-Wing Flight*. Washington: Smithsonian Institution Press, 1988.

Brooks-Pazmany, Kathleen. *United States Women in Aviation 1919–1929*. Washington: Smithsonian Institution Press, 1991.

Cadogan, Mary. *Women with Wings: Female Flyers in Fact and Fiction*. Chicago: Academy, 1993.

"For the Greatest Achievement in American Aviation." *National Aeronautic Magazine* (May 1931): 31–33.

Lavell, Edith. *Linda Carlton, Air Pilot*. Akron, Ohio: Saalfield, 1931. Cited as AP.

_____. *Linda Carlton's Hollywood Flight*. New York: A.L. Burt, 1932. Cited as HF.

_____. *Linda Carlton's Island Adventure*. Akron, Ohio: Saalfield, 1931. Cited as IA.

_____. *Linda Carlton's Ocean Flight*. Akron, Ohio: Saalfield, 1931. Cited as OF.

_____. *Linda Carlton's Perilous Summer*. New York: A.L. Burt, 1932. Cited as PS.

MacLeod, Anne Scott. "Nancy Drew and her Rivals: No Contest." *Horn Book Magazine*, 63 (1987): 314–22, 442–50.

"Miss Earhart Pilots Passenger in Autogiro." *New York Times* (20 December 1930): 3.

"Miss Earhart Sets Autogiro Record." *New York Times* (9 April 1931): 1.

Oakes, Claudia M. *United States Women in Aviation 1930–1939*. Washington: Smithsonian Institution Press, 1991.

Ovington, Earle. "The Airplane and Autogiro Compared." *Popular Aviation* (November 1931): 36.

Rehak, Melanie. *Girl Sleuth: Nancy Drew and the Women Who Created Her*. Orlando: Harcourt, 2005.

Spencer, G.K. "Pioneer Women of Aviation." *Sportsman Pilot* (May 1930): 16–17, 49.

Vaughan, David K. "Girl Fliers in a World of Guys." *Dime Novel Roundup* 68 (1999): 16–27.

Woloch, Nancy. *Women and the American Experience: A Concise History*. 2nd ed. Boston: McGraw-Hill, 2002.

Wosk, Julie. *Women and the Machine: Representations from the Spinning Wheel to the Electronic Age*. Baltimore: Johns Hopkins University Press, 2001.

The Girl Sleuths
of Melody Lane

H. Alan Pickrell

It is, perhaps, more than self-evident to point out that the Melody Lane teen-age sleuth series, which ran between the years of 1933 and 1940, is an anomaly in the lexicon of teen sleuth literature. Authored by Lilian Garis of the famous Garis writing family, the series (if it truly is a series) is unique in a number of ways. First and foremost among the series' differences is the matter of name. Customarily, series are referred to by the names of their nominal leading characters: i.e. Nancy Drew, Beverly Gray, Judy Bolton, the Dana Girls, Connie Blair, and Penny Parker, to name a few of many, many others. Melody Lane, however, is not the name of an individual, but rather the name of a street or section of town (and that changes over the course of the series) in what is probably New Jersey, near the state line.

This premise offers the hope of diversity and freshness. The possibility of stories based on buildings and localities rather than personalities offers a promise of a unique usage of the series concept. However, that potential of creativity never develops, since the series quickly settles down to introduce teenage ghost buster Carol Duncan and her friends and family. Rather than creating a fresh approach to the mysteries by utilizing a setting as the focal point of the story, this use of a major figure is the accepted, and even hackneyed, approach to teen sleuth stories. In this series, however, characters are as mutable as the settings, since Carol's sister Cecy takes over as detective at one point in the series. This instance is unique in series literature. No teen sleuth had ever abandoned detection to another. George and Bess were always Nancy Drew's sidekicks and never attempted to take over the case or strike out on their own, and sister crime fighting teams, like Jean and Louise Dana of the Dana Girls, always worked together. Occasionally, as in the Dana Girls' mysteries or the Kay Tracey mysteries, an archenemy of one of the girls might try to steal a case from them, but no teen sleuth worth her salt would simply abandon a case.

Also, after the first few volumes, the Melody Lane series leaves Melody Lane. This means that the Melody Lane series is no longer about Melody Lane; therefore; since the series so readily deserts its namesake, one is compelled to ask, why is it called the Melody Lane series? The area originally received its name from the massive organ that was built into the upper floor of Oak Lodge. The instrument was so powerful that it could be heard outside the mansion almost as easily as inside. Evidently though, there were only a limited number of mysterious buildings or geographic features along that stretch of road, and those that were there were quickly exhausted, so Carol is forced to leave Melody Lane in search of further adventure, and eventually even abandons the role of detective itself. In a particular way, this geographic restraint calls to mind late Victorian/early Edwardian author H. Rider Haggard and his popular Allan Quatermain character. In the second Quatermain book, *Allan Quatermain*, Haggard killed his character at the end of the book. Later on he regretted that decision; consequently, for fourteen or so novels, Haggard had to find ways to allow Quatermain to speak from beyond the grave through devices such as the discovery of a lost manuscript. Likewise, Garis eventually found a way to return Carol as detective to Melody Lane, via the device of a fresh-air camp, after a four book hiatus.

Undoubtedly, the confusion over the series' name, geography, and main character only serves to highlight the confusion which surrounds the Melody Lane books themselves. Consequently, given a series that abandons its original premise and changes leading characters, readers might well ask if this collection of volumes is, indeed, truly a series at all, and if it is, once it leaves the locale of the series behind, what might the name of the series actually be?

Despite a plethora of mystery and detection series for young women that featured teenaged sleuths, not all of those efforts were successful. The most popular efforts seemed to be those published by Grosset and Dunlap, and, in the case of Nancy Drew and the Dana Girls, written by the Stratemeyer Syndicate, which seemed to have had a formula for material that worked and sold. Other popular series more or less dated themselves out of existence, but not the adventures of Nancy Drew. Nancy never dated herself by referring to calamities, wars, or social tragedies. Most tellingly, the Drew books did not need to be read in sequence. Circumstances didn't change enough from volume to volume to make it necessary for readers to peruse Volume 35 before reading Volume 36. Stratemeyer had learned his lesson from his popular Ruth Fielding series in which schoolgirl Ruth grew up, went to college, had a career, married, and had children, taking her well past the teen sleuth age range and status. He had done the same thing with his popular series for boys, The Rover Boys. Later, Stratemeyer tried to revive the series by bringing it back as a series about the sons of the original brothers. Melody Lane, however, was the creation of Lilian Garis without the guidance of the syndicate, for whom she had a written a number of books under various pseudonyms. Despite its illustrious pedigree, it is an example of a series that failed for a number of reasons.

In the event that the reader decides to go along with the concept that the Melody Lane books *are* a series (as it was touted by the publisher), most readers would be forced to admit that they are one of the most ill-conceived and poorly constructed series around. Most series books like to give the readers the impression that one adventure follows hard on the heels of the previous one. In the Melody Lane series, though, many things happen between the volumes that go unexplained: for example, one book concludes leaving the Duncan family in fairly desperate financial straits — near poverty, in fact. Then, the next book opens with the family living, once again, if not in luxury's lap, then at least quite comfortably. Few explanations for this reversal of fortune are given; consequently, readers are left feeling dissatisfied and uninformed, especially about the lives of characters central to the books.

Having accepted and advertised the books on the basis of the three volume "breeder" set, the use of which Stratemeyer popularized as a merchandising ploy, the publishers were faced with the problem of what to do with a number of books that turned out to be related by characters and intent, but really had nothing much to do with a connecting quotient within the volumes themselves. Some were connected by their location on Melody Lane and some were connected by association with the Duncan family, but the connection is not consistent. "Series" is really the most convenient and familiar way to designate the volumes; although, perhaps, more truthfully, the books are actually sequels one to the other rather than a "series" in the Stratemeyer sense. Juvenile readers might not understand the fine distinction between "sequel" and "series," and the term "series" is probably best understood and most frequently encountered. As Strate-meyer and his imitators created them, a series is a comfortable and famil-iar situation in which characters remain pretty much the same, as do the conditions surrounding them. In a sequel, however, frequently the con-ditions of leading characters do change, and often the position of leading character is passed along to another character. In fact, to confuse matters more, *The Secret of the Kashmir Shawl* is advertised as a sequel to *The Wild Warning,* though, of course, both books are part of the same series.

Still, the Melody Lane books do have some of the characteristics of other juvenile series books. Like the adventures of Nancy Drew, Judy Bolton, Kay Tracy, Penny Parker, and all of those other young sleuths, titles of the Melody Lane stories are sensationalistic or evocative with, in many instances, seemingly supernatural overtones. These titles certainly attract the interest and attention of a young audience and serve the purpose of titillating burgeoning readers, but in a number of cases, more sophisti-cated readers will find themselves aware of the hard work going on as the author attempts to conform the plot to the title of the book. To speak completely truthfully, the plots are often exceptionally awkward and con-trived, and in many cases, it seems a foregone conclusion that the author thought of the title first and then tried to manufacture a plot to fit. Strate-meyer had an outline for the next book in his series and announced the title of the successor at the end of the present volume, and that was accepted practice. Not all authors, however, had the next plot in mind when the title was announced. In *The Tower Secret,* for example, there happens to be an old tower on the property that a family friend has just purchased. The tower is not a part of the mansion that exists on the site, and is in no way physically connected to that building. On certain nights, a light shines from the tower. The problem, then, is to find the source of the light. This plot quickly degenerates into a confused smuggling plot and use of scientific technology to manufacture a light in the tower, and various people who appear and disappear in the vicinity of the tower, and the tower's value because of its visibility from the road. No good expla-nation of the original purpose of the tower is ever given, nor is any good reason given to justify keeping it on the property instead of tearing it down, as the owner wishes. Since the tower serves no purpose for the Bond family, and since it is not particularly historically distinguished, tearing the thing down seems an easy way to end the problem once and for all. Even after the solution of the mystery, no one is completely certain what to do with the tower.

The primary sleuth of the Melody Lane series, as before mentioned, is Carol Duncan. Like many of the girl sleuths who populate the juvenile and young adult mystery fiction genre, Carol is motherless. In general, except for Judy Bolton, Connie Blair, and several others, girl detectives lack one or more parents. It is this very lack of parental supervision that allows the sleuths to have the freedom they need to pursue the many mysteries that engross them. If their sole parent is a father, then he is usually extremely indulgent with his daughter. If the parent is a mother, then she tends to be somewhat fluttery and ineffectual. At any rate, either parent's presence seems to bring about the same predictable results: a lack of supervision and a remarkable amount of freedom for the young detective. In the case of Carol Duncan and her father, however, this indulgence is exercised to a ludicrous degree. It seems that Felix Duncan, Carol's surviving parent, is out of work and ill. Carol, like all girl sleuths, is a practical psychologist and suspects that the one factor might be causing the other, but the situation has become a chicken-and-egg dilemma. She also suspects that he might be depressed, since he has, for all intents and purposes, turned the reins of the family over to Carol, including the care and feeding of Carol's headstrong, spoiled, impetuous, and impractical younger sister, Cecy. This is a potentially interesting situation as sleuthing goes, since sibling sleuths are neither unheard of nor unknown. The Dana Girls are some of the most readily recalled, although the most intriguing sister snoops would be Connie Blair and her twin, a device that allows the detective to be in two places at the same time. Cecy, however, given her shallow nature, doesn't actually participate in solving the mysteries; she is far too flighty to concentrate her attention on serious matters. In fact, she doesn't even appear in all of the volumes until she assumes the magnifying glass and flashlight in *The Secret of the Kashmir Shawl*, when Carol more or less retires.

One of the greatest departures from the pattern of other teen sleuths is the fact that Carol is the major wage earner for her family. Indeed, although from an obviously privileged family formerly, Carol must compartmentalize her high school education while making a living for her family. Fortunately, like many teen sleuths, Carol has not only the determination to keep her family afloat, but the means to make it possible to do so. Carol is a talented organist and plays the musical scores to accompany silent films at the local theatre. Certainly, multi-abilities seem to be a hallmark of teen sleuths. Ruth Fielding wrote, directed and starred in her own films, and there isn't much that Nancy Drew cannot tackle and succeed at doing. While the author of the books is extremely coy about revealing the ages of either Carol or Cecy, readers can deduce that Carol seems to be between sixteen and seventeen years of age, and Cecy is probably around fourteen or fifteen, although somewhat young for her age. A possible mistake that Garis makes in developing the characters is in allowing the girls to age too quickly. This limits their mystery solving to summer vacation, and by the time the breeder books are finished, Carol is already out of high school and thus, technically, no longer a teen sleuth.

Besides Cecy, Carol has friends who attempt to aid her in her sleuthing interests. Foremost among those friends is Thalia ("Thally") Bond. It should be noted, however, that Thally is not a true sidekick in the same way George and Bess were sidekicks to Nancy Drew. Once, and only once, during *The Sign of the Twisted Candles,* did George and Bess desert Nancy, and that was largely because of a misunderstanding. Thally often abandons Carol, leaving her on her own to solve some real puzzles. It also should be noted that Carol is not simply a detective. She is a recognized ghost buster, although she is often referred to as a "ghost chaser." Of course, none of the ghosts with which she tangles are real specters, and actually, Carol doesn't believe in ghosts during daylight hours; however, when something unusually spooky happens after dark, Carol becomes as ready to seek help and company as anyone else would. Her company of choice is Glenn Garrison, who is always present when Carol needs rescuing. Glenn obviously thinks that Carol is the "cat's meow," and she seems to think well of him, too. In fact, their relationship shows a bit of promise of getting past the Nancy Drew–Ned Nickerson stages and becoming warmer and more sincere.

It is to Glenn that Carol turns when she is in need of advice, help, consolation, and general cheering up, and Glenn is more than happy to oblige. In *The Ghost of Melody Lane,* Glenn drives Carol to an interview for a job that she needs badly. She feels she can confide in him, and she does. His interest and sympathy cause Carol to slip over "closer to Glenn. He was protective" (Garis *Ghost* 29). Later on, to further cheer Carol and build her confidence, Glenn "secures her hand in a playful little grasp" (30). Still, the fact that Carol frequently reflects on how immature boys (and Glenn specifically) can act and how disgusted she can get over Glenn's acts of "larking around" with his friends sets Carol apart and above Glenn, at least in her own perspective. Their relationship, however, lasts until Carol moves to the city and Glenn goes away to college in *The Mystery of Stingyman's Alley.*

During the first book, Carol's family is languishing away in the midst of the Great Depression, but Thally and Glenn and their families seem to have retained their socio-economic status in the community. Still, Thally and Glenn are devoted to Carol, even though her family's fortunes have shriveled. In addition to her musical talents, which seem to disappear after the first three books, Carol, like most girl sleuths, is highly intelligent and logical. Additionally, she is exceptionally loyal to her friends, family, and ideals, but she is a rather introspective young woman, much more serious than her sister Cecy. Yet, Carol is a typical teenager, and when nothing else interferes, she enjoys having fun with her friends. There are situations, in fact, when Carol gets so involved with friends and fun that she forgets whatever case is at hand for extended periods of time, which suggests that she might not be quite as dedicated to sleuthing as some of her teenaged counterparts. Unfortunately, this very fact has the effect of slowing down the action of the book, rather than building suspense, as the device may have been intended to do.

The series author, Lilian C. Garis, was an experienced writer who, in addition to newspaper work, had written original books under her own name as well as a number of books for the Stratemeyer Syndicate under a variety of pseudonyms. Garis was extremely popular with readers and publishers, and it was she who involved her husband, Howard, with the Stratemeyer Syndicate. During her tenure with the Stratemeyer enterprise, Lilian wrote as Margaret Penrose, Laura Lee Hope, and probably other names as well. In his family memoir, *My Father Was Uncle Wiggily*, Roger Garis revealed that his mother and father sometimes worked on or wrote books for one another (74).

Lilian, however, like Howard, had published and was publishing numerous books without the benefit of the syndicate, and was considered to be an able writer of stories for juvenile girls. She was one of the first juvenile writers to have her picture published on the dust jackets of her books along with a list of her prior publications. In fact, the Melody Lane books were advertised on the jackets of the Nancy Drew books, even though they were not products of the Stratemeyer Syndicate. Such an occurrence seems to indicate that the publishers hoped that the cachet of the Drew books would establish some momentum for the Garis series. Given all of these facts, Garis' writing style, especially in the Melody Lane series, is both puzzling and, at times, disturbing.

While her son, Roger, said that she had an excellent writing style for not only juvenile but adult-oriented materials as well, critics such as Jennifer White and Joan H. Young have commented on Garis's lengthy sentences and "choppy, breathless style," which seem to contradict Roger's evaluation. As to sentence structure, two examples of awkward phrasing (from among many) include: "But the will will settle it" (*Alley* 206), or "What is the nursery over there closed for?" (161). Later, when Carol's father awakens her from a bad dream, he asks if she is having "the" nightmare. "The" seems a strange use of an article in this context. Surely, "a" would have been infinitely preferable, since "the" implies one of two things: (1) that this bad dream is the only bad dream Carol has and she has it repeatedly or (2) that there is only one bad dream and it is common to all humankind. In point of fact, the expression seems almost dialectal in nature, like a foreign speaker who has not quite grasped the nuances of English language articles.

Roger's memoir, while primarily about his father, presents a relatively complete picture of his mother as well. Without using these exact words and phrases, Roger depicts Lilian Garis as a complicated, complex, and somewhat neurotic woman who is competitive with her husband and son, and who is, in some ways, jealous of their respective successes. Once Howard began to experience the huge success of Uncle Wiggily and the attendant radio, promotional, and product income, Lilian suffered insecurity based on the difference between their incomes that had, before Wiggily, been almost equal (Garis *Wiggily* 159–185).

When Roger began to achieve some success as an adult writer, Lilian began to feel the need to compete with him as well (159). This sense of competition could very well be reflected in the Melody Lane books. If, for whatever reason, Lilian needed to prove her writing for children was equal to Roger's writings for adults, then Melody Lane could have been the venue in which she tried to make this transition. Certainly that could explain the vagaries of stylistics which various critics have observed. It might account for the overly ambitious plots that fail, somehow, to follow through to an exciting and creative culmination, and why Carol and Cecy age out of the series so quickly. In reading *Stingyman,* the reader is aware that it is a book about an adult young woman, and not about a teen sleuth. Ultimately, the books just seem to run out of energy and the somewhat contrived and, unfortunately, never very interesting plots do not live up to the excitement promised by the books' titles.

A general impression of the books is that the stories often seem more like separate books than a series. Since Garis' intentions for this series are impossible to guess or deduce, readers are left to wonder what the reasons for this lack of connection might be. While mother-son competition might be one explanation, Roger also mentions that his mother was frequently ill and his father stayed in her room with her until she recovered. Since the books seem to be so unrelated, could this sequence of books have been an example of those times when Lilian and Howard covered for one another and wrote one another's books? At this date, it is impossible to tell, but it could explain the lack of continuity and attention paid to some of the issues featured in the books.

In the first of the books, *The Ghost of Melody Lane,* Carol's father, Felix, has lost his job due to his poor health. At the end of the story, Felix and his daughters have been invited to live in the gate house of Oak Lodge. By the second book, Felix is healthy and recovered enough to return to work, although the Duncans continue to live at Oak Lodge. By the fourth book, *The Wild Warning,* the Duncans are financially recovered enough to hire a housekeeper. Also, Melody Lane, that rural lane of mansions, has become a town, and development is on-going. In the seventh book, *The Mystery of Stingyman's Alley,* the Duncans are, once again, plunged into dire financial straits. With no explanation, they have given up the gate house and the housekeeper, and moved to the city where Felix is working for a newspaper and Carol works for a charity operated day nursery. Glenn, Carol's "special" friend, is a part of the past, as is her friend Thally Bond, and Carol is now seeing a young lawyer.

The Secret of the Kashmir Shawl, book eight in the sequence, is all about Cecy and the mystery she solves (and it has nothing to do with Melody Lane either), so once again, the focus splits even more. In the ninth book, *The Hermit of Proud Hill,* both Carol and Cecy participate in a mystery set once again at Melody Lane, but Kay Findley, a hitherto unknown teen-aged resident of Melody Lane, is actually the central character this time. The change in central character fractures the focus of the series irreparably. Even though a tenth title (*The Clue of the Crooked Key*) was announced at the end of the book, the series stopped with volume number nine. By the time the series finished, it was far from where it had started. Indeed, the last books almost seem to have been written by someone who had only quickly scanned or was not overly familiar with the material in previous books.

Within the books, Garis is prone to the overall race and class prejudice and stereotyping that existed generally in the United States at the time these books were written: poor people were usually dirty and unkempt; black youths were usually dirty and ragged, with a tendency to take things that didn't belong to them. One of these racial generalizations is found in *The Dragon of the Hills* and is so offensive that it is difficult to imagine that a publisher let it stand. In the book, The Dragon of the Hills is the name of a tea shop, noteworthy for its famous cinnamon toast. Roadside inns that served tea and cinnamon toast were a staple ingredient in teenaged sleuth stories during the thirties and the forties, so this concept is not unique to Garis. (Incidentally, for this book, she seems to have researched what such a business would demand a bit more thoroughly than she has researched the subject matter for some of the other Melody Lane books.) However, in this particular tea shop, one of the characters in the story insults all Asians everywhere when she declares that a customer was either Chinese or Japanese — she can never tell the difference (Garis 24). The unspoken comment that accompanies this comment is that it really does not matter, either. This is probably the result of negative feeling about the Japanese deriving from World War II. Anti-Asian propaganda, while hurtful to many American citizens of Asian descent, was considered patriotic during that time. It also is the sort of thoughtless response that many privileged WASPs of the era would think to themselves, though without voicing it. Within the plot and details of the book, Garis reveals her own confusion about China and Japan and their cultures and peoples. She obviously hasn't bothered to consult any sources to help straighten out her misunderstandings, either.

It is also within this book that one of the strangest scenes in juvenile literature occurs. A neighbor child awakens Carol and her friend, Dorothy, to seek their help. The child has been unable to stir her grandmother and fears that she has died. While the child sobs uncontrollably, Carol and Dorothy question her closely, and then decide to make some coffee for her. The child insists that she is too upset to have anything, so the girls have a cup before managing to persuade the child that the stimulant will be good for her. At last, the girls decide to call the constable and a doctor. Following that, they dress and make-up for the day, and only then do they take the inconsolable child back to her home. The reader is left to ponder the enormous insensitivity of the two girls and further realize that, if the old lady wasn't dead when the child first arrived asking for help, she would be by the time those two girls managed to get themselves together to deal with the tragedy at hand. Seemingly, Garis experienced very few of life's emergencies. Certainly Roger gives the impression that she was cosseted and protected by Howard, when she was willing to listen to him.

Still, Garis may have revealed a good bit about herself in these texts without realizing what she was doing. First of all, Carol is embarrassed by any show of emotion from others; she demonstrates this by refusing to show any kind of sympathy or comfort to or for them. Time after time, we see Carol withdraw from people who are experiencing emotional distress rather than trying to soothe them. Next, in *Dragon of the Hills* and several other volumes, there is a recurrent incident: no one likes to touch anything that may have been touched by someone else — particularly a foreigner. Nor does anyone like to be touched by a foreigner. This causes the main characters to come across to a modern audience as rude, insensitive to the feelings of others, and uncaring beyond belief. They exercise any excuse to avoid taking someone's hand or accepting their card, not worrying if or how deeply they may offend another person. They pick up discarded items by using a tissue between their fingers and the object they are retrieving, and then wash the object and their hands thoroughly. This overt display of xenophobia is certainly one of the low points in the texts.

In point of fact, the books seem to ignore people from other cultures almost altogether, except to use them as possible villains or to make them counterpoints to white Anglo-Saxons. Much has been written and conjectured about the treatment of other ethnicities and races in these juvenile series books, but in many ways, Garis seems to show the worst aspects of this early form of profiling. African-American characters speak a pronounced dialect, are tremendously superstitious, frequently dishonest, often rather dirty, lazy, and are not very bright. Gypsies are swarthy in complexion, devious, dishonest, frequently soiled, show poor taste in clothes and jewelry, and are frequently sinister. Asian women are dainty and doll-like, without much sense of personal worth or confidence. Asian men, however, are of two types: those descended directly from Sax Rohmer's "yellow peril" novels or else rather comical fellows who say "l" when they mean "r"; still, in the Melody Lane books, the implications are clear: dark complexions equals not only social inferiority, but ethical, moral, and hygienic inferiority as well.

The character who provides most of the attitudes for the series is Carol herself, mainly because she appears in more of the books than anyone else. Carol is an interesting kind of central character, and might have grown out of Lilian's interest in women's rights. There is an almost stereotypical social worker aspect about Carol from her introduction in the first book, and she seems to have a basic need to care for others, which is a continuing strain throughout all of the books. Plus, with the Great Depression as a background (Abreu 4) and almost a setting for the books, there is a good deal of social work to be done. Between immigrants' "special" children, out-of-work circus performers, and destitute corn and dahlia farmers, Carol's care and concern for others manage to get her and her friends in trouble fairly often. Carol is, however, in neither the Nancy Drew nor the Judy Bolton mold. In fact, whereas Nancy welcomes opportunities to "observe" and "overhear" her suspects in revealing situations and conversations and where Judy frequently gets started on a case due to a word or phrase she overhears, Carol gets accidentally sealed in a cave trying to avoid spying. Of course, the cave has another opening, but since Carol brought no flashlight, she can't find it. If, however, she hadn't been quite so nice, she could have followed the other folks out the opposite entrance. Surely, Carol is one of the most reluctant teen sleuths in juvenile series literature. She doesn't enjoy detection; she simply does her sleuthing as she does anything else: because it has to be done. When out-of-work show people take up residence on Melody Lane and various homeowners complain, Carol wants to find them work and a place to live near-by. Judy Bolton would have given a big party and tried to reconcile the various disparate social elements, but Carol needs for everyone to find his or her niche in life and be useful and content.

Carol always seems to find herself responsible for numbers of different people, including her younger sister, Cecy, Cecy's friend Rosie, and total strangers such as Jeannette Ripley, daughter of a friend of Felix Duncan's. Jeannette is sent to stay with the Duncans for an "attitude adjustment." Unfortunately, Felix neglected to mention her forthcoming visit to either of the girls, and it is Carol who gets stuck with her. In this adventure, *The Dragon of the Hills*, Carol reveals a side of her character that is decidedly unattractive. Her propensity to be judgmental and unbending has always been a part of her personality, but it takes center stage in this book, and in succeeding ones as well. Just as when she decided that Glenn and other boys his age were silly for their adolescent caperings and posturings, Carol quickly decides whether or not another person is worth the investment of her time and energy. Not only that, but she deems herself the best judge of what is right for others. Yes, Jeannette *is* silly, self-centered, boy-crazy, and she smokes, but she's not a bad person at heart. Smoking is not a habit that is generally recommended for series book characters or their friends, but in this case, it simply demonstrates that Jeannette is anxious to appear sophisticated beyond her years. It makes her seem like the foolish, impetuous child that she is. Still, Carol can't seem to cut her any slack — and doesn't. "Then, there was Jeanette to be watched and perhaps to be sent home, for Carol was 'no policeman,' as she had often told Thally (141).... Jeanette was calling goodnight.... 'I wish Jeanette wouldn't shout like that,' Carol was thinking as the car groaned away and Jeanette's light step sounded on the porch. 'She never thinks that Mary Ellen might be sleeping now after having been up since five this morning'" (144).

Over time, Carol develops a type of Christian-martyr persona, refusing to explain what is bothering her and why it bothers her until everything eventually erupts in an outburst of moral lecture. Ashamed later on, she always modestly apologizes, making the object of her wrath feel even worse. Given that unpleasant turn to her character, it is amazing that the series made it through nine volumes.

Still, there is a nagging question that is never answered. In the first volume of the series, we are given to understand that Carol is the practical, intelligent, and logical sister. Cecy is given more to homemaking and has a real talent for cooking and baking, though not much interest in education. Yet, in the final volumes of the books, it is Carol who is teaching in a nursery school and doing social work without a college degree while she makes a home for their father, while it is Cecy who goes to college. Carol earlier admits that she is the world's worst cook, yet there she is, preparing breakfast and dinners when her father is there to eat them. Also, about this time (*Stingyman's Alley*), the author tells us that Carol's father calls her by a nickname, explaining that Carol was the sort of person just made to be called nicknames. Her new lawyer-to-be boyfriend also has a nickname for her, but oddly, before this book, Glenn was the only person who called Carol by a nickname, and then only briefly, and in only one book.

Then there's Cecy. In the volumes preceding the *Kashmir Shawl*, Cecy almost never manages to stick with the mystery to the end. She is easily bored and easily frightened, too. So, frequently, she leaves right in the middle of the action and suspense and takes off with her friends, leaving the mystery to Carol and Thally. Usually, as soon as Cecy departs, Carol gets down to business and the mystery is finally solved. The solution is always so completely obvious that the readers must find themselves wondering why it took so many people so long to solve it.

Cecy is blonde, flighty, and immature, so perhaps that is why she must get out of the way before Carol can get down to work. Consequently, it is decidedly odd that, after Carol solves the mystery concerning her Aunt Isabel's house, Moaning Cliff, Isabel decides to take Cecy, and not Carol, to live with her out West and send to boarding school. One can only assume that the *Shawl* story that reintroduces the character of Flinders from *The Wild Warning* is intended to display an older and more mature Cecy. Yet, in the *Shawl* novel, there is no mystery. Both the characters and the readers know from the very beginning what is going on and who is responsible. Cecy's new maturity seems have formulated from her constantly asking herself the question, "WWCD?" ("What would Carol do?")

All in all, the Melody Lane series must be one of the oddest girls' series ever and probably holds the record for a central lack of focus and character in a young people's series. With a teenage sleuth who is frequently unsympathetic, and who shifts identity from book to book, with volumes whose subject shifts from mystery to social work, and with characters, subjects, and a thematic that shifts from book to book as well, the series eventually had no recourse but to implode upon itself. Still, the series represents an interesting and noble experiment that succeeded for a time. Its setting in the Great Depression allows readers an educational insight into a period of history that is largely ignored by most series books of the period. Roger Garis pointed out that his family was neither hurt nor particularly influenced by the Great Depression. Their income varied little, and they hardly noticed the economic woes of the nation because of the popularity of their writing, so it is significant that his mother chose to detail the Depression in the series. Authors like Mildred Wirt, who felt the Depression more strongly, did not include it in the Nancy Drew series, for example. Perhaps that is why, even though the series seems to be weak by contemporary standards, it does appear to have been popular during its day. That contention can be borne out by the relative ease with which one finds copies of the volumes, even of the final title, *The Hermit of Proud Hill*. It may have proved to be inspiring to youngsters whose families were facing the deprivations that the Depression brought about, showing, as it did, how determined young women can carve a life and living for themselves and their families from their own talents and wits. The books also catered to the notion that a young woman can successfully take on the responsibility for her family and be successful.

Ultimately, it is the lack of cohesion both within the plots and within the succession of stories that makes the Melody Lane books a puzzle for readers and something of a failure as a series. Still, the books are the product of a famous and well-known author from a time when series books about teenage sleuths topped the sales charts. For that reason alone, the Melody Lane books — whether a true series or not — remain worthy of both critical and collector scrutiny and attention.

Works Cited

Abreu, John E. "Down Melody Lane with Lilian Garis." *Yellowback Library* 2.3 (1982): 3–8.

Billman, Carol. *The Secret of the Stratemeyer Syndicate: Nancy Drew, The Hardy Boy and the Million Dollar Fiction Factory.* New York: The Ungar Publishing Company, 1986.

Dizer, John. *Tom Swift, The Bobbsey Twins, and Other Heroes of American Juvenile Literature.* Lewiston, N.Y.: Edwin Mellen Press, 1997.

Garis, Lilian C. *The Dragon of the Hills.* New York: Grosset and Dunlap, 1936.

_____. *The Forbidden Trail.* New York: Grosset and Dunlap, 1933.

_____. *The Ghost of Melody Lane.* New York: Grosset and Dunlap, 1933.

_____. *The Hermit of Proud Hill.* New York: Grosset and Dunlap, 1940.

_____. *The Mystery of Stingyman's Alley.* New York: Grosset and Dunlap, 1938.

_____. *The Secret of the Kashmir Shawl.* New York: Grosset and Dunlap, 1939.

_____. *Terror at Moaning Cliff.* New York: Grosset and Dunlap, 1935.

_____. *The Tower Secret.* New York: Grosset and Dunlap, 1933.

_____. *The Wild Warning.* New York: Grosset and Dunlap, 1934.

Garis, Roger. *My Father Was Uncle Wiggily.* New York: McGraw-Hill Book Company, 1966.

Lilian Garis. 19 Oct.1999. Information and Facts About Girls' Series. 9 August 2007, http://users.tellurian.com/bksleuth/info.htm.

MacCann, Donnarae. "Nancy Drew and the Myth of White Supremacy." *Rediscovering Nancy Drew.* Carolyn Stewart Dyer and Nancy Tillman Romalov, eds. Iowa City: University of Iowa Press, 1995.

Rehak, Melanie. *Girl Sleuth: Nancy Drew and the Women Who Created Her.* New York: Harcourt, 2005.

Stratemeyer's Other Garis Ghost: Lilian C. Garis Etexts. 2002–2004. Authors and Books for Children. 9 Aug 2007, http://www.elliemik.co/lcgarisetexts.html.

White, Jennifer. *Vintage Series Books for Girls...and a Few for Boys.* 2003. The Melody Lane Mystery Stories by Lilian Garis. 9 Aug 2007, http://www.Seriesbooks.com/melodylane.html.

Young, Joan H. *Mysteries.* 1997. Melody Lane Mysteries. 9 Aug 2007, http://www.t-one.net-om/read/mystery.html.

Measuring Up to the Task: Cherry Ames as Nurse and Sleuth

Anita G. Gorman and
Leslie Robertson Mateer

Although not as well known as Nancy Drew, nurse-sleuth Cherry Ames appeared in novel after novel from 1943 to 1968, twenty-seven texts in all. The books, written first by Helen Wells, then Julie Tatham, and then again by Wells, suffered from a bit of an identity crisis as they evolved over the course of twenty-five years, leading to three distinct phases or identities. The first phase relates directly to the series' formation. Cherry Ames was created first as a response to World War II and the dramatic need for registered nurses in the United States. Although the focus in these early novels is on nursing, its demands and its rewards, they do involve at least some mystery, some secrecy, and some bravado on the part of the heroine; thus, they are not inconsistent with the later novels. After the war, when the wounded were healed and the country returned to a seemingly tranquil domesticity, these popular books had to find a new *raison d'être*. This second phase, the post-war Ames novels under the authorship of Julie Tatham, took Cherry to a variety of nursing positions in various venues and made her more of an amateur sleuth, à la Nancy Drew. These novels also saw subtle changes in interpretations of Cherry's character as well as in writing style. The third phase sees Wells returning as author, bringing with her a more confident, proficient Cherry in smooth, entertaining, and somewhat formulaic novels. These last novels see Cherry move away, ever so slightly, from dependence on patriarchal authority and emphasize a more glamorous lifestyle.

While the three unique identities the Cherry Ames books manifest are not enough to disrupt the unified sense of series the books exhibit, they are distinct enough to merit critical attention. Changes in authorship, Cherry's character, Cherry's vocation and relationships all reflect the shifting paradigm of a series adapting to changing conditions in both the world around it and the world it so assiduously portrays.

Cherry Ames: War Nurse

More than 150,000 women served in the military during World War II, with more than one-third as army nurses. Army Nurse Corps recruiting literature, according to Joanne Rosenberger, portrayed "these women as pretty, probably virginal, and usually delicate," no doubt because of "the uneasiness that the patriarchal culture had with women in uniform and in positions of authority" (Parry 130). Although nurses had to endure many of the same ordeals as men, to a large degree "popular culture representations of military nurses tended to minimalize their contribution to the war effort" (Parry 132). The Cherry Ames stories, on the other hand, show nurses to be an integral part of the war effort, women who often had to appear stronger than the wounded men they cared for and comforted.

Born in 1910, Wells was a young child during World War I. According to her brother Robert, he would dress up in an old army uniform during the war so that Helen and a friend could pretend that they were Red Cross nurses tending the wounded ("Helen Wells"). Although her family carried on their Jewish and European traditions, Wells also absorbed a sense of allegiance toward the United States, in part from her early environment in Danville, Illinois, and in part from an uncle whose ancestors had fought in the American Revolution ("Helen Wells"). When Grosset and Dunlap needed a bright, young author to create a wartime series, Wells seemed the right person for the job.

The World War II novels —*Senior Nurse, Army Nurse, Chief Nurse, Flight Nurse*, and *Veterans' Nurse*— all written by Wells, focus on characteristic themes: the demands and joys of nursing education, Cherry's infractions, antagonistic authority figures, love interest, "lessons in life" for young girls, patriotism, and at least some dabbling in both feminism and mystery.

The first novel, *Cherry Ames, Student Nurse* (1943), in which the reader meets Cherry and rest of the series' recurring characters, outlines the demands of nursing education. Miss Reamer, superintendent of nurses, teaches the students at Spencer Nursing School that "the first duty of a nurse ... is always to her patient" (30), and that the students will need "good health, intelligence, unselfishness, patience, tact, humor, sympathy, efficiency, neatness, plus plenty of energy for hard work" (32). In this book, as in the second novel, *Senior Nurse* (1944), Cherry worries about measuring up and being able to successfully complete coursework and perform proficiently in the various wards of the hospital. She uses psychology to convince Mrs. Thompson, a patient, that she should return home, and she spends extra time with sick and injured children. Later, as an Army nurse, Cherry practices holistic nursing, though she believes she knows little about "psychoneurological nursing — except that the ancient Greek word, taken to pieces, meant the nursing of soul, nerves, and reason" (*Army Nurse* 127).

One reason Cherry doubts her ability to succeed as both a student and a registered nurse is her propensity for bending the rules. The hierarchies of nursing schools, hospitals, and the military all demand obedience, yet, as a student nurse, Cherry smuggles a large doll, normally used as a patient in demonstrations, into the room of a little girl who wants a playmate, and she takes a child with a burned face to the orthopedic ward to look at a Christmas tree, thereby incurring the wrath of a doctor. In *Army Nurse*, while the soldiers and nurses are playing what the army calls "war games," Cherry comes upon a child whose little brother has been injured. According to the rules, Cherry is not to help the child. Of course she does break the rules, and — temporarily — gets into trouble with a superior. Her infractions generally emanate from her compassion, her playfulness, and the curiosity that will eventually contribute to her success as a sleuth.

Protagonists need antagonists, and for Cherry these usually appear as authority figures. Dr. Wylie, a prominent surgeon, more than once castigates Cherry for using rouge, though she wears none. In *Student Nurse*, he also scolds Cherry for entering the room of a mystery patient when she has been ordered to keep out; yet, because she also helps to get Dr. Joe Fortune's new medicine to the mystery patient, a general, Dr. Wylie eventually admits that the general would have died if she had not disobeyed orders. Other authority figures disapprove of Cherry, including the appropriately named Colonel Pillsbee, who considers Ames "almost too popular" with the sick and injured soldiers, her youth and attractiveness counting as disadvantages in his opinion (*Chief Nurse* 71).

Cherry's attractiveness and vitality attract men, among them Dr. Lex Upham and Captain Wade Cooper, both of whom appear in multiple volumes. Cherry likes them, too, but she avoids any immediate or serious commitment. This carefree attitude may be a lesson for young girls: marriage remains in the future, but nursing remains the more rewarding option for the present.

Delaying marriage is but one of the "lessons in life" embedded in these early (and many other) Ames novels. The first two novels show Cherry — and the young reader — how to overcome hostility from another young woman. She learns that her fellow students have hidden reasons for being unfriendly, and that they are needy. Another lesson involves body image: Cherry tells Midge Fortune, her young neighbor in Hilton, Illinois, to "look and act natural," not like "a third-rate movie-queen" (*Veterans' Nurse* 77), and in *Chief Nurse*, she encourages Bessie, a nurse anesthetist, to stand tall and proud and not to injure both her health and disposition by strenuous dieting.

Patriotism also informs the early Ames novels. When Cherry graduates from nursing school, her entire class enlists in the Army. Later, a torpedoed transport ship and hundreds of Army casualties provide the stage for Cherry to show her mettle: "That night and even the less turbulent nights that followed tested Cherry's idealism and her worthiness to be an Army nurse to the utmost. For all the tragic things she saw, there was no horror ... she only felt, more strongly than ever before, the glory, the beauty almost, of the service she could give" (*Army Nurse* 193). As the war continues, Cherry also comes to see war as "the most horrible thing in the world" (*Chief Nurse* 139); "shaken at the awful human waste of war," she can "only keep these men from getting worse, give a little comfort, until she got them to a hospital and surgeons" (*Flight Nurse* 109). War means danger, but it also means camaraderie, dedication to an ideal, and sacrifice.

Since nursing in the 1940s was a female profession, the early Ames novels include threads of feminist thought. In *Senior Nurse*, an obstetrician, Dr. Walker, turns out to be a woman, though no particular importance is placed on this fact. Cherry's teachers and supervisors in nursing school are mostly women, and on more than one occasion male authority figures receive their comeuppance. *Veterans' Nurse* exposes a male physician as a thief reprimanded by a tough female, Colonel Brown: "She snorted and tossed her white head. 'I've known unscrupulous men before.... I can handle you, my smart-alecky lad,'" a remark that leads Cherry to conclude that "there was something to be said in favor of battle-axes, after all!" (*Veterans' Nurse* 198–199). When suitor Wade Cooper loses his balance in a canoe, both he and Cherry end up in the water, but it is Cherry who saves Wade, a non-swimmer. His masculine ego somewhat bruised, Wade states, "I'm going to marry a soft, helpless feminine little girl who'd let me drown!" (*Veterans' Nurse* 162). His sexism and desire for a compliant wife are presented in a humorous way, though some truth underlies Wade's outburst. Feminism also permeates these books in the portrayal of a protagonist who chooses a career, places herself in danger, and oversees the care of injured and sick soldiers.

In these early novels, Helen Wells lays the groundwork for Cherry's later career as a sleuth. Qualities such as curiosity, intelligence, and courage provide the needed foundation for detective work. Mystery happens from the very first novel with the "mystery patient," later revealed to be a sick general. In *Senior Nurse*, a theft occurs and is solved by Cherry and another student disguised as cleaning women, but the novel remains less about detection and more about nursing as a noble and demanding career, a career necessary to the war effort. In *Cherry Ames, Army Nurse* (1944), Cherry solves a medical mystery — the source of a Panamanian Indian's malaria — but that hardly qualifies as a puzzle worthy of Nancy Drew.

In *Chief Nurse*, Cherry and her twin brother Charlie use their powers of deduction to conclude that the Japanese have a new weapon and that they have reached Island 20 or 21 in the Pacific, close to the Allied base. *Flight Nurse* involves a conundrum — whether Mark Gardiner spies for the Germans or the British — but Cherry does not solve the puzzle; Mark simply tells her the truth. *Cherry Ames, Veterans' Nurse* (1946) involves a few more ingredients of the classic mystery: the hospital's medical storeroom has been robbed of a new drug, an amino acid medication needed to accelerate recovery. Jim (one of the recovering veterans) accompanies Cherry to the storeroom at night to wait for the thief, who turns out to be Margaret Heller, in league with Dr. Orchard; she was a suspect for Cherry and Jim as soon as they saw her picking the lock of her own house (another in a long list of coincidences throughout the series). Cherry is beginning to enter Nancy Drew territory.

With *Private Duty Nurse* (1945), Cherry Ames says goodbye to World War II and its aftermath, and nursing becomes less significant than detective work. *Private Duty Nurse* features unscrupulous, fraudulent fortunetellers, a famous concert pianist (Scott Owens), and a gang of bona fide thieves intent on blackmailing the pianist. Melodrama dominates: Scott has a heart attack; he screams out clues in his sleep; Cherry breaks into an apartment via the fire escape, hides behind a sofa, and is caught by the thieves; finally, she foils the culprits inside a bank vault. The focus has now shifted; using one's wits and courage to find and overcome the bad guys now trumps caring for the sick, even if it takes a series of coincidences to do the job.

Searching for Post-War Identity, or The Tatham Years

In 1948, Wells decided to abandon the Cherry Ames and Vicki Barr series to write for television and radio. Julie Tatham (also Julie Campbell) took the reins and wrote the next eight Cherry Ames novels. Julie Tatham was no novice to juvenile literature, as she was the highly successful author of the Ginny Gordon and Trixie Belden series (the latter still in print today).

Tatham's time as author lasted from 1948 until 1955. Her novels include *Cherry Ames, Cruise Nurse*, the cover of which credits Helen Wells, but which was ghostwritten by Tatham; *Cherry Ames, At Spencer; Cherry Ames, Night Supervisor; Cherry Ames, Mountaineer Nurse; Cherry Ames, Clinic Nurse; Cherry Ames, Dude Ranch Nurse;* and *Cherry Ames, Country Doctor's Nurse.*

Tatham effectively moves Cherry even further from her war experience and establishes her firmly as a girl sleuth. The original Wells-created cast of characters, including Cherry's parents and brother, Dr. Joe and Midge, and the Spencer Club women, find places again in Tatham's work. Tatham, who considered herself an "ardent feminist," continues the emphasis on Cherry's career and her penchant for bending the rules ("Julie Campbell Tatham"). Yet, as might be expected, the change in author also signals at least a subtle change in tone for the series.

Tatham's novels have a snappiness to them: they are often marked by non-stop action and the interweaving of several plotlines, maintaining interest and suspense up to the very end. Tatham also eliminated long-time boyfriends in favor of one romantic interest per book. Tatham prefers that Cherry's beaux linger only as long as the mystery remains unsolved; once we move on to another book, the romantic interests are rarely, if ever, mentioned again. As might be expected, these more expendable boyfriends tend to be less developed as characters.[1]

Perhaps Tatham's interpretation of Cherry's character is the most disconcerting of the differences between the authors. Tatham's Cherry remains sharp, observant, fun-loving, and dedicated to her work, yet as she struggles with putting pieces of a mystery together, she too often exhibits errors in judgment that one would not expect Wells's Cherry to make.

Several other distinctly Tatham characteristics are evident in these "middle" novels. Tatham exhibits an ability to effectively weave Cherry's nursing and sleuthing activities with multiple plotlines. For instance, in *Rest Home Nurse*, Cherry's work in a rest home, or a recuperating center for new mothers and other convalescents, is complicated by several factors. First, Cherry tries to facilitate the romance of a young man and woman who met at the home but who never get a chance to be alone because Ricky, a mischievous teenager with a leg injury, will not leave them alone. In steps Midge, recruited to distract Ricky, but who develops a crush on Dan Clyde, the handsome young lieutenant who prefers to woo Cherry. Dan gives Cherry reason to suspect, however, that he is blackmailing Mr. Stanley, the secretive and demanding patient who literally collapses at the rest home door. Enter Gwen and Josie, longtime Spencer Club members and fellow staff, who notice missing items and nighttime noises. Upon confrontation, Cherry finds that Dan actually suspects Mr. Stanley of stealing his father's patent for a kitchen gadget, called Open Sesame, and his own resulting fortune.

Possibly the most telling plotline in this same book is the one involving spoiled heiress Nanine Underwood. Nanine is at the rest home recovering from the birth of her daughter, but her diva-like behavior, the absence of a husband, and her refusal to have anything to do with the baby raises questions about her past life. As it turns out, Nanine and her husband have separated because she was raised an heiress and never taught to cook and clean. He, feeling threatened by her fortune, ridiculed her for her lack of housewifery skills. So Cherry and the rest-home staff take on the task of making Nanine more acceptable to her husband — by teaching her to cook, garden, and change diapers. By the end, Nanine has learned her gender-specific role: she agrees to contribute only as much as her husband's salary to the household expenses, and not a penny more, to save his pride. Not incidentally, it is discovered that Nanine's fortune is from the company that bought the patent for Open Sesame.

Tatham often overstresses Cherry, mentioning, in tense situations, how rushed Cherry's meals are and how her sleep is interrupted. Tatham shows the negative effects stress has on Cherry, trying to accomplish the dual purpose of increasing tension and, at the same time, inserting information about proper diet and nutrition. This is to be expected, as these novels are directed towards young girls and include an educational aspect. Though the novels were written well before current concerns about body image, eating disorders, and obesity, several mentions are made of overweight patients (*Chief Nurse, Dude Ranch Nurse, Rest Home Nurse*) and the deleterious effect of too much weight. Underweight patients are also a cause for concern. As a nurse, Cherry understands the importance of proper diet and taking care of herself. Mentioning what she eats certainly can be seen as setting a good example for young girls, though Tatham's use of this tactic to also increase tension may cast doubt on its educational success.

Nonstop action and multiple plotlines seem to be Tatham's strengths. Strong characterizations often are not. In *Mountaineer Nurse*, Cherry sets up a nursing station in a poor Kentucky mountain village. Stereotypes abound: the people are superstitious and backward, a feud is in place between the two most prominent families, and, of course, the youngest members of the two families are victims of a forbidden love. Yet the two matriarchs, or "grannies," who govern the families with an iron hand, seem to be, if not particularly original, certainly compelling. Alternately grizzled and tender, tough but wise, enlightened yet even to the end unwilling to let go of time-honored superstitions, they stand in sharp relief to the cookie-cutter characters surrounding them. Tatham also cannot be seen as much of a wordsmith: she repeatedly employs standard, clichéd phrases such as "had a stroke" and "packed like sardines," and copious uses of the word "cope." Whenever Midge Fortune is around, she is invariably described as a "fiend" or "imp."

Though Tatham effectively moved Cherry further from her war experience and did an admirable job of continuing the series, it was up to the return of Wells to deepen and strengthen the character of Cherry into the confident, proficient nurse and sleuth depicted in the earlier Wells novels.

Confidence and Coincidence, or The Return of Wells

Boarding School Nurse, published in 1955, marks the return of Helen Wells to the series. It is also one of the last novels where Cherry worries about her abilities. The final Cherry Ames novels, all written by Wells, reflect a more mature, self-assured, and well-established Cherry. Yet Wells seems to struggle at first with establishing plotlines that do not overly strain credibility.

All of the plotlines in the series, as one might expect, depend a great deal on coincidence to move the story along. Yet in *Cherry Ames, Department Store Nurse*, and *Cherry Ames, Camp Nurse*, the leaps of faith the author asks her readers to take are almost "above and beyond." In *Cherry Ames, Department Store Nurse* (1956), Wells has Cherry working in New York City, tending to the needs of various customers and the store's employees and using her sleuthing abilities to clear a store employee, Anna Julian, a young widow, of having stolen a jade Ming vase, a highboy, and even her own music box. The book involves many coincidences: The "large, masculine" woman on the Long Island Railroad train turns out to be the wife of one of the real thieves, Anna Julian's employer; Cherry's friend amazingly receives an invitation to a private gallery that turns out to be the home of the thieves; Cherry and an older woman, Aunt Kathy, visit the gallery in disguise and hear the missing music box's tinkle; Cherry just happens to be in the right place at the right time when one of the thieves is on his way to steal a diamond necklace. Although the final chase to and in Idlewild Airport includes moments of tension, the novel ends with too lengthy an explanation of the elaborate fraud executed by the thieves.

Coincidences abound as well in *Cherry Ames, Camp Nurse* (1957), wherein Cherry becomes a nurse at a camp in northeastern Pennsylvania. On a train, Cherry Ames spots a newspaper headline about a New York loan company robbery. Coincidentally (of course), a suspect in the robbery is seen near the camp. In addition to the usual subplots and incidents dealing with nursing, Cherry Ames meets a young man named Mac Cook, who seems to fit the description of the robbery suspect. Mac avoids meeting Purdy, a local photographer, who is later revealed as the thief. That both the actual perpetrator and the prime suspect show up at the camp where Cherry works does strain credibility. As it turns out, Purdy had "set up" Cook, whose real name is Jack Waldron, to be the suspect. When she finds footprints from "rope-soled sandals" (135), Cherry concludes that Purdy has taken out a stolen camp boat. A series of events leads Cherry and Reed, Cherry's current beau, to Purdy and the evidence. Although Cherry worries for a few seconds that she will be in the line of fire when the police confront the armed Purdy, the bullet Purdy fires conveniently enters the ground. The reader then learns Purdy's motivation; he was angry at a loan company for buying the building that housed his photography studio and raising the rent. Although the loan company offers Jack/Mac his previous job, he decides to live on the farm with his half-brother Fred Epler, the person he was seeking when he decided to vacation in Pennsylvania.

Reed Champion, head counselor at a nearby camp for boys, is by far the least aggressive of Cherry's suitors. This novel also includes "lessons in life" for young girls. For example, Cherry uses her psychological abilities to determine the real reasons for a camper's hurting ankle, namely that the girl is used to the comforts of home and fears playing tennis with better players. As in other Cherry Ames novels, families are close and loving, and the thief is a bad guy, but never a thoroughly evil one. Finally, nursing again takes a back seat, coming to the surface here and there, e.g., when an outbreak of influenza is feared, but not directly connected to the mystery.

As if to make up for the preeminence mystery has been taking over nursing, Wells firmly intertwines the two in *Cherry Ames: At Hilton Hospital* (1959). Here the sole plotline centers entirely on a single patient. A young man, "Bob Smith," is brought into Cherry's orthopedic ward with a broken leg, but it soon becomes evident that he has completely lost his memory. Who is he? Why is he here? What deep-seated trauma forced amnesia on him? Cherry works closely with a psychiatrist to unravel the mystery of his past.

As in *Flight Nurse*, Cherry is called upon to exercise patience, steadiness, and ingenuity to help Bob recover. Wells works hard in this novel to de-stigmatize mental illness, making it clear that mental illness is just as real as physical illness. She also, perhaps too optimistically, states that mental illness, with steady care, is just as completely curable as, say, a broken leg.

Another remarkable aspect of *At Hilton Hospital* is a complete lack of romantic interest for Cherry. Cherry doesn't date or even flirt, though she is surrounded by men, both as doctors and patients.[2] Perhaps Wells wants to reinforce her character as a serious professional. Yet even without a romantic character, gender roles are enforced: Cherry rubs Bob's feet and holds his hand; her doctor compliments her often as a "good girl."

The last five novels of the series — *Cherry Ames, Staff Nurse*; *Cherry Ames, Companion Nurse*; *Cherry Ames, Jungle Nurse*; *Mystery in the Doctor's Office*; and *Cherry Ames, Ski Nurse* — all reflect a writer in firm control of her character and her genre. Cherry grows up; her proficiency as a professional is no longer questioned, either by herself or by other characters. Though they could be seen as formulaic, the last five novels are presented with a confidence and smoothness that makes them a delight to read.

It is in these novels that the reader can most clearly see how Cherry fits into what Bobbie Ann Mason termed the "glamour girl" (99). Mason is speaking of the popular career girl sleuths, including Cherry Ames, Vicki Barr, Connie Blair and Beverly Gray. Mason alludes to a "tourist mentality [that] pervades the career-sleuth stories" and comments on how girl sleuths with careers pursued romantic locations as "dressed up substitutes for grander ambitions" (101). Certainly the last five novels have Cherry, confident and well-dressed, smoothly dispensing care and solving mysteries in a series of romantic locations, including England, Africa, and Switzerland. Though Mason condemns the "glamour girl" prototype as an attempt to water-down and circumvent real achievements by women (99), the series does end with Cherry taking at least small steps towards increased independence from patriarchy.

Perhaps the most marked characteristic in the last five books is the growth in the perception of Cherry as a complete professional. Though some word choices that grate on today's ears show up repeatedly in the novels (such as the ubiquitous "Yes, Doctor" and the constant references to women as "girls," most particularly in the use of the seemingly patronizing "good girl" as a compliment), Cherry has grown up as a character. No longer is anyone questioning her competence and, perhaps more importantly, she is not questioning her own ability. Father figures abound in the series, but, beginning in *Staff Nurse*, Cherry Ames moves away from them as a source of validation. Most importantly, there seem to be fewer attempts by the males and father figures in her life to take care of her. In *Staff Nurse*, she decides finally that the best way to apprehend the perpetrator of an investment scam is to travel to Chicago by herself, somehow locate him, and confront him. Her father declines to go with her, as "he had confidence in Cherry's ability to take care of herself" (117). In spite of the apparent dangers, taking care of herself is precisely what Cherry does.

Wells frequently seems to be ambivalent about judging people by their looks, often reinforcing stereotypes on one hand while trying to tear them down with the other. Appearances mean a great deal in these novels — one can often pinpoint a "bad guy" by how the author describes him or her. Perhaps the pinnacle of judging a book by its cover occurs in *Staff*

Nurse, when with one look Cherry assesses a man's whole life: "he looked like a man who usually would be friendly and self-controlled, a stable-looking man, well dressed, probably a small-town businessman, probably married and the father of two or three small children, and a member of his community" (128–129). Yet Wells sometimes plays with visual stereotypes, as in *Companion Nurse*, when Cherry tells her romantic interest, an "extremely pleasant-looking young man," "I was surprised to hear you're a professor.... Aren't professors supposed to be old and solemn?" Peter replies, "I'm only an assistant professor" (40).

These last novels also see an increase in violence. In previous novels Cherry had been kidnapped more than once and occasionally found herself on the receiving end of an unfired or misfired gun, but never had Cherry been physically hurt. In *Companion Nurse*, Cherry races after a criminal on foot and on trolleys. After entering a lone building, she is captured, gagged, dragged up three flights of stairs, and slapped across the face. Tied to a chair, she "was in so much physical discomfort she almost cried ... the harsh ropes confined her to one rigid, aching posture" (160). Perhaps this increase in violence reflected the growing violence in the media of the day.[3] Yet also, as the text now depicts Cherry as a mature, professional woman, it must also demonstrate that she operates in a real, and sometimes cruel, world.

Throughout the Cherry Ames series, overt racism is avoided, largely because black characters are rare. The very few that do exist are relegated to minor roles. One perhaps could see *Jungle Nurse*, set in Africa, as a possible remedy to the dearth of black characters, but it is no such thing. It is startling to realize the relative lack of prominent black characters even in Africa. When Cherry arrives in the small village to help set up a hospital with a white American doctor, she finds white American workers already there. The "bad guys," a fake photographer, a safari guide and an airplane pilot, are all white. The black characters consist of two female assistants whom Cherry is to train. Kavarondi is described as "exceptionally handsome" with "features more Caucasian than African" (59). Cherry wonders if her African ancestors intermarried with white Crusaders who got lost in Africa. Sara is described as "unmistakably African," with ears "pierced in the Kikuyu fashion ... distended by wooden plugs" (59–60). The only other black characters are Toma, the camp cook; Kandi, a young patient who develops a crush on Cherry and sticks around (he later plays an important part in solving the mystery); and Tom Gikingku, the Abercrombie Foundation's African official. Gikingku certainly is the highest-ranking black character in any Cherry Ames novel, but he is mostly absent in *Jungle Nurse* and only steps in to help resolve the mystery at the very end. Although there are "native workers" helping to build the makeshift hospital, the foremen are white Americans.

Another interesting motif in *Jungle Nurse* is a recurrent dialogue on the presence of white foreigners in Africa. With typical optimism, Wells presents the British and American presence in Nairobi in a favorable light. Africa is described as beautiful and haunting, yet also "primitive" and "uncivilized." British colonization is presented as having provided many benefits to Kenya — particularly in health care — benefits that departed with the British when Kenya became independent. In the story, white health care workers "white-wash" the inside of each hut so that "when it was finished, the interiors were gleaming white and the gloominess of the huts had been replaced by a cheerful brightness" (*Jungle Nurse* 81). Cherry instructs the village women on how to plant flowers outside their doors, the goal being to turn the village into a "model town" "with happy people in it" (84–85).

That Wells takes this approach is not surprising, considering her emphasis on the positives of all things modern (especially in medicine and technology). Yet Wells cannot allow herself to be as simplistic as that. Wells questions, though rather tentatively, the role of the white man in Africa. On a picnic, Kandi picks up a stone he thinks is a diamond:

> Bob said reflectively, "that was how the first African diamond was found — by a boy playing along a riverbank. And it was that diamond rush that caused the rush of European settlers, and built Africa up to the great country it is becoming now."
> "Maybe Africa would be better off today," Jeff said, "if the boy had thrown the diamond back into the water and white men had never come here at all" [105].

Cherry runs into the constant problem of not being taken seriously when she voices her suspicions about a mystery, but in *Jungle Nurse*, perhaps for the first time, she takes a clear lead over a man when it comes to solving the mystery. After completely figuring out on her own how diamonds are being smuggled out of the country, she sits down, tells Bob her suspicions, outlines a plan, and challenges him to follow her lead with a confident "Are you game?" (141).

The last two novels in the Cherry Ames series are *The Mystery in the Doctor's Office* and *Ski Nurse*, published in 1966 and 1968. By this time, Wells (and Cherry) have hit their stride, and the mysteries are presented with confidence. In *The Mystery in the Doctor's Office*, Wells uses the plot-line to further question Cherry's unblinking devotion to the ethics of those dedicated to the medical profession. When Cherry finds out the office manager used her cachet with the physicians to get the previous nurse fired, she is skeptical: "She doubted that any RN would permit a medical secretary to drive her off a job" (67). Later, when Cherry learns that the previous nurse, a Nurse Colt, was accused of being "unkind" to patients, she is even more surprised: "Unkind! A nurse?" she exclaims (68). Yet, although Cherry's faith in medical professionals is tested, eventually her beliefs are validated — she is able to prove that Nurse Colt was falsely accused by the insidious Mrs. Wick and restores her reputation, as well as her job, to her.

Ski Nurse is pure escapist entertainment. Here Cherry secures her reputation as an expert sleuth, professional nurse, and glamorous jetsetter, not to mention dandy skier, when she travels to Switzerland for a little nursing and a lot of sleuthing in a luxurious ski resort town. Wells uses both *Mystery in the Doctor's Office* and *Ski Nurse* to instruct her young readers on the importance of honest work and self-reliance. In *Mystery*, she comes down hard on the embezzling office manager, and the consequences of her serious crime are clear. Yet Wells is also careful to point out that another employee's unauthorized "borrowing" of a small amount of cash was just as wrong — though the consequences not as severe. In *Ski Nurse*, a likable young man, Toni, is an expert skier who covets the status of a ski instructor yet disdains the tedious process required to get his legal license. This sense of entitlement and lack of respect for the rules lead him to even greater errors of judgment: he gets involved as a pawn in a smuggling operation that eventually leads to jail time and, of course, many lessons learned.

Like many other girls' series of the time, the Cherry Ames novels derived their initial inspiration from the Nancy Drew novels as well as the wartime need to fill a nursing shortage. Strongly influenced by the mores of the day, the novels nevertheless broke ground by depicting a woman with a career, a woman who did not see marriage as her immediate or ultimate goal, a woman who showed some independence and insubordination as well as the more conventional qualities of beauty, compassion, and adherence to hierarchical organization. To a certain degree the novels are outdated; sulfa is no longer the drug of choice for infections, for example, and today's nurses no longer clean their patients' rooms or prepare their food. Though not as offensive in their stereotypes as the original

Nancy Drew novels, the Ames books do reflect the racial and cultural biases of their time.

Yet, despite changing authors and vast upheavals in society, medicine, and technology over a period of twenty-five years, the Cherry Ames series remained popular and relevant enough to lead to the reissue of the first eight novels, without significant revision, in 2005–2006. The holder of the rights to the Wells novels, Harriet Forman, Ed.D., R.N., intends to reissue all twenty-one of the novels written by Helen Wells, "assuming buyer interest continues:"

> When these books first were published, they motivated many young readers to select nursing as their life's work. I and many of my nurse colleagues are among those readers. I tested the waters, so to speak, and asked a number of young people I know to read some of the novels. They liked them and all asked many questions about nursing. I know you can't replicate the past but I'm hoping some readers will be interested enough to think of nursing as Helen Wells thought of nursing — and frankly as I think of nursing.
>
> Given the opportunity, I'd do it again! [Forman].

Perhaps the reissue of the Cherry Ames novels will again inspire young women to consider the nursing profession — and even to consider amateur sleuthing as a logical companion activity. Both, after all, require intelligence, training, logic, and the ability to question, analyze, and care for and about our fellow human beings.

Notes

1. Tatham does allow Dr. Lex Upham and Wade Cooper a short reappearance in *Country Doctor's Nurse*. Wells also makes a brief mention of Wade Cooper in *At Hilton Hospital*, but later Wells-penned novels follow the Tatham-inspired trend of a different romantic interest per book.

2. The hospitals Cherry works in have "wards" or large open rooms with beds or cots separated only by curtains, segregated by gender. Occasionally a special patient is given a separate, private room.

3. *Companion Nurse* was published in 1964.

Works Cited

The Cherry Ames Page. 1996. Netwrx Consulting. 10 February 2007, http://www.netwrxl. com/CherryAmes/book16.html.

Forman, Harriet. "Re: Question About the Cherry Ames Novels." E-mail to Anita G. Gorman. 7 February 2007.

"Helen Wells." *Contemporary Authors*. Literature Resource Center. Slippery Rock University of Pennsylvania. 13 July 2007, http://galenet.galegroup.com.

"Julie Campbell Tatham." *Contemporary Authors*. Pennsylvania State University. 3 January 2007, http://galenet.galegroup.com.

Mason, Bobbie Ann. *The Girl Sleuth: A Feminist Guide*. Old Westbury, N.Y.: Feminist Press, 1975.

Parry, Sally E. "'You are needed, desperately needed!': Cherry Ames in World War II." *Nancy Drew and Company: Culture, Gender, and Girls' Series*. Ed. Sherrie A. Inness. Bowling Green: Bowling Green State University Popular Press, 1997, pp. 129–144.

Tatham, Julie. *Cherry Ames, Clinic Nurse*. New York: Grosset, 1952.

_____. *Cherry Ames, Country Doctor's Nurse*. New York: Grosset, 1955.

_____. *Cherry Ames, Dude Ranch Nurse*. New York: Grosset, 1953.

_____. *Cherry Ames, Mountaineer Nurse*. New York: Grosset, 1951.

_____. *Cherry Ames, Night Supervisor*. New York: Grosset, 1950.

_____. *Cherry Ames, Rest Home Nurse*. New York: Grosset, 1954.

_____. *Cherry Ames at Spencer*. New York: Grosset, 1949.

Wells, Helen. *Cherry Ames, Army Nurse*. New York: Grosset, 1944.

_____. *Cherry Ames, Boarding School Nurse*. New York: Grosset, 1955.

_____. *Cherry Ames' Book of First Aid and Home Nursing*. New York: Grosset, 1959.

_____. *Cherry Ames, Camp Nurse*. New York: Grosset, 1957.

_____. *Cherry Ames, Chief Nurse*. New York: Grosset, 1944.

_____. *Cherry Ames, Companion Nurse*. New York: Grosset, 1964.

_____. [Julie Tatham]. *Cherry Ames, Cruise Nurse*. New York: Grosset, 1948.

_____. *Cherry Ames, Department Store Nurse*. New York: Grosset, 1956.

_____. *Cherry Ames, Flight Nurse*. New York: Grosset, 1945.

_____. *Cherry Ames at Hilton Hospital*. New York: Grosset, 1959.

_____. *Cherry Ames, Island Nurse*. New York: Grosset, 1960.

_____. *Cherry Ames, Jungle Nurse*. New York: Grosset, 1965.

_____. *Cherry Ames, Private Duty Nurse*. New York: Grosset, 1945.

_____. *Cherry Ames, Rural Nurse*. New York: Grosset, 1960.

_____. *Cherry Ames, Senior Nurse*. New York: Grosset, 1944.

_____. *Cherry Ames, Staff Nurse*. New York: Grosset, 1962.

_____. *Cherry Ames, Student Nurse*. New York: Grosset, 1943.

_____. *Cherry Ames, Veterans' Nurse*. New York: Grosset, 1946.

_____. *Cherry Ames, Visiting Nurse*. New York: Grosset, 1947.

_____. *The Mystery in the Doctor's Office*. New York: Grosset, 1966.

_____. *Ski Nurse Mystery*. New York: Grosset, 1968.

Puzzles, Paternity, and Privilege: The Mysterious Function(s) of the Family in Trixie Belden

Steven J. Zani

Trixie Belden, a middle-class fourteen-year-old tomboy girl sleuth, is one of the more popular serialized female adolescent figures of the twentieth century. In her thirty-nine novels, she solved crimes and mysteries with the help of her wealthy friend Honey Wheeler and a group of sleuthing chums called the "Bob-Whites of the Glen." Several elements of her narrative compare to others in the girl sleuth genre, but there is a family-oriented agenda in the Trixie Belden books that makes the series distinct from the focus and agenda of Nancy Drew and other girl sleuths. In Trixie Belden, comfort, security, and identity are constructed and found in the family dynamic, and a meticulous look at the texts of her series, their origins, history and narrative arcs can reveal not only an otherwise unnoticed arena of girl sleuth scholarship, but an ideology of family that was complicit with many other narratives of class, labor, privilege and status, codependent networks of power and knowledge in American culture of the twentieth century.

The first six books of the Trixie series were written by Julie Campbell, while later additions were by multiple in-house writers for the Golden Press division of Western Publishing (Random House currently owns the copyright for reprints), all written under the pseudonym "Kathryn Kenny."[1]

In contrast to the preeminent girl sleuth model of Nancy Drew, Trixie is neither refined nor confident. She is not "quirky" like many of her contemporary counterparts such as Sammy Keyes, and she's not as witty as contemporary television sleuths such as Veronica Mars. While mysteries are obviously a focal point of her stories, and every one of the thirty-nine Trixie books contains the word "Secret" or "Mystery" in the title, these books are not detective narratives in the traditional sense, and while there are often real criminals, villains are much more likely to lock Trixie in a remote closet than they are to provide a direct physical threat. In fact, this lack of violence and suspense places the novels into the critical sub-genre known as "cozy" detective fiction.[2] However, her books have seen many reprints, there is an annual conference held by fans of the series, and she has a visible fan base on the Internet. Scholar Bobbie Ann Mason calls Trixie "the most liberating" of girl sleuths (98). The author of "The Trixie Belden Homepage" (one of several devoted to Trixie) remarks, in favorable comparison to Nancy, that Trixie "just seemed more real to me" ("Trixie Belden Homepage"). Yet what is it that makes Trixie "more real"? How does she differ from other girl sleuths? What the Trixie Belden series has, instead of refined feminist confidence or direct physical confrontation, is a constant focus on families, whether literal or figurative. Looking at Trixie, then, is a look both at the question of the family as it was understood during the production of the series, and a look at female identity in relation to the community that produced it.

How is "family" created as an agenda in the Trixie series? Harriet Stratemeyer Adams remarked that one of the essential qualities of Nancy Drew was that she follows the paradigmatic motto of Wellesley College, which Adams herself attended. That motto is *Non Ministrari Sed Ministrare*, which translates as "Not to be ministered unto but to minister to" (Rehak 32). Like Nancy, Trixie does "ministering," but with a difference, and this difference is what makes her valuable for study; her ministering to others is almost exclusively for others in her immediate family or community, or to help establish or strengthen families that she has encountered in her narratives. The plots of many of the novels, and virtually all the stories from early in the series, focus on issues of wealth and inheritance, and particularly on the question of familial problems and obligations that accompanies such wealth. While Nancy Drew stories also contain inheritance narratives — the first in the series, *The Secret of the Old Clock*, is an example — it is arguable that the entire Trixie series is centered on them. Unlike Nancy Drew, where the class status and wealth of the heroine is implicit, in Trixie narratives it is her lack of wealth and overt status that is her welcome feature, and money functions in entirely different ways. The abiding lesson of these novels is that wealth, while it may solve problems, does not provide happiness; the comfort of family does. Furthermore, if there is a goal for individuals, and for the communities that they inhabit, it is to support families as an active social agenda.

To make sense of wealth, class, and the function of family in the Trixie series, one must first have some sense of how these terms operate in the culture of the girl sleuth novel, and in twentieth century America in general. As critic Kathleen Chamberlain notes in her analysis of the Isabel Carleton novels, "We must go beyond a conception of class based solely on income" (38). A number of critics in recent years have begun to explore the ways that class has become a dominant, if often understated, cornerstone of American culture, although the relation of class to actual economic hierarchies is more complicated than one might assume. Paul Fussell, in *Class*, his shrewd and somewhat lackadaisical analysis of American class structure, relates the following: "At the bottom, people tend to believe that class is defined by the amount of money you have. In the middle, people grant that money has something to do with it, but think education and the kind of work you do almost equally important. Nearer the top, people perceive that taste, values, ideas, style, and behavior are indispensable criteria of class, regardless of money or occupation or education" (3).

Fussell's key insight is that the class that people literally hold is less important than the issue of what those occupants themselves *think* makes them occupy that class. Each class has a different ideological perspective of what constitutes the term itself. The insight is useful here because it reveals that Trixie Belden does not occupy her class primarily based on her economic status. Instead, she occupies her class because of the ideas promoted in the novels, which support one version of class ideology over another. In Fussell's sense, Trixie Belden is the quintessential middle-class heroine regardless of her family's economic status, because the novels promote the middle-class understanding of class and the social obligations that come along with it. Trixie promotes a credo that combines ideas of wealth with a sensibility that both education and labor must be channeled into appropriate avenues, the "work you do" along with the knowledge of what to do with it, rather than simply the money that one has.

Trixie Belden novels promote another traditional American ideology of class, the idea that class is essentially unimportant or irrelevant in society. Stanley Aronowitz argues, in *How Class Works*, that the term for this ideology is "American exceptionalism," explaining that Americans eschew class associations because of the supposed utter fluidity of their lives — the dream that citizens have that they have equal opportunity to rise or fall in their class status based solely on their ingenuity and labor: "Exceptionalism is not merely an intellectual construct; class denial is woven into the fabric of American life. American culture rests on the proposition [of] unlimited opportunity ... with a combination of luck and hard work — whether that means earning educational credentials, starting a small business, or hitting the lottery — they can get rich or at least achieve economic security" (15).

Eventually, Aronowitz makes an argument about American and global politics with one specific suggestion. If one is to make useful political struggles and understand how class and economics affect everyday life, then this is a time for "analysis and speculation as much as organization and protest" (229). The need for careful analysis, in part, can be seen exactly in addressing Trixie Belden, for if one is to see how girl sleuth studies provide a small but important avenue for understanding American culture, one must do it by uncovering its implicit messages, such as the idea that wealth can be generated by a combination of pluck, luck, and hard work.

The idea, however, that class status is not important, or in fact detrimental to a fulfilled life, is one that is pursued through a "family" agenda in the novels, sometimes in a very specific fashion. For example, in the fourth book in the Trixie series, *The Mysterious Visitor*, Trixie's newest friend, Diana, has trouble adjusting to her family's shift from middle to upper-class when they become wealthy. Simply put, wealth and class status create anxieties. On some level, however, the issue is not limited to one or two books and is the latent argument of the entire history of Trixie Belden in general. Every book of the series includes at least some gesture in this direction with the relationship that exists between Trixie and her friend Honey. Honey is consistently disappointed by her wealthy but absent mother, and a repetitive component of the text is Honey's complaint that some activity (which Trixie has access to or knowledge of) has been denied to her because of wealth. This dynamic between them is revealed, in fact, on the first page in which Honey is introduced into the narrative, in the introductory novel, *The Secret of the Mansion*. Trixie at first assumes that Honey is "stuck-up," and asks without much hope if Honey rides horses:

> Honey smiled, then, "Oh, yes," she said. "Do you?"
> Trixie shook her head ruefully. "No, but I want to learn like anything.

The only thing I have to ride is a babyish old bike. But I'm earning the money now to buy a horse just as soon as I can."

"A bike?" Honey's smile widened ... "I wish I had a bike," she said wistfully. "Mother wouldn't let me have one in the city because of the traffic, and the rest of the time I was at boarding school and camp, where they're not allowed" [23].

This selection demonstrates an element that will repeat itself in virtually every novel of the series, with Honey's wistful desires to have a life like Trixie's, desires which are often forbidden or impossible because of wealth, or because of Honey's absent family, who travel constantly for business purposes. Honey, however, is only the most obvious and repetitive example of an entire series that is virtually obsessed with an agenda of creating and sustaining family units, through inheritance, adoption, donations or otherwise, to support and nurture the activities of children.

The plot of the first novel is especially revelatory of this concept. The story revolves around an old, abandoned mansion near Trixie's house. When Trixie and her newfound friend Honey investigate, they discover a young runaway, Jim. He is a distant relative of the deceased owner of the mansion, and he is hiding from his cruel stepfather, who only wants to use Jim to acquire the supposed fortune (the "secret") hidden inside the house. Ultimately, there is little money hidden inside the house, and there is really no secret to the mansion at all, and everyone discovers that Jim is entitled to the entire half-million dollar inheritance that was put in trust. In short, the novel seems less interested in addressing how one finds clues or uncovers information as it is in making sure a displaced orphan finds his appropriate home. The novel ends on a tantalizingly incomplete note, with Jim missing, and the girls on a mission to track him down and let him know about his money.

In the second novel, *The Red Trailer Mystery*, the girls travel. Perhaps the "logical" necessity of so much travel in girl sleuth literature is because of the lack of repetitive mysterious crimes in any single non-metropolitan area. Yet it is worth mentioning that another function at work is that of empowering young adults, particularly women, in that these girl sleuths are appropriating roles traditionally pursued by adults or men. In this case, the travel is accomplished entirely by women, as Trixie and Honey are driven from campsite to campsite by Honey's governess, Miss Trask, ostensibly taking a vacation, while really looking for Jim. Feminist or not, along the way, the girls are given plenty of training in how to sustain a family and a home:

"I always wanted to fool around in the kitchen," Honey said wistfully, "but none of our cooks would ever let me touch anything."

"Well," Miss Trask said briskly, "I think every girl, no matter her
position, should learn how to cook and keep house...."

"I can cook," Trixie said proudly. "I fixed homemade baked beans for
Dad's supper tonight. It's a cinch," she admitted with a grin.

"Sounds divine," Honey said admiringly [19].

This scene illustrates that Honey's wealth is not something that the novel
finds positive. Having servants and a wealthy family is often portrayed
detrimentally. Compare Honey, with her wealth, to Trixie, whose absence
of wealthy parents allows her to connect with her father by cooking to sustain the family.

The mystery of the novel begins when the girls encounter a red trailer
that houses a very strange family, the Darnells, consisting of a mother,
father, two daughters and an infant. They are all wearing threadbare clothing, the father inspires fear and has unkempt hair, and they appear under-
fed, yet they are driving an expensive trailer, and mysteriously keep the
windows closed and shuttered to prevent peering inside. Their difference
from others is immediately noticed. Honey remarks, "Did you ever hear
of such a peculiar family?" (31). Thus begins the mystery, which will be
solved only by reclaiming and normalizing the Darnell family. Slightly
later in the narrative, Trixie is awakened by sounds of sobbing from within
the trailer, and overhears an argument between the parents.

"A fine thing," the man grumbled. "My own family turning against
me! You were all for it in the beginning, Sarah."

"I know, I know," the woman moaned. "But I didn't realize then ...
what its doing to Sally and Joanne. I can't bear it." ... Then there was
silence — a silence that made Trixie remember how, earlier, the family had
sat together, staring vacantly into space.

"What's the matter with that family?" she wondered [36–37].

The matter with "that family" (why they are turning against one another)
is that Mrs. Darnell has been ill, and could not take care of the children
alone while her husband traveled to work as a farmhand, an unfortunate
event that prompted him to steal the expensive red trailer from an employer
so the family could travel together. The plot is complicated by two real
thieves who are stealing trailers in the same area and who eventually
threaten Trixie and Honey before being caught by the state troopers. A
critic focusing on the detective elements of this narrative might dwell more
on the dangers of those two men, the real criminals of the narrative, but

the criminal narrative of this story is beside the point. In some "real" sense, Trixie Belden stories aren't about criminals, they are about families, promoting and sustaining the idea of them. The narrative suggests that readers should have some sympathy for the Darnells' plight, since their crime was necessitated by their desire to sustain a tight family unit, a detail that Trixie herself argues. When Trixie discovers the reason the trailer was stolen, she says the following: "You haven't got a thing to worry about Mrs. Darnell.... I know Mr. Lynch, and he's just about the kindest man alive. He'll understand why you had to borrow his trailer. Why, he's got four or five children of his own.... I'm going right back ... and call him up and tell him the whole story" (211).

Trixie is correct; the Darnells are not only forgiven by Mr. Lynch (who is a family man, and hence more understanding), the state troopers also thank them for their help in catching the real trailer thieves. In a two-page extended discourse that shortly follows Trixie's proclamation, the troopers explain that they'll provide an escort home when the Darnells are returning the trailer, and they even slip Mrs. Darnell twenty dollars on the side and explain to her that her husband can have a job with them if he is so inclined.

The narrative of the novel ends as the Darnell family finds a permanent home to live in with a kindly old lady, Mrs. Smith, encountered earlier in the narrative. Everything in the plot has moved towards the direction of helping this family. The teleology of the story is that a family in trouble is discovered, and then helped, and in fact it even becomes clear that helping one family always seems to help another at the same time, as both the Darnell family and the Smith family are overjoyed to be brought together: "Mrs. Smith dabbed at her eyes with the corner of her apron. 'I declare,' she said to her husband. 'The Lord certainly is looking out for us'" (228).

Likewise, Jim — the young boy Trixie and Honey were searching for in the first place — ends up finding family in multiple locations. Not only does kindly Mrs. Smith offer him a home, but Honey's parents want to adopt him (they are already wealthy, it should be mentioned, so they are ostensibly adopting him for genuine reasons, not for his trust fund, a fear mentioned on more than one occasion in the Trixie series). The novel concludes with Jim's adoption, and Trixie's final words, "Sometimes dreams *do* come true" (236).

If the entire dream of Trixie Belden is preserving family, surely the authors would have run out of narratives in the series soon. There are only so many times that people can be adopted or get an inheritance, and a new family cannot be introduced into the plot with every novel. The mysterious crimes committed in Trixie Belden aren't enough to sustain narrative interest just by themselves, or rather they do tend to wear thin after thirty-nine books — it is nearly impossible to count the number of things that get stolen. A non-exhaustive list includes emeralds (Book 14), necklaces (Book 23), gold lockets (Book 2), antiques (Book 7), and other variations of burglary (Books 8, 9, 17, 18, 19, 22, and 38). Although the issue of heirs and inheritance appears multiple times in the series, one way the authors of Trixie Belden kept their focus on families, without specifically introducing new families, was to circumvent this problem in the third novel, *The Gatehouse Mystery*, by forming the detective group "The Bob-Whites of the Glen" (B.W.G.s), Trixie's gang of friends who serve as a mini-family of camaraderie and community.

The B.W.G.s are easy to conceptualize as nothing more than an extended version of Trixie's friendship with Honey; they are a demonstration that every child should have friends, or a community of friends, to sustain and interest them. However, there is more going on in the creation of this extended community than a simple admission of the need for "friends," which becomes more evident when understanding the B.W.G.s in the context of American ideology of community service and group labor. Susan Ostrander's work *Women of the Upper Class*, an analysis of actual social practice and activity of upper class women, argues that such women of the upper class carry a sense of obligation in forming social clubs to accomplish community service: "This 'noblesse oblige' reflects the extent to which class is used as a context to make sense of volunteerism. Their volunteer work, as they themselves define it, justifies their existence as members of the privileged class. It staves off the charges ... that their privileges are unearned and undeserved" (96).

This ideology of the necessity to work in order to demonstrate value does, however, coincide with Fussell's earlier comments about middle-class ideology, revealing that in part the lines drawn between various classes in American society are blurry in certain places. Similarly, one can contextualize Ostrander's documentation of upper-class obligation with the understanding that the female lower classes, too, have a history in twentieth-century America of participating not only in labor (that is, in joining the workforce, particularly during and after World War II), but in subsequently forming labor unions and in working not only to promote individual feminist goals, but to promote the traditional goals of social improvement accomplished by labor unions through the years; or, in short, in performing public service through means of communal organization.[3] The relation to Trixie Belden is obvious. That is, with a shift in the novels towards not simply individual "sleuthing," but community-oriented projects and activities, Trixie Belden novels are ostensibly middle-class, meaning that they promote an ideology understood across the entire spectrum of American female (and male, for that matter) class divisions.

Before citing specific instances in the novels where the B.W.G.s fulfill this role of promoting community work, one caveat is wise. In saying that the B.W.G.s are an extended family, I am perhaps opening myself up to criticism that they might be much more as well. After all, critics such as Michael Bronski, in "Sex and the Teenage Sleuth," argue that the young adult detective genre is "smoldering with unmistakable eroticism" (31–32). Perhaps these sub-narratives of group identity are offering a primer for young teens, lessons on emergent sexuality and social interaction, rather than promoting an early form of either upper- or lower-class service or union activity? Bronski doesn't address Trixie Belden specifically (nor, frankly, do any other critics on this issue), but I would argue that notwithstanding the potential for a reading of the B.W.G.s as explicitly sexual, the primary function of the group is far less sexual than it is communal. The B.W.G.s can be understood most easily as an organization supportive of family, in that they themselves always discuss their purpose as humanitarian. They are a social organization of teens interacting with one another, which of course has potential for sexuality, but in the narrative of Trixie Belden that potential is never explicitly addressed and certainly never develops. Instead, the group is exclusively interested in promoting family-oriented goals, and in promoting the idea that groups of people, when they work together in some system of shared governance, can accomplish far-reaching ends. For example, the fifteenth novel in the series, *The Mystery on the Mississippi*, ends with the group deciding what to do with the reward money in the "Bob-White fund for charity" they've just received for stopping international arms smugglers. The passage is formulaic in that it is representative of a great number of final B.W.G. conversations at the end of most of the books in the series:

> "What'll we ever do with that much money?" Honey wondered in a dazed voice.
> Mart laughed. "Golly, that won't take too much thinking. We have half a dozen places to put money. There's always the United Nations Children's Fund."

"And CARE," Brian added.

"Red Cross Relief, the United Fund," Dan suggested.

Honey's eyes shone like stars. "Do you do know what I'd like most of all in the world? I remember pictures of little Korean orphans I saw in a magazine. They were in an advertisement asking for people to adopt one of them ... not really bring them to this country, but send money every month to take care of them. Do you think the Bob-Whites could do that?" [253].

Of course everyone agrees (the complete unreality of this situation can be understood best by thinking of all the other things that young adolescents might have wanted to do with extra money in this situation — buy themselves clothes, vehicles, etc. — something these novels fail to address in any sense whatsoever, even as a passing desire by one of the children), and Trixie ends the novel beaming that she can go home happy, because, as she says, "This was one of the most exciting trips ever — and I guess we really have some worthwhile things to show for it" (254).

Ultimately, if readers have something to "show for" reading Trixie Belden, it is that we have a greater understanding of the mechanisms of how class, family, and adolescent female identity combine in very particular ways in twentieth-century American literature. Perhaps what is most interesting in Trixie is that things are not always what they appear to be. Joel Shoemaker, commenting on the popularity of the girl sleuth genre in being adopted by libraries nationwide, explains that these novels have been promoted not only for their comforting, stable qualities — the promotion of traditional relationships and conservative values — but also for their subversive qualities, that a girl sleuth "does things that the adults around her can't do and that empowers kids to go beyond expectations, too" (125). Trixie and her friends might take several novels to work up to it, but eventually their actions result in actual international influence, as the example of Korean adoption demonstrates.

While on the one hand these books maintain the status quo and promote an assortment of orthodox ideologies that one would expect from middle class, democratic America, on the other hand, Trixie reveals herself as a heroine who, despite character anxieties, lack of wealth, and general uncertainty about life, still manages to accomplish the goals she sets for herself. Perhaps this is what makes her "more real" to her reading public; the fact that a girl who is neither particularly privileged nor particularly superior can nonetheless — through constant reliance on, and attention to, family — produce and sustain a happy, complex world and community for herself.

Notes

1. Authors include the following: Nicolete Meredith Stack, Virginia McDonnell, Gladys Baker Bond, Carl Henry Rathjen, Owenita Harrah Sanderlin, Laura French, Joan Chase Bowden, and Kathleen Krull. For an easy reference, with brief biographical accounts of these authors and their relation to the series, see the Trixie-Belden.com Web site, http://www.trixie-belden.com/books/KathrynKenny.htm. Information there was collected from an article written by James D. and Kimberlee Keeline, "Trixie Belden, Schoolgirl Shamus," which contains an extensive amount of background information on the entire Trixie Belden series, and which can be found at the authors' personal Web site, http://www.kee line.com/Trixie_Belden.pdf. The original version of the article was a presentation of the same title at the 1998 Popular Culture Association Conference.

2. For a brief article that addresses "cozy" fiction in relation to Nancy Drew, see Jeffrey Trachtenberg's "Eccentric Sleuths, Off-stage Murders and Very Little Sex" in the *Wall Street Journal* (full details in Works Cited).

3. See Cobble, Dorothy Sue. "Recapturing Working-Class Feminism: Union Women in the Postwar Era" from the book *Not June Cleaver: Women and Gender in Postwar America, 1945–1960* (full details in Works Cited.) Cobble argues that the postwar era (when not coincidentally many Trixie Belden texts were written) saw growing recognition by the female labor force that union work was one of the most effective means of accomplishing their ends, and female participation in unions was far more widespread than previously understood.

Works Cited

Aronowitz, Stanley. *How Class Works: Power and Social Movement.* New Haven: Yale University Press, 2003.

Bronski, Michael. "Sex and the Teenage Sleuth." *Gay and Lesbian Review Worldwide* 9.5 (September 2002): 31–32.

Campbell, Julie. *The Red Trailer Mystery.* Racine: Western Pub., 1977.

_____. *The Secret of the Mansion.* Racine: Western Pub., 1977.

Chamberlain, Kathleen. "Gender, Class and Domesticity in the Isabel Carleton Series." *Nancy Drew and Company.* Ed. Sherrie A. Inness. Bowling Green: Bowling Green State University Press, 1997, pp. 37–58.

Cobble, Dorothy Sue. "Recapturing Working-Class Feminism: Union Women in the Postwar Era." *Not June Cleaver: Women and Gender in Postwar America, 1945–1960.* Ed. Joanne Meyerowitz. Philadelphia: Temple University Press, 1994, pp. 57–83.

Fussell, Paul. *Class.* New York: Random House, 1983.

Inness, Sherrie A. "Girl Scouts, Camp Fire Girls, and Woodcraft Girls: The Ideology of Girls' Scouting Novels, 1910–1935." *Nancy Drew and Company.* Ed. Sherrie A. Inness. Bowling Green: Bowling Green State University Press, 1997, pp. 89–100.

Johns, Jenni. Trixie-Belden.com. September 18, 2001. January 14, 2007, http://www.trixie-belden.com.

Johnson, Deidre A. "Community and Character: A Comparison of Josephine Lawrence's Linda Lane Series and Classic Orphan Fiction." *Nancy Drew and Company.* Ed. Sherrie A. Inness. Bowling Green: Bowling Green State University Press, 1997, pp. 59–73.

Kenny, Kathryn. *The Mystery of the Headless Horseman.* Racine: Western Pub., 1979.

_____. *The Mystery on the Mississippi.* Racine, Wis.: Whitman Pub., 1965.

Mason, Bobbie Ann. *The Girl Sleuth: A Feminist Guide.* New York: Feminist Press, 1975.

Mitchell, Claudia, and Jacqueline Reid-Walsh. "The Case of the Whistle-Blowing Girls: Nancy Drew and Her Readers." *Textual Studies in Canada* 13/14 (Summer 2001): 15–24.

Ostrander, Susan. *Women of the Upper Class*. Philadelphia: Temple University Press, 1984.
Rehak, Melanie. *Girl Sleuth: Nancy Drew and the Women Who Created Her*. Orlando: Harcourt, 2005. 32.
Shoemaker, Joel. "Series Books and Competing Mandates in the School Library." *Rediscovering Nancy Drew*. Ed. Carolyn Dyer and Nancy Romalov. Iowa City: University of Iowa Press, 1995.
Trachtenberg, Jeffrey. "Eccentric Sleuths, Off-stage Murders and Very Little Sex." *Wall Street Journal*. 20 January 2004, eastern ed.: A1–A12.
The Trixie Belden Homepage. 01 July 1997. 14 January 2007, http://barbln.org/trixie/.

Not Nancy Drew but Not Clueless: Embodying the Teen Girl Sleuth in the Twenty-first Century

Marla Harris

The teenaged girl sleuth emerged in fiction with *Bobs, A Girl Detective* in 1928, soon to be eclipsed by the popularity of the Nancy Drew series, which debuted in 1930 with *The Secret of the Old Clock*, and the host of series that followed, chronicling the adventures of girl detectives like Judy Bolton, Kay Tracey, and the Dana Girls. Bobbie Ann Mason has suggested that one reason for the longevity of the girl sleuth is that it is "the role which allows more freedom than any particular career.... Detecting allows her [the heroine] to use her brains" (123). By the late-twentieth century, however, female-centered detective fiction had usually come to mean either fiction for younger (grade-school) readers or for adult women, possibly because greater freedom for teens in real life lessened the appeal of this particular fantasy, and because teen girls have long tended to read adult women's fiction. The term "girl detective" has persisted nonetheless, often used in a self-deprecating or satirical way to refer to a woman detective.

Yet, the twenty-first century has seen a renewed interest in the teen girl sleuth, in young adult novels such as Libby Sternberg's *Uncovering Sadie's Secrets* (2003), Bennett Madison's *Lulu Dark Can See Through Walls* (2005), Peter Abrahams's *Down the Rabbit Hole* (2005), Alane Ferguson's

The Christopher Killer (2006), and Michelle Jaffe's *Bad Kitty* (2006), as well as on television, with the *Veronica Mars* series (UPN 2004-6, CW 2006-7).[1] One reason may be that for its female readers (and viewers), the genre validates their attention to social relationships, to clothing, and to appearances generally, redefining as valuable what has been undervalued or mocked by the culture at large and by male characters within the texts. For example, Lulu Dark's boyfriend Charlie accuses her of being "way too wrapped up in clothes and appearances and shallow stuff like that," but the attention to detail(s) that is part of the socialization of contemporary girls prepares them for becoming detectives (*Lulu Dark* 248). The genre also taps into girls' anxieties about their bodies as viewed objects; how they look matters. Drawing on the observation of sociologist Liz Frost that "policing and self-policing is a dominant feature of feminine subjectivity" for adolescent girls, I want to suggest that there is a correlation here between social spectatorship and surveilling suspects, reading the social scene and reading a crime scene, and that being a teen girl is (like) being a girl detective (195).

The themes of disguise and deception central to detective fiction resonate with the adolescent's search for his or her own identity. As Roz Kaveney remarks, "*Veronica Mars* uses detective tropes to point out that the truth of who you are and how you got to be that person is at once a necessary discovery and a painful one" (180). However, this identity crisis is even more problematic for adolescent females coming of age in a society that demands that they pay constant attention to their bodies, but criticizes them as superficial; that aggressively markets to them as consumers, but chides them for being materialistic; that encourages girls to equate self-confidence with sexiness, but constructs them as potential victims of sex crimes both in real life and on television. Joanna Webb Johnson argues that teen girls "are constantly bombarded with images in the media that seem bent on destroying their already fragile egos. Just as adult women are under constant physical scrutiny, girls also must struggle with inflexible guidelines typically not followed by their male counterparts" (148).

In the late 1990s Joan Jacobs Brumberg noted with concern that the girl's body was "regarded as something to be managed and maintained, usually through expenditures on clothes and personal grooming items, with special attention to exterior surfaces — skin, hair, and contours" (xxi). In the twenty-first century Ingrid Levin-Hill, the heroine of *Down the Rabbit Hole*, reflects on how much alteration that body requires to be presentable: "Waiting in the wings are the orthodontist, the dermatologist, the contact lens guy, the hair-tinting guy, maybe even the nose-job guy" (*Rabbit* 1–2). Dr. Moore's patronizing advice to seventeen-year-old Cameryn Mahoney, the apprentice pathologist of *The Christopher Killer*, to "Go play with your Barbies!" is, of course, ridiculous, but a continuing reminder that the teen girl's body, like the adult woman's body, can never measure up to Barbie's idealized figure, at least without surgical enhancement (*Christopher Killer* 101). More recently, Sharon Lamb and Lyn Mikel Brown have amply illustrated in *Packaging Girlhood: Rescuing Our Daughters from Marketers' Schemes* (2006) how twenty-first century girls are encouraged through music, fashion, books, magazines, and television to locate their self-esteem in dressing and accessorizing the body. As Bianca Balducci asks rhetorically in *Uncovering Sadie's Secrets*, "Doesn't every good story start with a trip to the mall?" (2).

In dramatizing the pressures to conform, these texts raise questions about what makes a girl unique or authentic. Lulu, whose adventures in detecting begin with a quest for her stolen handbag, itself a knockoff of an expensive brand, finds her own identity usurped by a classmate who mimics her hairstyle and clothing. Dismissing the other girl as "a cheap copy," Lulu nonetheless wonders, "If you get your driver's license stolen, or you put it through the laundry one too many times, or you never bother to get one in the first place, are you still you? If you have nothing to prove it to anyone, how can anyone be sure of who you are? Is it your clothes, or your hairdo, or your voice, or what?" (*Lulu Dark* 232, 118). How does one reconcile being an individual with the pressure to look like everyone else, to buy the same clothes, the same shoes, the same haircut, the same bags, the same music?

And what if a girl does not look like everyone else? Jas Callihan's self-consciousness in *Bad Kitty* about having darker skin, being nearly six feet tall, and wearing size ten shoes corroborates Frost's claim that "young women may experience a damaging sense of shame if they cannot reproduce the necessary version of beauty for whatever reasons: if, for example, they are not a fair-skinned, blue-eyed blonde but a young black teenager, or if they have a disability, or even a very common 'variation' of appearance, such as glasses or a brace on their teeth, or are a little too tall or too broad" (196). Furthermore, in Jas's all-white world, her "exotic," racially marked body is misread as sexually available.

The figure of the girl detective exposes the contradictory messages of empowerment and disempowerment that surround the adolescent female body, giving her agency and authority, on the one hand, while emphasizing her vulnerability, on the other. Blurring the boundaries between female victim and female detective, the girl detective genre supports Brumberg's assertion that "Contemporary girls *seem* to have more autonomy, but their freedom is laced with peril" (197).

Like teen chick lit, another genre for teen girls, popularized by authors like Megan McCafferty, Meg Cabot, Louise Rennison, and Ann Brashares, these novels and television programs are often narrated in the first person, and marked by a chatty, informal tone and a self-mocking humor. Like chick lit, these texts, too, are rich in allusions to contemporary popular culture — slang, music, fashion brands, and communication technology (technology proves a liability when Cameryn, hiding under a murderer's bed, is given away by her cell phone's ill-timed ring-tone). Typically the heroine is an attractive middle- or upper-middle-class white heterosexual girl who is at the top of her class academically, highly independent and resourceful, and living in a one-parent household with her father, her mother being absent or dead. There are exceptions, of course: Cameryn works with her father, as does Veronica Mars. Bianca lives with her mother, sister, and brother, and Ingrid, the youngest of these girls, lives in a two-parent household. Half Jamaican, Jas is the only non-white detective in these texts, where economic, racial, ethnic, and sexual diversity tends to be relegated to sidekicks or displaced onto other characters in need of the detective's help.

Johnson's remarks about teen chick lit being "an engaging guidebook" for girls that maps "a world that cannot be *controlled* but can be *negotiated*" also apply to the girl detective genre (148,149). But whereas girls in chick lit devote themselves to getting along socially and romantically, girl detectives transform specifically "feminine" knowledge — about subjects like cosmetics and clothes — into tools of the detecting trade. Jas cleverly improvises a fingerprint kit, using a make-up brush covered with green eye shadow, explaining that "This is long-wearing eye shadow. It works by adhering to the oil in the skin. Since fingerprints are oily deposits left on paper, it adheres to them" (*Bad Kitty* 119). Jas's friend Polly's fashion sense helps her analyze a female victim's closet for clues about her state of mind: "Half the clothes are like two years old, while the other half were practically purchased yesterday. They still have tags on them and everything. If they were different sizes, like she'd gained weight or something, I would understand, but they aren't. Absent extenuating circumstances, that kind of binge shopping is a warning sign, a cry for help" (*Bad Kitty* 203).

For pragmatic Polly, an outfit is not just something "to die for," but something to die in, reminding Jas, "What you wear always matters. You should dress every moment like it could be your last" (*Bad Kitty* 183). Thus looking at a female corpse, "The first thing she [Cameryn] noticed were the shoes — regular Nikes like Cameryn and all her friends wore.... From her size and the kind of clothes she wore, Cameryn guessed her to be about her age. About her age and dead" (*Christopher Killer* 82–83). Later it is her furtive perusal of Dr. Jewel's oddly mismatched wardrobe that convinces her that he is not who he claims to be.

Female clothing and accessories, from Lulu's handbag to Ingrid's shoes, repeatedly figure in the plots. In *Down the Rabbit Hole*, for example, Ingrid accidentally leaves her "bright-red Puma cleats with the glittery red laces almost bright enough to hurt your eyes ... the fastest shoes on earth," at a murder victim's house, where they become police evidence (58). Later Ingrid is embarrassed when she contrasts her worn-out Skechers with the Manolo Blahniks of her nemesis, rich, spoiled Chloe, but Ingrid's shoes enable her to sprint across town in the middle of the night to investigate a crime scene. Her footwear even saves her life when she and Vincent Dunn, who has already committed two murders, grapple above the falls, and he plunges to his death, having caught hold of her shoes rather than her legs.

As these girl detectives illustrate, dressing for success in detecting requires merging style and function. Lulu explains that my "shorts gave me the freedom of movement to run if I needed to.... And the steel-toed cowboy boots were my self-defense" (*Lulu Dark* 154). Jas becomes a walking undercover kit, with hot red peppers in her pocket, a belt to tie up an assailant, a watch that plays a tune by NSYNC to draw attention in an emergency, a ring whose sharp points can cut through ropes, and boots stuffed with perfume, "completely debilitating if sprayed near the face," while Polly's stiletto heels are simultaneously fashion must-haves and lethal weapons (*Bad Kitty* 122).

As much as these girl detectives claim to be in control, however, their bodies threaten to betray them. Frost's choice of the word "policing" underscores the extent to which girls' bodies are treated as "problems." The genre "acknowledges that which may seem trivial (and yet is not) and validates a young woman's sense of insecurity and self-doubt" (Johnson 148). In Jas's pursuit of a runaway cat, and her accidental catapulting of a wedding cake into a swimming pool, she muses that "Five million people, or however many were at the pool, all stopped to stare at me. And all probably saw the place behind my knee that I missed shaving" (*Bad Kitty* 17). Cameryn is mortified when she throws up after seeing her first corpse — and is seen doing so by the handsome deputy sheriff Justin Crowley. Ingrid dramatically dubs her acne breakout "a one-in-a-million dermatological freak show" (*Rabbit* 55), and Lulu frets about her own imperfect complexion: "I felt my face flush. I didn't think anyone had noticed my zit — I'd been doing such a good job of covering it up!" (*Lulu Dark* 9). Cameryn feels acutely that she is not who she seems to be, that she herself is guilty of a cover-up: "What was she doing here? Her father thought she was a forensic genius because she found a baggie in a telephone book, believed she had nerves of steel because the second time around she didn't puke at the sight of a decaying body. But she knew the truth. She was a high-school student who didn't know anything except what she'd found in books" (*Christopher Killer* 97). Like criminals, these heroines share the sense of being impersonators and imposters, the feeling that they have something to hide, whether it is bad skin, a bad haircut, or a flat chest.

At times the girl detective is placed in the position of looking like a criminal herself. Ingrid's math teacher charges her with cheating; Neptune High's principal accuses Veronica of manufacturing the fake IDs that have been planted in her locker; Hattie calls Lulu a thief; and hotel security interrogates Jas. At other times, she actually engages in questionable activities that cross the line into criminality. Thus Cameryn breaks into and searches a man's hotel room; Bianca breaks into the school to search confidential files; Ingrid lies to her parents and the police, skips school, removes evidence from a crime scene, and drives a car although she is underage; and Lulu makes up a false story to get into another girl's house to search her bedroom. Veronica regularly disguises herself in order to extract information: she mimics the Swedish accent of Sheriff Lamb's receptionist, dons a black wig and uniform to pose as a caterer, and infiltrates a rival high school using the alias "Betty."

Yet girls in these texts cannot always control how their bodies or images of them are interpreted or exploited by others. Lulu discovers that the mysterious Hattie, like a male stalker, has created a photo collage of her in her bedroom; worse, Charlie thinks that it is Lulu, not Hattie, who has been seen at clubs dancing on tables without underwear and making out with strange men (*Lulu Dark* 218). As Frost describes the phenomenon of girls living "with the sense of body as something not themselves, as something at a conceptual distance from them," so Veronica, slowly recovering memories of her rape, feels detached from what her body has experienced, as if she is watching a film of someone else's life (81). So, too, her classmate Carmen is blackmailed by her boyfriend with a video of her drunk and naked with a Popsicle in a hot tub, while Lilly Kane quarrels with Aaron Echolls about ownership of a sex tape that he has made of the two of them. In *The Christopher Killer*, Dr. Jewel, who claims to be a psychic detective, kills teen girls and then later exhibits their bodies on his popular television show. The most explicit objectification of the teen girl's body occurs when Cameryn's friend Rachel is murdered; in the autopsy suite, a kind of mock-bedroom where she is undressed, examined, and dissected, she is redefined as a medical specimen (*Christopher Killer* 80).

The motif of the double is another way that these texts express the girl's split or divided consciousness, at the same time highlighting the interchangeability of teenaged (white) girls. In *Lulu Dark*, Hattie adopts Berlin Silver's name and identity after she watches the real Berlin die in a drowning accident. Veronica's friend Mac discovers that she and the super-pretty, super-rich, and super-spoiled Madison Sinclair were switched at birth at the hospital, and that Madison's privileged life, doting parents, and little sister should have been hers instead. Veronica's own double is her best friend Lilly; not only does Veronica temporarily believe that Lilly's brother Duncan is her brother too, and that she might be Jake Kane's daughter, but she also dates Logan Echolls, Lilly's former boyfriend. Cameryn has a double in Rachel, her friend and fellow waitress at the hotel. Realizing that Rachel was selected simply because she was the last one to leave the restaurant, she muses that "it could have been me out in that field" (*Christopher Killer* 94). Aspiring actress Ingrid uncovers an unlikely double in Cracked-Up Katie, a middle-aged alcoholic bag lady who is murdered shortly after letting Ingrid into her house to use the telephone. When she sees a photo of Katie as a young girl, she realizes that they were "Not just the same age, but there was a bit of a physical resemblance between them, Katie and Ingrid. Katie had braces on her teeth, for one thing. Hey. Two granddaughters who wore braces. Wore braces and loved acting" (*Rabbit* 329).

Identifying with the victim, Veronica, Cameryn, and Ingrid all occupy the place of potential murder victim themselves at the hands of Aaron Echolls, Dr. Jewel, and Vincent Dunn, respectively, who all happen to be professional actors. Having made careers of controlling and manipulating their images in relation to the camera and the audience, these villains try to direct the girls' deaths. However, the girls refuse to play the part of passive and powerless female victim: Cameryn melodramatically warns Dr. Jewel that if he kills her, "I'll be all through this room — they'll find me! I'll be on the walls and in the carpet. I'll be on the bed. My blood will be evidence you can't get rid of" (*Christopher Killer* 259).

The girl detective also reverses the male gaze that is directed at her in other ways. That reversal may be comic, as in the case of Ingrid, who resents her orthodontist's invasive scrutiny of the inside of her mouth. While he is looking at her, he is unaware that she is looking back at him, seeing him grotesquely magnified: the "white hair poking out of Dr. Binkerman's left nostril; the sleepy seed, lima bean colored, in the corner of his right eye; the pinprick-size blackhead on the end of his nose, a millimeter off-center" (*Rabbit* 4). However, girls also regard boys as (sex) objects: Lulu becomes infatuated with a male singer because of his toned body "like the statue of David if he wore tight jeans and a black tank top" (*Lulu Dark* 16), and Jas casts an appraising gaze at would-be boyfriend Jack, "a dark-haired, lightly tanned, moss green-eyed,/worn-in jean-ed, green suede Adidas-ed, white-shirted package," as if he is a commodity to be purchased (*Bad Kitty* 59–60). Later, undressing him after he has been drugged and is unconscious, she describes him as "a Jack doll you could do whatever you wanted with," her words a reminder of how girls (like Veronica) in a similarly powerless position risk being raped (*Bad Kitty* 212).

Not only do girls objectify boys, but they also "appraise and rate girls: models, actresses, and television personalities, teachers, mothers, and classmates, unknown girls in city streets and on buses and trains," visually and verbally sizing up other females in ways that eerily reproduce the dismembering gaze of the male murderer or rapist (Frost 133). Jas's stepmother Sherri, for example, identifies women with their breasts, pointing out "the different brands of breast implants on display around us in the pool" (*Bad Kitty* 2). Her profession as a Hollywood body double exposes media images of women as unreal or unnatural constructions, the result of editing either in the cutting room or through literal surgery. Even Jas's father's anthropological research involves fetishizing women's body parts, for he and Jas once "spent a year traveling around Europe looking for all the pieces of St. Catherine's body" (20).

As school photographer and as detective, Veronica regularly turns her camera on others. Her eye for details leads her to notice Lilly's shoes in the police photographs and video, proving that the sheriff arrested the wrong man for her death. Cameryn takes photographs at Rachel's autopsy, where she notices a brown stain on Rachel's hands, which along with the smell of garlic, alerts her to the presence of dimethyl sulfoxide with which the murderer drugged Rachel before killing her, and which is overlooked by the crusty male pathologist. Ingrid, as an actress herself, spots the *Dial M for Murder* playbill in Katie's house, which holds a vital clue to the murderer's identity. With Ingrid, Veronica, and Cameryn, their emotional involvement gives them a privileged position as investigators, enabling them to see what is invisible to the more detached and objective males around them.

However, despite, or because of, Nancy Drew's reputation, the twenty-first century girl detective rejects her as a role model; the name has become synonymous with a particular kind of sanitized, asexual, goody-goody heroine. Lulu's detecting success leads to her being labeled a "Real-life Nancy Drew" in the local newspaper, but she remains adamant that "I am *not* a girl detective.... They've got no personality, no social lives outside of their obviously gay boyfriends, and absolutely no sense of style.... Girl detectives are prissy busybodies who investigate the disappearance of stolen brooches for old heiresses" (*Lulu Dark* 41). Instead, these girl detectives identify with fictional male detectives. Ingrid, for instance, wants to be a female Sherlock Holmes. Veronica's name and Season 1 haircut may conjure up actress Veronica Lake, but she models herself after the hard-boiled no-nonsense male detectives of 1940s and early 1950s film noir (although she and her father mockingly introduce themselves as Carson and Nancy Drew in the third season episode "The Mourning After"). Similarly, Bianca sees herself as a female Sam Spade "in trench coat and fedora finding Maltese falcons and kidnapped heiresses" (*Finding the Forger* 33).

Perhaps Nancy Drew has also fallen from favor among these girls because good and evil here are less clear-cut, whereas "The formulaic adventures of Nancy Drew appeal by their consistent and concrete enactment of the defeat of evil by good" (Lundin 125). When Lulu finally corners Hattie, she determines that Hattie is mentally ill, but no murderer. Bianca's sister Connie, a professional P.I., warns her that "it's not all Nancy Drew skulking-around, you know" (*Sadie* 150). Bianca discovers that detecting interferes with her social life (and ruins her hairdo and clothing) when she breaks a date with her boyfriend Doug in order to help a client, and Doug thinks she has stood him up. She also has ethical qualms, wondering if "by uncovering Sadie's secrets, I could be jeopardizing her happiness" (*Sadie* 146). Cameryn learns that real dead bodies can look and smell awful, as she encounters a maggot-filled corpse: "The eyes were open and sunken; more flies crawled over the vacant pupils that stared like bits of dusty glass.... Tiny larvae wiggled out from beneath his eyelids like grains of crackling rice" (*Christopher Killer* 36).

And Veronica repeatedly finds in Season 1 that solving mysteries does not always produce happy endings. She tries to help her erstwhile boyfriend Troy get back his stolen BMW, only to discover that he is a drug dealer with a steady girlfriend; she locates her missing mother, an alcoholic who steals her college fund; and she defends her history teacher from charges of seducing his students, learning too late that he lied to her and that one of her classmates is pregnant by him. "Are there some things better left buried?" is a question that she keeps asking herself and others.

Not only do these texts question the idea of happily-ever-after endings, but as serial fiction they also expose closure as a convenience; endings or conclusions are tentative, subject to revision. In Season 2 of *Veronica Mars*, for example, Veronica learns that her first-season "solution" to the crime perpetrated on her/body was only partially correct, and that sex with her boyfriend Duncan occurred after her real rape by Cassidy Casablancas. Unlike the eternally-eighteen-year-old Nancy Drew, and more like Judy Bolton, aging throughout her series, these girls are in the process of growing up, their perspectives shifting as they gain new insight into themselves and their families.

If being a detective is in some ways an unsuitable job for a girl, it also acknowledges what girls in general, and these girls in particular, experience every day, where "surveillance" is a fact of life, at school, work, and home. From Bianca complaining about how difficult it is to eat in front of boys, to Cameryn trying not to be intimidated by Dr. Moore's "pinprick eyes, weighing her value, judging her," to Veronica facing down a gauntlet of snickering 09ers, the girl detective, it seems, cannot escape being a viewed object (*Christopher Killer* 102). Her ability to step outside her identity, to regard her own body as Other, prepares her, however, to interrogate others' identities and bodies, and to appreciate how outward appearances can be distorted or deliberately deceptive. In the refusal of its heroines to be passive objects of the (male) gaze, prying instead into the lives of others — classmates, teachers, parents, and other adults — without permission, the contemporary teen detective genre can be read as subversive. It is also highly critical of law enforcement, as innocent individuals are arrested in *Veronica Mars*, *The Christopher Killer*, and *Down the Rab-*

bit Hole. In addition, the genre offers a thinly veiled attack on paternal authority. Jas and Ingrid, in particular, both resent being pushed by their ambitious fathers, who have definite ideas about how a model daughter should act. In pursuing detective work, they are disobeying their fathers, especially Jas's father, the anti–Carson Drew, who tries to persuade her that being a detective is "unhealthy" and "unnatural" (*Bad Kitty* 32). Veronica's challenging of her father is made explicit when she vets one of his girlfriends, and he retaliates by compiling a damning dossier on her boyfriend Troy.

Although more morally ambiguous than the Nancy Drew books, in some ways these texts are no more realistic than Nancy's River Heights, "hermetically sealed off" from economic depression, war, and social change (Rehak 117). Despite the potential of texts like these to challenge the classification and stereotyping of girls, these heroines do not reflect the range of economic, sexual, racial, religious, and ethnic diversity explored in recent women's detective fiction. It can be argued that *Veronica Mars* foregrounds class conflict, but Veronica herself, despite her father's precarious social and economic status, never entirely forfeits the perks of her 09er connections. So, too, racism is present early on in *Bad Kitty*, when Jas is harassed in a bar, but subsequently it is never mentioned again, suggesting that Jas's (white) father's high socio-economic status serves to render her racial difference invisible.

With occasional exceptions the authors of these texts are complicit in constructing a conservative female fantasy. Girls may be the ones to figure things out, but ultimately Jas, Veronica, Cameryn, and Ingrid require rescuing — by males. In addition, each girl detective not only solves the case, but also gains a boyfriend, confirming her desirability and heterosexuality, as if romance is her real reward. In what must surely be intended as an ironic coda, Bianca quaintly sums up her adventure as "an etiquette lesson" and describes her own behavior as a detective in terms of bad manners: "It is preferable to ask one's friends directly if they have a problem rather than resorting to spying on, and speculating about them" (*Sadie* 203). It seems that being a girl detective, like being a girl, is about decoding society's mixed messages.

Note

1. This selection of texts is not meant to be exhaustive, but representative. As I write this, *Veronica Mars* is concluding its third (and final) season; however, in this essay I am

only considering Season 1. In addition, while Ferguson, Sternberg, Madison, and Abrahams have each written a second book in their respective series, I am restricting my discussion to these earlier texts.

Works Cited

Abrahams, Peter. *Down the Rabbit Hole*. New York: Laura Geringer Books, 2005.
Brumberg, Joan Jacobs. *The Body Project: An Intimate History of American Girls*. New York: Vintage, 1998.
Ferguson, Alane. *The Christopher Killer: A Forensic Mystery*. New York: Penguin, 2006.
Frost, Liz. *Young Women and the Body: A Feminist Sociology*. Houndmills, Basingstoke: Palgrave, 2001.
Jaffe, Michele. *Bad Kitty*. New York: HarperCollins, 2006.
Johnson, Joanna Webb. "Chick Lit Jr.: More Than Glitz and Glamour for Teens and Tweens." *Chick Lit: The New Woman's Fiction*. Eds. Suzanne Ferriss and Mallory Young, New York: Routledge, 2006, pp. 141–157.
Kaveney, Roz. *Teen Dreams: Reading Teen Film and Television from Heathers to Veronica Mars*. London: I.B. Tauris, 2006.
Lamb, Sharon, and Lyn Mikel Brown. *Packaging Childhood: Rescuing Our Daughters from Marketers' Schemes*. New York: St. Martin's Press, 2006.
Lundin, Anne. "Everygirl's Good Deeds: The Heroics of Nancy Drew." *The Lion and the Unicorn* 27.1 (2003): 120–30.
Madison, Bennett. *Lulu Dark Can See Through Walls*. New York: Penguin, 2005.
Mason, Bobbie Ann. *The Girl Sleuth: A Feminist Guide*. Old Westbury, N.Y.: Feminist Press, 1975.
Norton, Carol. *Bobs: A Girl Detective*. New York: A.L. Burt, 1928.
Rehak, Melanie. *Girl Sleuth: Nancy Drew and the Women Who Created Her*. Orlando: Harcourt, 2005.
Sternberg, Libby. *Finding the Forger*. Baltimore: Bancroft, 2004.
_____. *Uncovering Sadie's Secrets*. New York: Smooch, 2003.
Veronica Mars (television). Dir. Rob Thomas. UPN 2004-5; CW 2006-7.

Hermione Granger
as Girl Sleuth

Glenna Andrade

Trap doors, wardrobes with concealed compartments, secret rooms, and mysterious maps: these are just a few examples of similar items found in both the Nancy Drew mysteries and in the Harry Potter series. More important, appearing in the tradition of girl sleuth is Hermione Granger in the role of young female detective. As such, Hermione evolves from a long history of girl sleuths that zenithed with the Nancy Drew series, which codified the independent girl detective in juvenile fiction (Craig and Cadogan 149). Like Carolyn Keene's Nancy, Hermione is a superior girl sleuth of intelligence and action. She uses her wits to detect clues, unravel riddles, expose suspects and their motives, and solve mysteries, often more skillfully than Harry Potter himself. Although not as athletic as Harry, she takes individual action not only to track down research and pursue adventures, but also to fight energetically against villains.

Because the sleuth and the fantasy-adventure hero genres are intertwined in J.K. Rowling's Harry Potter books, Hermione's role as Nancy Drew sleuth complicates the series. Since genre is both a literary focus and a social construction (Bishop and Ostrom xiii), both types of heroes are part of a literary tradition constructed by cultural conventions over a long period of time. Even though many stories incorporate elements of other genres, such as when a romance includes detective elements or when historical fiction integrates adventure hero qualities, each hero remains central within the formula of his or her genre.

While various definitions of the detective and the hero abound, the following descriptions provide a beginning to compare the heroes of both plot-driven formulas. Detective fiction has always placed its focus squarely on the central investigating figure; the texts are plot driven, but the plots are often formulaic enough to allow the sleuth figure to shine through as the cynosure of the text. Readers remember Sherlock Holmes, Miss Marple, and Hercule Poirot, not the random murders that made up the plots of their individual mysteries. This identification as central subjectivity within a text has created a unique position for the girl sleuth, who as a teenaged character now rises to the forefront of a genre heavy on action and dependant upon the independence and valor of its protagonist. Thus, within this girl detective genre, Hermione takes on the sleuth role as the independent young female whose curiosity and intelligence induce her to take action in solving mysteries even when she must break rules, all the while showing confidence and competence while avoiding distractions, yet keeping her femininity as she tracks down research, pursues adventures, and fights villains, thereby restoring justice to society.

Like the girl sleuth protagonist who acts as the cynosure of her narrative, the male fantasy hero is very often the central identificatory figure in his series, a swashbuckling figure who saves the day with powers, daring, and might. This contrasts the main tools of the girl sleuth, whose intellect, perseverance, and guile are often the best tools of her trade. Another contrast between the two figures is in their settings; the sleuth works in the "real world," but the male adventurer inhabits fantastical realms; thus Harry may be seen as the hero who is the brave male youth with magical powers who begins as an outcast, but who is quickly called to the quest, during which he leads helpful companions in his adventures, overcomes various supernatural villains and beasts, and frequently descends into an underworld with the purpose of defeating evil so as to re-establish stability in the world.

In part because of his wizarding lineage, Harry stars as the adventure hero of the fantasy; alternately, Hermione's non-wizarding origin, or "Muggle-born" status, situates her in the relatively realistic realm of detective fiction. Both share the heroic quest to fight injustice and evil to restore order to society, and each uses the traditional methods — sleuthing and magic — inherent to their genre. Yet when the genre boundaries overlap in the Potter series, the competing sleuth role — the role occupied by the female character — becomes suppressed, though still managing to remain disruptive. It is this interaction, this suppression and disruption, which both essentializes Hermione's character and renders her less important than Harry at the same time.

Just as Nancy Drew initiates action in her own realm of River Heights, when Hermione takes agency in the Potter series, she intervenes in Hogwarts' culture. The concept of "agency," which is to advocate for oneself, includes the capability of both the internal capacities for making choices and the external conditions that permit them (Nussbaum qtd. in Gardiner 13). Clearly, the showcasing of the male-fantasy-adventure hero is one external condition that constricts choice. In other words, when Hermione performs as a girl detective in the Potter novels, the emphasis on the male adventure inhibits her agency. Nevertheless, as Hermione's character develops during the series, she begins to defy the stereotype of the hero's female sidekick when she evolves into an independent thinker and an active sleuth whose talents often undercut the focus on Harry Potter; moreover, Hermione continues to grow in subjectivity and agency even after her part is lessened and the series refocuses on the male-driven fantasy genre.

At the start, Hermione earns her role as sleuth in *The Sorcerer's Stone* through her quest for knowledge and her intelligence. Like Nancy Drew, Hermione's acumen runs the gamut from being perceptive to analyzing clues and to preparing in advance for upcoming adventures. For instance, attempting to retrieve the Sorcerer's Stone during the attic scene, Hermione is the first of the Harry-Ron-Hermione trio to spy the trapdoor to the subterranean realm, thus demonstrating Nancy Drew's keen power of observation (MacLeod 444). Later in *The Sorcerer's Stone*, Hermione identifies its creator and connects it to the object being protected by the dog in the attic (*SS* 220). Even before the adventure, she plans ahead by looking up enchantments they may need to break (*SS* 271). Thus, Hermione, like Nancy Drew, is "serious, competent, disciplined, and determined" (MacLeod 446). Whereas Harry is sometimes impulsive, Hermione provides the role model of the hero who is keenly observant and who anticipates consequences. Akin to Nancy, Hermione conforms to the sleuth of girl detective fiction who uses intelligence to solve mysteries, in contrast to earlier heroines who depended upon mere hunches and intuition (Craig and Cadogan 237). Not too incidentally, the boys thank Hermione for her knowledge of herbology after she saves them from the Devil's Snare during the attic scene (*SS* 278).

After her introduction as sleuth in *The Sorcerer's Stone*, Hermione's detective qualities strengthen in the *Chamber of Secrets* when she uncovers suspects, reads clues, and plans ahead. Instead of following Harry's lead, she initiates the plan to uncover suspects by volunteering to make a Polyjuice potion so the trio can impersonate the henchmen of the young villain Draco Malfoy to gather information surreptitiously (*CS* 155–166). In fact, the ability to create clever disguises is a signature Nancy Drew trait (Craig and Cadogan 79). Furthermore, at the Chamber of Secrets' entrance, Hermione deduces that whatever petrified a cat could not be human, and discovers the clue that the spiders are marching, showing, like a proper girl sleuth, no fear of spiders, whereas Ron is terrified (*CS* 154).

Accepting that some rules must be broken for a higher purpose, Hermione leads the boys to infringe upon them. Moments after the spider discovery, Hermione persuades Ron and Harry to defy the prohibition against entering the girls' bathroom to investigate the mystery further (*CS* 155). Later, Hermione violates numerous school policies, as when she steals a teacher's signature, pinches a restricted library book (*CS* 162–164), and even steals ingredients from a professor's office (*CS* 186). She is like a Nancy Drew who will eavesdrop, break and enter, and even search someone's room to pursue a higher cause.

When questioned about the Polyjuice potion, Hermione makes the moral decision that breaking the rules is better than doing nothing about the threat to the students (*CS* 165–166). While Hermione's rule-breaking in *The Sorcerer's Stone* does reinforce the status quo of the female who disobeys authority to further the males' goals rather than her personal ones, as Ruthann Mayes-Elma points out (93), Hermione is not punished by an authority figure in *The Chamber of Secrets*, thus avoiding "the traditional construction of gender" (Mayes-Elma 94). Additionally, in resisting Hogwarts' patriarchal culture, she actually orders the boys to create a diversion so as to steal ingredients (*CS* 186), a trait of independence reminiscent of Nancy Drew (Caprio 51). Plus, while some subjugated women feel "remorseful and ashamed afterwards" for rule-breaking (Mayes-Elma 94), Hermione experiences neither in *The Chamber of Secrets*. This change from companion to co-conspirator becomes a major turning point in Hermione's development as the sleuth who decides what must be done and how to do it, regardless of the rules. Hence, the emerging focus on Hermione's qualities as smart girl sleuth begins to undercut the primacy of Harry's position as male fantasy hero. Because readers can engage in "distancing" (Bennett qtd. in Smith 319) to distinguish between the sleuth and the fantasy genres whenever boundaries shift, readers can admire Hermione's increasing independence and agency as well as Harry's fantasy-hero character traits.

Just as it motivates Nancy, curiosity inspires Hermione to set off on her first separate adventure in *The Chamber of Secrets*. Although the escapade is told in retrospect, Hermione has succeeded in identifying the Basilisk that terrorizes Hogwarts. Granted, she is found petrified, and she may have been intrepid to the point of foolishness, yet she retains her Nancy-like self-possession (Craig and Cadogan 152) when she awakens and explains her actions, undaunted by the experience. The scene is even reminiscent of the many times Nancy is rendered unconscious by some dastardly villain. Again, Hermione had prepared for the adventure beforehand. When discovered unconscious, Hermione is holding a mirror that averts the effects of the monster's stare (*CS* 157). In her hand are still further clues. She clutches the library page that describes the Basilisk's traits and that explains the spiders' march as a retreat from the monster's presence. The page contains her handwritten clue "Pipes," which identifies the entrance of the Chamber of Secrets in the girls' bathroom (*CS* 291). Therefore, while Hermione was unsuccessful in confronting the monster, readers can admire her curiosity, research, and initiative to act alone — all substantiating Hermione's Nancy Drew–like qualities. She neither asked for help, nor admitted she was wrong in initiating her adventure, just as Nancy Drew would not (Caprio 51). Hermione does not apologize for failing, and this lack of repentance seems to be more typical of a "man" who is "not supposed to give [rule-breaking] enough thought to be sorry or regretful" (Elma-Mayes 94).

As Hermione's character grows in capability and assertiveness, she functions more adeptly as a co-leader in the later novels. In *The Prisoner of Azkaban,* she not only receives praise (346) for her quick thinking during the werewolf fray and for solving the werewolf mystery, but also exhibits increasing assertiveness. As she chides Hagrid for his drunkenness, she is not simply a rule-enforcer in word, but vigorously dumps out his tankard (*PA* 121). She breaks the passive female role when she slaps Draco Malfoy for insulting Hagrid (*PA* 326). She even resists adult male power when she interrupts the authoritarian Professor Snape during a highly charged event (*PA* 359). Confidence and assertiveness affirmed, Hermione emerges as a main leader during the Time-Turner episode. She tells Harry what to do and then must restrain him when he begins to act impulsively during a precarious moment (*PA* 395–409). Because they alternate leadership, Harry acknowledges their shared agency to Dumbledore when he says, "We did it" (*PA* 418), which is not so much a usurpation of the female as it is admiration for her intellectual powers, decisiveness, and action.

Hermione's shared leadership continues in *The Order of the Phoenix* when her actions verify her invention, persuasion, and even fighting ability. When she, Harry, and Ron are in a tight spot, Hermione spontaneously concocts a plan to deflect Professor Umbridge from the trio's real purpose of saving Harry's godfather (*OP* 749–52). She misdirects the villainous Umbridge into the Forbidden Forest and pleads for Harry's and her own release boldly and effectively (*OP* 757). As a co-leader, Hermione's quick wit and persuasion rescues the pair from what could be a failed adventure. Equally important, Hermione embodies a new role as a vigorous fighter during the conclusion of *The Order of the Phoenix*. Though as usual she casts spells, assesses dangers, and reacts quickly when she accompanies Harry and others on their rescue of Sirius at the Department of Mysteries, she now engages in actual combat. Rather than suggesting Hermione as a token presence of the female in the action scene who fails (Heilman 225), Hermione's new role as the intrepid fighter in the battle for justice demonstrates that she has far outgrown any girlish terror.

In addition to leadership and action, Hermione shows herself to be a deep thinker. Just as she has insight into some villains' intentions, a trait comparable with Nancy Drew, Hermione has examined even the hero's motivation and has the temerity to speak candidly. She articulates what she sees as Harry's weakness. When Harry is about to act impulsively to save Sirius, Hermione questions him: "Don't you think you've got a bit of a — a —*saving-people thing?*" (*OP* 733). Although Harry avoids this possibility, he does pause and adopt Hermione's plan of rescue. Therefore, while Hermione may tell white lies to save the day or to accomplish a mission with a greater purpose, she evolves into a truth-teller, the independent co-leader who does not shirk from speaking out honestly so the other hero can assess his own vulnerability. In fact, her personal introspection has come earlier than Harry's. Although both the sleuth and fantasy genres tend to preclude self-examination because they are mostly plot-driven, Hermione has already recognized her fear of failure (*PA* 319), whereas Harry shows little introspection until two novels later, when he admits to himself that he must be independent from protectors and mentors (*HBP* 645). In the parabola of both plots, Hermione's self-recognition peaks earlier than Harry's, suggesting she has matured sooner and is thus wiser.

In spite of Hermione's maturation through the Potter series, her sleuth role lessens dramatically in *The Goblet of Fire*, but reappears qualitatively in *The Half-Blood Prince*. Even though she has no separate adventures, Hermione continues to refine her sleuth capabilities. In contrast to the usual female associate who asks questions of the male detective that propels the plot (Craig and Cadogan 85), Hermione continually makes connections that Harry overlooks. To prevent him from following a red herring, she corrects him about a previous encounter during which Draco Malfoy was interested in the Vanishing Cabinet (*HBP* 254). Even as Harry is confused by the Marauder's Map, Hermione explains why it could not depict Malfoy's presence. Moreover, it is she who solves the identity of the Half-Blood Prince as Snape, the most compelling mystery in this novel, and even works out his motive (*HBP* 637–638). Hermione's deductions are akin to the young girl detective's instant assumptions that are always accurate (Craig and Cadogan 155); Harry's mistakes reveal his incapacity as a sleuth. In addition, Hermione appears to be a better co-leader than Ron. More often than not, Harry tests out his theories on Hermione, who confirms them, corrects them, follows with further ideas, substantiates them with research, or even pursues her own solitary adventures for more information. In short, Hermione contributes more thoughtfulness and wisdom to the shared agency than the sidekick Ron, who frequently just listens and wonders.

Appropriately, Hermione's role diminishes when the series steers away from realism to re-center upon the fantasy hero's adventures, such as in *The Half-Blood Prince*; nonetheless, Hermione resumes her role as sleuth with even more expertise in *The Deathly Hallows*. Once again, she plays the Nancy Drew character who steals books, but now from Dumbledore's personal library (*DH* 101). She not only plans ahead by packing camping equipment in her magical beaded bag, but also creates several clever disguises that work well (*DH* 522) instead of backfiring as during her first attempt (*SS* 271). Certainly readers must applaud Hermione for her continuing focus in *The Deathly Hallows* when she insists early on that Harry should concentrate on destroying the Horcruxes (objects containing pieces of Voldemort's soul) (100) and when she steers the boys back on this track during the battle at Hogwarts (640). She not only anticipates Voldemort's presence in Godric's Hallow, which had not occurred to Harry (100), but also acts quickly to give Harry a flask to save Snape's memories in when Harry did not know what to do *(DH* 657). She even shows a greater loyalty to the quest than Ron, who leaves Harry mid-way during their sufferings in the wilderness.

Finally, Hermione's best trait, her unwavering logic, is admired by Xenophilius Lovegood, who praises her for pointing out his fallacy when she replies that someone "could claim anything is true if the only basis is that nobody proved otherwise" (*DH* 411). Therefore, Hermione's finer

Nancy Drew qualities help compensate for Harry's impulsiveness, tendency to distraction, and occasional slip in decisiveness in the final novel. In fact, near the novel's conclusion, Dumbledore admits that he had always counted on Hermione's presence to slow down Harry's impulsiveness (*DH* 720).

Eventually, though, Hermione reconfirms her independence when she returns as sleuth and now succeeds in a personal adventure. Targeted by a sleazy journalist for dating Harry's competitor in *The Goblet of Fire*, Hermione not only tracks down the journalist (*GF* 548) and solves the mystery of how the spy illegally recorded private conversations, but also captures her in a glass jar sealed with a spell (*GF* 727–728). In contrast to previous misadventures, Hermione triumphs that she has succeeded in solving her own mystery separately (*GF* 728), and she even replicates the role of justice hero, specifically helping others who have endured Rita Skeeter's gossip mongering. Moreover, Hermione continues as a smart sleuth when she convinces Rita to publish an article revealing the conspiracy to hide the problem of Voldemort's return (*OP* 567). Hence, Hermione demonstrates agency in persuading a former scoundrel to use the newspaper for the political benefit of denouncing evil. In this way, the realism of the girl sleuth genre contributes to solving a specific social problem in the wizarding realm.

Where Hermione breaks more clearly free of the classic Nancy Drew role is when she becomes a social activist for the house elves in *The Goblet of Fire*. Outraged by their enslavement, Hermione begins a grass-roots organization called the Society for the Promotion of Elfish Welfare or S-P-E-W (*GF* 224), confronts the Hogwarts' students about the elves' working conditions (*GF* 239), approves the now-freed Dobby as a new role model (*GF* 383), begins a movement to educate the students, and even addresses the elves collectively about their right to wages (*GF* 538). Thus, Hermione assumes agency in advocating for the rights of the oppressed, a role in keeping with modern feminism, since campaigning for other marginalized groups is "closely tied to the oppression of women" (Warhol and Herndl x). Simply put, when Hermione follows feminism's more general goal of bringing positive social changes to the world, readers of Rowling's popular novels can learn which behaviors "to emulate or shun" and so help reconfigure "the social and political order," as Jane Tompkins describes the potential cultural applications of fiction (Tompkins xvii). The detective plot becomes a space where readers can try out Hermione's activism in preparation for re-entry into the world outside the text. Unlike Nancy

Drew, who is often a "vigilante, but not a reformer" (Craig and Cadogan 158), Hermione facilitates social improvement through political means.

As *Order of the Phoenix* progresses, however, Hermione's well-meaning activism is less significant to the story line. Readers hear only a scattering of Hermione's abolitionist plans. Whereas Hermione's efforts are mocked and the elves remain impressed under a conservative hegemony (Heilman and Gregory 245), at the very least Hermione's activism has changed other people's minds. Dumbledore admits that the elves' enslavement has caused discontent and even rebellion (*OP* 852) and offers them wages for their work at Hogwarts. While SPEW is rarely mentioned again in the next novel, *The Half-Blood Prince*, Hermione's influence emerges in Harry's new sympathy for the house-elves' conditions (439). Further, in *The Deathly Hallows*, Ron's mind has changed to wanting to protect them from Voldemort *(DH* 625), whereupon the elves join forces against the villain in battle *(DH* 734). In contrast to one feminist critic who views Hermione's fight for the house elves as another form of female, sacrificial behavior (Bradshaw "Hermione as Sacrificial Lamb"), Hermione's intervention supports the feminist goal of bringing positive social changes. It may be that Hermione's social intervention is necessarily downplayed because in pushing beyond the boundary of the girl sleuth genre, the theme of political activism begins to threaten the formula's familiarity and stability, and even further destabilizes the focus on the fantasy hero's adventures.

However, not all readers and critics appreciate Hermione's role as intellectual girl sleuth in the Harry Potter series. Some say that as the "know-it-all," she only preserves the typical female role in *The Sorcerer's Stone* (Mayes-Elma 97). Nonetheless, Hermione's aptitude and pursuit of knowledge become essential to Harry and Ron. Their initial disapproval of her knowledge confirms her role as the smart girl sleuth who is generally mocked for her intellect, and even reflects badly on the boys' behavior. On the positive side, Hermione's intelligence does break the stereotype of the tag-along, dumb female companion in the action-adventure genre, undermining the image of the passive female. Typecasting Hermione as a "know-it-all" is not unlike saying that all boys who are facile at computers are "nerds." Additionally, when Harry and Ron criticize Hermione as "bossy and nosey" (*SS* 164) early in the first novel, their displeasure can be understood as criticizing Hermione's behavior rather than her brains. Her bossiness may evolve from feeling insecure in a new social milieu where she has not yet confirmed her position.

Hermione suffers from other emotional pressures too. As a Muggle-born, she is especially conscious of the amount of learning she must acquire about wizarding. Hermione must study diligently because she attends boarding school based on her aptitude in contrast to those students from wizard families. She even suffers from prejudice as a "Mudblood" (an insult to those born with magical powers, but without wizard ancestry). Clearly, Hermione must prove her worth to be socially acceptable. On the one hand, her quest for knowledge is like that of Nancy Drew's interest in serious reading, in contrast to her sidekicks, who often prefer games (MacLeod 445) or sports. That Hermione is teased for perpetually reading and studying sets up a contrast to the boys, who only do enough to get by. Her difference is a convention that actually serves to distinguish her from main characters in other detective stories (MacDonald 70). On the other hand, Hermione eventually recognizes that her exaggerated need to achieve stems from great fear of failure (*PA* 319) and that her self-imposed stress was not worth the agony (*PA* 430). In a more serious vein, Hermione, like Nancy, must resolve this personal inner mystery (Caprio 105) so as to become a more enlightened person (Caprio 126).

In contrast to one critic, who postulates that Hermione gains acceptance through her alliance with Harry's own high status (Dresang 226 quoted in Bradshaw), Hermione earns her position through her thinking and actions, to the admiration of Harry, Ron, and others. Much like the conventional male adventure hero, Hermione begins as a Muggle-born "outcast" so that her virtues will later shine. Thus, while some critics perceive that women are marginalized in the Hogwarts world, others champion Hermione's efforts to prove her subjecthood as a capable young woman in this new realm.

Hermione's quest for knowledge is, as Mayes-Elma points out, a necessary part of her identity (92). Undoubtedly Hermione is introduced as a "know-it-all" to contrast her change from submissive to assertive and from competitive to cooperative. Clearly, Hermione is frightened and submissive during the mountain troll event in *The Sorcerer's Stone*. When she is discovered "shrinking against the wall opposite, looking as if she [is] about to faint" (*SS* 175), Hermione's behavior in the bathroom scene is stereotypical and does suggest that women are ruled by their emotions, as Melissa Bradshaw points out ("Hermione as Sacrificial Lamb"). That this behavior happens "frequently" is an overstatement by Bradshaw, since Hermione changes through the series. Bradshaw does make a good observation when she points out that Hermione could have saved herself from the troll, because she had earlier taught Ron the levitation spell he uses to rescue her ("Hermione as Sacrificial Lamb"), but anyone, male or female, might react with terror when surprised by an evil monster, especially for the first time. (After all, Harry and Ron were forewarned before the confrontation.) Perhaps Rowling began with the stereotype of the "wimpy girl" so Hermione could transcend it; in fact, Hermione changes at the scene's conclusion. She immediately decides to disobey the rules at Hogwarts, thus beginning her journey to adventure, mystery solving, and justice.

Later in the same book, Hermione moves beyond the superficial knowledge of book learning to demonstrate her intellect and to participate in a shared agency that challenges Harry's predominance. For one, she serves as a foil to Harry's best friend Ron. In the "underworld" below the attic, Ron demonstrates his skills as a strategist during the Wizard Chess battle, whereas Hermione reveals another intellectual aptitude — logical deduction — when solving the riddle of the potions (*SS* 283–285). Hermione's detection of the correct potion is essential to the quest. Although criticized by some for stepping aside to let Harry finish the mission, Hermione's sacrifice is equal to Ron's during the Wizard Chess battle. When she says that friendship and bravery are more important than "Books! And cleverness!" (*SS* 287), her modesty is no less than Ron's.

Hermione not only exhibits her own subjectivity, but also learns that in a well-working multiple agency, some must stay back while others continue, as is typical in a hero-centered adventure. Similar to other fantasy stories where heroes form a triad, each sidekick contributes some quality that the main hero must eventually acquire, in this case, Ron's strategizing and Hermione's logic. In fact, Mimi Gladstein sees the triad as containing friendship partners, where Hermione is "an equal and essential member" (50), in contrast to other feminist critics who see Hermione as subordinate when "she ... downplays [her] intellect" (Mayes-Elma 95), though this happens only in *The Sorcerer's Stone*. Looked at another way, Ron's supposed gift for strategy is overshadowed by Hermione, who more clearly illustrates the skill during the rest of the series when she continually plans ahead, anticipates potential consequences, and forms alternate plans. Perhaps a better contrast between each one's specialized knowledge is that Ron understands the history and background of the wizarding world while Hermione contributes her expertise in research, strategy, and logic.

Many feminist readers criticize Hermione's anti-feminist traits, although they admit to her agency and composure. One feminist reader who disapproves of Hermione as a mere enabler of male action in *The Sorcerer's Stone* does grant Hermione's agency when she works for the greater good beyond her immediate gain (Mayes-Elma 92). Mayes-Elma relegates Hermione to the helpmate or "rule-enforcer" and even castigates Hermione's rule-breaking as supporting the patriarchy in the first novel (91).

Nevertheless, Hermione's rule-breaking is essential to the pursuit of justice in accordance with her role as sleuth. Hermione's power to choose when to abide by or break the rules is a confirmation of her feminism within the genre: it is her space to act however she determines according to the circumstances. Likewise criticizing Hermione, Melissa Bradshaw admits that Hermione remains "composed" throughout the novels and gives the example of Hermione's action in *The Sorcerer's Stone* when she rescues the boys by casting a spell to open a locked door, preventing their school expulsion; on the other hand, Bradshaw chides Rowling for failing to credit Hermione's capability after the event ("Hermione as Sacrificial Lamb"). Nonetheless, Hermione is not without commendation: she is thanked by the boys for rescuing them from the Devil's Snare during the attic scene (*SS* 278), is recognized by Dumbledore at the end of *The Sorcerer's Stone* for her "use of cool logic" (305), is praised by Professor Lupin for deducing he was a werewolf (*PA* 346), earns recognition of her "genius" from the boys in *The Deathly Hallows* (425) and is admired for her brains by her husband Ron in the epilogue of the same book (*DH* 756).

Generally, Hermione is so self-confident that she never appears to need any sort of praise. Moreover, most of these criticisms of Hermione, like many others, are justified in the first novel that sets up Hermione's character change; however, it is a mistake to censure Hermione's character without acknowledging her growing confidence and competence in the later novels. In addition, her sleuthing even destabilizes the male fantasy adventure when she transgresses the boundaries between the two genres. When Bradshaw condemns the series as being popular with girls "because they sympathize with Hermione and her oppressed situation," the critic too quickly dismisses the strength of Hermione's character, diminishes her finer girl-sleuth qualities, and fails to acknowledge that Hermione exhibits many feminist ideals within her own space in the girl sleuth genre ("The Sacrificial Lamb in Harry Potter"). That Hermione's actions tend to support the patriarchy is predetermined by the generic formula that requires the hero to return the world to stability, an ending that is equally essential to the plot of the fantasy adventure hero.

For readers sympathetic to feminism's more progressive goals, the diminishment of attention on Hermione can signify her suppression. The stronger Hermione gets in the series, the less predominant her character. Some critics, like Bradshaw, may be disturbed that Hermione's role is sacrificed for marketability ("The Sacrificial Lamb in Harry Potter"). Similarly, readers may justly affirm that Hermione's own adventures often end poorly, are inconsequential, or succeed against female, rather than male, villains. Rather than see these as flaws, however, readers must realize that Hermione's role diminishes whenever the fantasy genre supplants the girl sleuth genre, thus returning her to the intelligent female helper at times where her choices are constricted and her complete agency is inhibited, although she continues developing her attributes as a smart sleuth.

Still other readers will approve of Hermione, who, like Nancy, is the feminist in popular culture (Craig and Cadogan 163). Along the way, Hermione certainly fulfills some feminist aspects of the Nancy Drew sleuth who, as Anne Scott MacLeod points out, wants to be taken seriously, to earn credit for accomplishments, and to be accepted without restraints, prejudice, or any limitations of her gender (450). Whatever way a reader wants to see Hermione, as either a sidekick or a competing hero, Hermione's double role in the Potter series is facilitated by the formulas of fiction that permit readers to explore their own "self definition" (Tompkins xvi) as the hero in each genre.

Whenever Hermione works for the benefit of others, however, she undercuts her Nancy Drew role to further engage feminist principles. Whereas Nancy rarely helps change people's minds and tends to seek justice for single individuals, mostly of good families or of a high social standing (Parry 145–156), Hermione engages in social activism to pursue the goals of supporting truth in journalism and for the political goal of abolishing elf slavery. In these ways, her agency carries the conscience of feminism in correcting injustice and in subverting dominant values within the wizarding world to match feminism's more humanistic values. Further, unlike Nancy Drew, who stays frozen in her role of young girl detective, Hermione grows chronologically during the series and even matures to plan ahead for a future occupation in which she can do something worthwhile for others (OP 228), an intention in accord with feminism. Thus, in transcending her Nancy Drew role, whether as a romance heroine or a social reformer, Hermione continually interferes with Harry's position as the central male hero.

The intermingling of the two genres not only provides tension between the two heroes, but also results in a mix of non-gendered clues.

The commonplace objects such as the trap door in Hogwarts' attic, the Vanishing Cabinet with a hidden compartment, the unknown door in the Chamber of Secrets, and The Marauder's Map all link the sleuth and adventure genres; nonetheless, other clues are more gender neutral than those in the Nancy Drew series. While Nancy's clues are typically quaint, feminine, or sentimental objects, such as ballet slippers or pieces of jewelry (Craig and Cadogan 155), the clues in the Potter series are not gender linked. For example, Hermione is not squeamish about spiders or the petrified cat, and Harry decodes Voldemort's diary in *The Chamber of Secrets* and even the retrieves the clue of the locket in *The Half-Blood Prince.*

In inserting a girl sleuth into the Harry Potter series, Rowling ran into an invisible barrier in developing Hermione. There are few models of girl sleuths who follow feminist alternatives. Even the newer female adult detective genre is still in search of protagonists who transcend male domination and sexism (Klein 221). Although the author may have tried to counterbalance the focus on the male hero, if Rowling had strengthened Hermione's position too far, the violation of the conventions would construct a completely different kind of text. In short, the competition between the sleuth role in the realistic mode and the hero role in the fantasy adventure suggests that both genres co-exist uneasily between their fluctuating boundaries in the Harry Potter series.

In the end, Hermione proves her growth into a keen detective much like Nancy Drew. With increasing facility, Hermione has detected clues, unraveled riddles, solved mysteries, and uncovered suspects and their motives. She asserts her own subjectivity when she changes from rule-enforcer to rule-breaker. Her agency expands from assertiveness, forthright speech, and leadership into forceful action for justice. Changing from companion to co-conspirator and co-leader, Hermione develops into the sleuth who breaks the rules to do whatever must be done for a higher cause. She is more thoughtful and strategic than Ron, and more perceptive, logical, wise, and cool-headed than Harry. Readers who concentrate only on *The Sorcerer's Stone* may well complain that Hermione is submissive to the patriarchal hegemony, but those who read further in the series will witness that because of her take-charge personality, she often shares agency with Harry or pursues her own sleuthing adventures. Like Nancy Drew, Hermione Granger claims her own feminist space as a girl sleuth of intelligence and action within the parameters of formula fiction that requires the happy ending of restoring justice and order to society.

Works Cited

Bishop, Wendy, and Hans Ostrom. "Introduction." *Genre and Writing: Issues, Argument, Alternatives.* Ed. Wendy Bishop and Hans Ostrom. Portsmouth, N.H.: Boynton/Cook, 1997, pp. ix–xv.

Bradshaw, Melissa. "The Sacrificial Lamb in Harry Potter: A Glance Through the Lens of Feminist Theory." Kerrville, Texas: Schreiner University, 19 July 2007, http://organi zations.weber.edu/metaphor/OldSite/metaphor2004online/pg083.html.

Caprio, Betsy. *Girl Sleuth on the Couch: The Mystery of Nancy Drew.* Trabuco Canyon, CA: Source Books, 1992.

Craig, Patricia and Mary Cadogan. *The Lady Investigates: Women Detectives and Spies in Fiction.* New York: St. Martin's Press, 1981.

Gardiner, Judith Kegan. "Introduction." *Provoking Agents: Gender and Agency in Theory and Practice.* Ed. Judith Kegan Gardiner. Urbana: University of Illinois Press, 1995, pp. 1–20.

Gladstein, Mimi R. "Feminism and Equal Opportunity: Hermione and the Women of Hogwarts." *Harry Potter and Philosophy: If Aristotle Ran Hogwarts.* Eds. David Bagget and Shawn E. Klein. Chicago: Open Court, 2004, pp. 49–59.

Heilman, Elizabeth E. "Blue Wizards and Pink Witches." *Harry Potter's World: Multidisciplinary Critical Perspectives.* New York: Routledge Falmer, 2003, pp. 221–239.

Heilman, Elizabeth E., and Anne E. Gregory. "Images of the Privileged Insider and Outcast Outsider." *Harry Potter's World: Multidisciplinary Critical Perspectives.* New York: Routledge Falmer, 2003, pp. 241–259.

Klein, Kathleen Gregory. *The Woman Detective: Gender and Genre.* Second Edition. Urbana: University of Illinois Press, 1995.

MacDonald, Janice. "Parody and Detective Fiction." *Theory and Practice of Classic Detective Fiction.* Eds. Jerome Delamater and Ruth Progozy. Contributions to the Study of Popular Culture, 62. Westport: Greenwood Press, 1997, pp. 61–71.

MacLeod, Anne Scott. "Nancy Drew and Her Rivals: No Contest." *Horn Book* 63 (1987): 422–450.

Mayes-Elma, Ruthann. *Females and Harry Potter: Not All That Empowering.* Lanham: Rowman and Littlefield, 2006. 8 April 2007, http://www.ohiolink.edu/etd/send-pdf.cgi? acc_num=miami1060025232.

Parry, Sally E. "The Secret of the Feminist Heroine: The Search for Values in Nancy Drew and Judy Bolton." *Nancy Drew and Company: Culture, Gender; and Girls' Series.* Ed. Sherrie A. Inness. Bowling Green: Bowling Green State University Popular Press, 1997, pp. 145–158.

Rowling, J[oanne] K[athleen]. *Harry Potter and the Chamber of Secrets.* New York: Levine-Scholastic, 1999.

_____. *Harry Potter and the Deathly Hallows.* New York: Levine-Scholastic, 2007.

_____. *Harry Potter and the Goblet of Fire.* New York: Levine-Scholastic, 2000.

_____. *Harry Potter and the Half-Blood Prince.* New York: Levine-Scholastic, 2005.

_____. *Harry Potter and the Order of the Phoenix.* New York: Levine-Scholastic, 2003.

_____. *Harry Potter and the Prisoner of Azkaban.* New York: Levine-Scholastic, 1999.

_____. *Harry Potter and the Sorcerer's Stone.* New York: Levine-Scholastic, 1997.

Tompkins, Jane. "Introduction: The Cultural Work of American Fiction." *Sensational Designs: The Cultural Work of American Fiction 1790–1860.* New York: Oxford University Press, 1985, pp. xi–xix.

Warhol, Robyn R., and Diane Price Herndl, eds. "About Feminism." *Feminisms: An Anthology of Literary Theory and Criticism.* New Jersey: Rutgers, 1991, pp. ix–xvi.

Teen Sleuth Manifesto

Melissa Favara and
Allison Schuette-Hoffman

In this work of creative nonfiction, writer chums and lifelong Nancy devotees Melissa Favara and Allison Schuette-Hoffman perform a literary liberation raid. The essay — part cultural criticism, part critical encomium, part stand-up act — explores the impact of Nancy and her friends on the girls who grew up loving her. In the tradition of syndicate writing, they have not identified their separate contributions.

We will keep fresh batteries in our flashlights. We will not go to bed. We will look for the secret compartment. We will befriend the exiled heiress. We will brush aside the skeleton and by torchlight search the attic. We will practice the art of disguise. We will rise to the occasion. We will dive without fear into the wreck. We will be the meddling kids without whom bad men would have gotten away with everything.

❑

January 2003. The front of the calendar showcased the cover of Nancy Drew's very first mystery, *The Secret of the Old Clock*. Nancy sits on her hip, legs modestly tucked beneath her, in the wild grass. The evening around her settles ominously; the bare branches of trees project black silhouettes against the darkening sky. With her right hand she steadies the clock. With her left (ambidextrous, of course), she has pried open the face. She still grips the screwdriver but something has distracted her. Was that a noise she heard in the scrub? She glances over her shoulder, not afraid, but cautious, poised and ready. It all came back to me then. The row of yellow bindings, the page turning, the hunt, the longing. I bought the Nancy Drew calendar.

179

One day, changing January to February, I got the itch to reread Nancy. I punched her name into the university library's search engine, doubting much would come up. That was my first surprise. Scholarship. Among titles like *The Hidden Staircase* which I recognized from childhood, I found other titles like *Nancy Drew and Company: Culture, Gender, and Girls' Series*. Immediately, Nancy rose in my estimation. I rose in my estimation. My childish impulse to return to an adolescent hero apparently held weight. If others saw fit to research, analyze, and publish about Nancy, I must be onto something.

The library had two copies of *The Secret of the Old Clock*, the one I recognized from childhood, the one that graced January on my calendar, and another edition put out by Applewood Books. I quickly pulled out the copy and inspected the back cover.

> They're Back Again...
> Just as You Remember Them
> Nancy Drew® and The Hardy Boys®
> The original editions are back — the way they were first written.
> Beginning in 1959, the Hardy Boys and Nancy Drew stories
> were updated, rewritten, and condensed,
> and these old editions went out of print.

I caught my breath. What was this? Nancy had a life before the yellow spines?

I hastily opened the book to read the inside flaps. The world began to crack at its edges. I discovered — *no way!* — Carolyn Keene did not exist.

> Who Is the Author?
> The author whose name appears on all the Nancy Drew books, Carolyn Keene, was a pseudonym of Edward Stratemeyer.
> The company that he founded in the early part of this century, the Stratemeyer Syndicate, produced over 1200 books, including Tom Swift, the Bobbsey Twins, Nancy Drew, and the Hardy Boys.
> In 1929, prompted by the success of the Hardy Boys series, Stratemeyer sent plot outlines of a new girls' mystery series to a ghost-writer who completed the books. In 1930, *The Secret of the Old Clock, The Hidden Staircase,* and *The Bungalow Mystery* appeared. That same year, Edward Stratemeyer died.

Oh, Carolyn. I took you for granted. I swallowed you whole. I accepted your corporeality without a second thought. And you were nothing but a shade. A front for a man named Edward (and later, I learned, a woman named Mildred). A spirit, a specter, a spook.

If you lacked substance, you the author who should know flesh and blood, what of Nancy, the created, the imagined? Was she nothing more than a figment? If I couldn't trust in you, how could I trust in her?

❑

Notes from the Editor, Copyright 1931, facsimile reprinted 1994:

> Much has changed in America since the Nancy Drew series first began in 1930. The modern reader may be ... extremely uncomfortable with the racial and social stereotyping, the roles women play in these books, or the use of phrases or situations which may conjure up some response in the modern reader that was not felt by the reader of the times.
>
> For good or bad, we Americans have changed quite a bit since these books were first issued. Many readers will remember these editions with great affection and will be delighted with their return; others will wonder why we just don't let them disappear. These books are part of our heritage. They are a window on our real past. For that reason ... we are presenting *The Mystery at Lilac Inn* unedited and unchanged from its first edition.

❑

I rediscovered Nancy in 1997, when I wandered out of the literature section at Powell's City of Books and caught the familiar yellow wall that marked her territory in children's lit. I bought a copy of *Secret of the Old Clock* for five dollars second hand, one with a different cover than my mother's hand-me-down I'd left in Michigan. The story began to ring untrue to my memory of it on the second page, when I read the dialogue that was to set off the action of the story, a chat Nancy had with her father, the attorney Carson Drew. The publication date of the book in my hand was 1930.

On page three of the novel, Carson Drew asks Nancy her opinion of the Topham family. Her answer reads: "Who could like them, father? Richard Topham is an old skinflint who made his money by gambling on the stock exchange. And Cora, his wife, is nothing but a vapid social climber. The two girls, Isabel and Ada, are even worse. I went to school with them, and I never saw such stuck-up creatures in all my life. If they fall heir to any more money, this town won't be big enough to hold them!" (3).

The storyline: an eccentric uncle has died, and his last will and testament leaves all of his money to the horrible Tophams. But there are a handful of poor relations that the uncle promised to remember, and the case is afoot. Nancy swears to find the subsequent will Josiah Crowley promised to write, and of course she does. She does so in both books —

the 1930 original edition, and the edition I read when I was eight years old. Something felt different, reading the novel in Portland, Oregon, in my grownup life, in my rented room. This "original" Nancy wasn't the girl I remembered. I had my mother rifle the attic for my books and send them out to me in Oregon. Here's how the exchange goes in the 1959 reissue of the book, the one my mother read as a girl and passed on to me: "Nancy did not answer at once. She had been taught never to gossip. But finally she said tactfully, 'Ada and Isabel were in high school with me. They were never my close friends. We — uh — didn't see eye to eye on various things'" (7–8).

I held both books in my hands. I felt betrayed. Why doesn't she tell the questioner her answer to the question? And I felt disloyal for the enthusiasm I felt for this new old Nancy. The calm, mannered sleuth I grew up with slowly backed away, an image of the flapper-esque, slightly obnoxious teenager stepped between us.

❏

We will meddle. We will be of assistance. We will clean up. We will ruin our cashmere sweaters.

❏

In December, I made my mother talk to me about Nancy Drew. Actually, she volunteered. She wanted to. She knew about my off and on interest in the series we both loved over the past few years, and having begun to do a formal investigation of Nancy, I wanted her to weigh in. We had discussed my amazement at the fact that two entirely different versions of Nancy Drew had been published, and I vaguely remembered her saying years ago something to the effect that she had "liked the old ones better." I wanted to press her to talk about her experience. I wanted her to be outraged along with me about what had happened to our girl. I was shocked when she was.

I chain smoked on the porch while we talked.

"Do you remember giving me my first Nancy Drew?"

"I think I gave you some of mine. I bought you *Secret in the Old Attic* because it was one of my favorites, but I had liked the old one."

"Do you remember when you realized that there were two Nancy Drews, and how you felt about it?"

"When I got some of my own in the 5th or 6th grade for Christmas or whatever, I noticed right away that they had a different tone, and I didn't like them as well. But the old ones weren't available anymore. I was dismayed. I didn't understand why they had changed them. They weren't as exciting, and she didn't seem like as much of an individual as before. Maybe it was the period when the old ones were set, but they had a greater sense of mystery. And she was more adventurous then. And don't put this in there, but you know the popular rich kids in school? The new Nancy seemed like she was supposed to appeal more to them. She was never in a clique in the early ones. She seemed later to care more what people thought of her. The old Nancy cared more about people."

"Okay, I have to put that in there. It's exactly what I want to talk about. Can I put it in? Listen to how it sounds." I read the answer back.

"Sure. I just didn't think it applied."

I didn't say anything about this then, but I was curious about why the "don't put this in there." Was she afraid of whining? Why was it taboo to talk about Nancy Drew's change in relationship to her own class status, and how it made my mother feel about not being one of the popular rich girls? And at what point did I know that we weren't the Drews but the unfortunates that they tried to rescue?

❑

Notes from the Editor, The Secret of the Old Clock, *Copyright 1959*

"This new story for today's readers is based on the original of the same title."

❑

"Mom, do you remember when your mom gave you your first Nancy Drew?"

"My first Nancy Drews weren't given to me."

I'm talking to my mother on my cell phone on the walk home from campus; she's driving from school in Detroit back to Saginaw.

"My grandmother had my mother's on her bookshelf and I took them down and read them."

I perked up: I had such warm memories of my mom giving me the books; I had felt like the standard bearer of a tradition, the next in a line. I assumed my grandmother had done the same thing, but not so: my mother, left to raise herself, had gone snooping.

The Tuesday after our first phone interview, my mother called me twice, both times to add things to our Nancy discussion that she thought were important. The first call:

"Okay, don't put this in there, but I used those books at my grandma's house as an escape. We'd visit my grandparents on the weekend, and the adults would drink, and I would be disgusted, and I would hide in my grandma's bedroom and read."

"Okay," I said, "but that's really interesting. I kind of want to get into Grandma and Grandpa's alcoholism. I think it's important."

"Well, no one I know will ever see this, right? You could talk about it some."

She called again that night. "You have to put something in about how the books felt. The old ones. The paper was yellow and it *smelled* good. It smelled *old*. It smelled like *mystery*."

❑

Notes from the Editor, The Bungalow Mystery, *Copyright 1930*

"This book, while produced under wartime conditions, in full compliance with government regulations for the conservation of paper and other essential materials, is complete and unabridged."

❑

I know just what my mother meant — the history this physical book has lived through, the history it brings with it — the marks of a distant past on the book must have made it a better portal for getting the hell out of there the minute she opened it.

❑

Message in the Hollow Oak (1935)

> "Behold your property, Miss Drew!"
> With a feeling akin to awe Nancy permitted her gaze to sweep over the vast expanse of territory.
> "All that — mine ...?"
> "I feel like a feudal lord surveying his vast domain," Nancy smiled (131).

When Nancy wins a tract of land in Canada's "rough country," she quickly finds herself embroiled in the tricky politics of private property. Set in 1935 at a time when "the wild West" found modernity encroaching, Nancy's adventure situates her in the tension between vengeance and law, between those who believe that might makes right and those who won't proceed without evidence. Nancy quickly discovers that the aristocratic privilege of the feudal lord holds no power in the wilderness. Soon after "surveying her vast domain," claim jumpers from the shady Yellow Dawn — "Is that a company or a disease?" (135) — fly in to trump Nancy's title to the land. Before she can even adjust her hatpin, Nancy discovers Yellow Dawn has set up camp and begun mining a vein of gold. Norman Ranny, a kind and wise lovelorn prospector who's never been quite the same since he returned from the war, wants to fight for Nancy's right to the land, but Nancy holds him back. "She realized that it would be useless for her to enter into physical combat; if she wanted to defend her right, she would have to go to court" (135).

So Nancy wires her father, who quickly flies in with the sheriff of Wellington Lake and an expert surveyor in tow. But the wily men of Yellow Dawn know how to play it cool. They keep the peace until the sheriff and his men grow restless. When Nancy accidentally provides them with false information, they turn huffy and pull out. Nancy must face the fact that without hard evidence, the law is as useless as vigilante justice.

What's a teen sleuth to do? Why use her feminine wiles, of course! Knowing that the womanizer Raymond Niles, who guards the shack where the gold is kept, finds Nancy disarmingly attractive, Nancy, Bess and George approach flirtatiously. They sweet talk, they wheedle, they bat their eyelashes, but Niles refuses to let them near the shack. Nancy plies her final tactic.

> "Oh, please let us go inside," she pleaded, grasping him by the hand.
> A foolish grin spread over the young man's face.
> "I wish I could, Miss Drew, but I have to obey orders" (206).

No matter, for when Nancy coyly slips her hand away, the key belongs to her.

Later, Nancy sneaks back to the shack and quickly locates the sack of gold. In haste, she hurries back to her father and friends, thrusts the sack into her father's hands and tells everyone to ready their horses. Before anyone can stop her, she rushes off again, this time to locate dynamite. She carefully selects a large stick and carries it gingerly to the dam where she places the dynamite "in the most advantageous place." She lights it and races back to her father and friends, yelling, "Mount and ride for your lives!" (210).

When the dynamite explodes and the water, released from the dam, floods Nancy's property, Carson begins to rein in and shouts, "What was that?" (210).

But Nancy knows. She knows that you'd better not mess with a woman who puts her property and her body on the line because that woman takes risks. She might make sacrifices but in the end she turns them to her advantage. And so, striking the flank of Carson's horse, she cries out to her father, "Don't stop now...! Ride on! Ride on!" (210–211).

❑

In America, 37 years pass.

❑

By 1972, publishers apparently decided the lust for gold and the brouhaha over property rights no longer resonated with young readers. And so, in the revised version of *The Message in the Hollow Oak*, the sinister Buck Sawtice is replaced by the creepy Kit Kadle. The infinitely dupable Raymond Niles is replaced by the harmless college boy Art Budlow, who immediately forms a devastating crush on Nancy. And the kindly, lovelorn prospector Norman Ranny is replaced by the "tall, blond, attractive" leader of an archeological dig, Theresa Bancroft, "who looked very trim in her pale-blue dungarees" (29).

A trace of the "wild west" remains, however. Though the story now takes place in southern Illinois, the ethos of America's settlement is represented by the artifacts taken from the Hopewell Indian burial mounds and by the history behind Nancy's case. Her task: to find the treasure left behind by the French missionary Père Francois, who died shortly after the "powerful Iroquois swarmed down and nearly annihilated" (8) the Algonquin Indians he was attempting to convert. Luckily for Nancy, he'd managed to hold out long enough to write a note, place his valuable possessions in a metal box, hide the box in a hollow oak, and attach a lead plate to mark the tree. He also happened to have the foresight to alert the treasure seeker to a nearby Indian burial mound. "It is large, overgrown, and the rounded top is gone. I dug into it from the side and found fine objects. Then war came. I put them back and filled the hole" (175).

Nancy, then, not only solves the perplexing mystery. She also ensures that Theresa Bancroft can perpetuate the re-colonization of indigenous people by the desecration of their sacred sites. But, hey, no one said a teen sleuth's hands would always be clean.

❑

Plot Summary for *The Mystery at Lilac Inn* (1961), as voiced by Gay Moreau, the Antagonist

Call me Mary. Call me Jean. Call me Gay, any of my aliases. They all work. I am Nancy Drew's evil twin. I was a pretty good actress before I got busted for check forgery. They put me away. When I got out, I waited tables at the Lilac Inn. Like Nancy, I was curious. Off hours, I tapped the walls, found the secret panel in the dining room, a good place to hide when old Aunt Hazel presented the family diamonds to her niece, Nancy's friend Emily, a good place to tap once on the floor, to signal my boyfriend Frank to douse the lights so I could swipe them. I hid them in a tube of lipstick.

I never knew my father. I looked for another, everywhere. The first time I saw Carson Drew, I was wearing handcuffs — it was he who prosecuted me for fraud, in his good suit, and his salt and pepper, his fine, sympathetic brows, his good daughter seated behind him in her pillbox hat. Once, there was an old man who was nice to me, one of the people whose checks I kited, the one who wouldn't press charges. After a shift at the inn, biding my time and going by Jean, I stole the innkeeper's pipe to send to him.

After I got out, before the jewel heist, I broke into the Drew home, lifted a picture of Nancy and her Burk's charge card. I am so fucking good with makeup, a wig. I called myself by her name, and everyone bought it. I walked out with a watch, a mink stole, a half-dozen dresses I'd have been able to maybe afford in hell. We had another scheme going, Frank and me, selling stolen Navy equipment to an Enemy Agent, but none of that is important. I tried to kill Nancy in the end, first with a time bomb, then by sinking her in our submarine. But she broke free, the two of us were there, she in flippers, and I in my flawless disguise. Then Carson showed up. There on the dock, he didn't know who to save at first, but Nancy, Nancy was there to tear my wig and smudge my face just as I was about to throw myself into his arms.

❑

The Clue of the Velvet Mask (1953)

George snapped her fingers. "That gives me an idea. It will make everything safe as a bank vault!"

Nancy was folding the black velvet mask into the open traveling case, but she looked up startled.

"What's your idea?"

"I'll masquerade as you!" [66].

Dear George,

How ever did you choose which Nancy outfit to wear? The pink-flowered dress with the matching hat and black velvet bow. The olive-green knit with matching shoes and beige accessories. The yellow blouse and skirt with matching slipover. The powder blue sweater and skirt. How many did you try on before you felt just right, before you felt like her, like Nancy? Did some part of the costume still have to resonate with the

George in you? Or did you wish to erase her altogether? Who did you see when, standing next to Nancy's suitcase, blond wig affixed, you studied yourself in the mirror? I imagine it was in that moment — when you looked and saw your old chum staring back — that George actually slipped away, that the internal shift took place, that the cells, the tissues, the muscle and bone accepted a new idea of themselves. Did you ever worry that George would be lost to you forever?

When I was a young girl reading Nancy Drew, my parents, my teachers, the Girl Scouts — they all offered models of the girl I should be. If she excelled (and I *was* so encouraged), she excelled within boundaries. She excelled to the heights of an average girl. Her perfection remained steadfastly normal. Nancy offered a different model. Yes, she was perfect yet she hardly fit the norm. She didn't measure herself against the criteria of worth set by others. In fact, she didn't measure herself at all. She had no use for self-consciousness; she simply directed her own course in the world. I needed to see that.

But how useful is a hero one cannot become? When does the benchmark stop serving as a means of resistance to the status quo and start becoming a measure of one's own failure?

Your thoughts, George?

❏

We are recording devices. We will not self-destruct. We will become intimate with our engines. We will change our own oil. We will wait for a sign: one candle in the window, two candles in the window. We will drive like hell, and tell our passengers to hang on for their lives.

❏

I remember my mother trying to articulate the concept of a pen name when as I child I asked whether I could meet Carolyn Keene. I wish that I could remember how she explained it. What I do remember is that I felt a great sadness, as though I had ferreted out yet another of the dark secret conspiracies adults were in on together, like the jackalope, or confession, or anything that happened when my parents had people over and sent me and my sister upstairs to bed where we sat at the top of the steps and listened to the clink of glasses. Just as it bothered me then that Carolyn Keene wasn't a woman I could picture anymore, pensive at a noisy black typewriter like the one my dad brought home from the dump where he fixed the garbage trucks, it bothered me as an adult that the character who comprised my childhood fantasy of agency, independence, and heroism was in fact a watered-down version of a girl who the Stratemeyer Syndicate had invented, and then hidden from me. But almost immediately, I knew that I didn't want to erase the 1950s Nancy, I didn't want to call her a fraud. I wanted to find a way to remind her who she was when it wasn't communist to badmouth the stock market, when the wealthy were suspect, when it was okay to shoot off her mouth. I wanted to rescue her from that bad decade, find her in a closet with her flashlight batteries dead, bound with clothesline, sneezing from the dust. I wanted that Nancy 1930 and I should break in and seize her up. That we should make trouble.

❏

Mildred Wirt Benson wrote twenty-three of the fifty-six Nancy Drew Mystery Stories. She was the most popular ghostwriter for the series.

Dear Mildred,

As a reader, it's hard to know where Stratemeyer ends and you begin, and later, where you end and Stratemeyer's daughter Harriet Adams begins. How did you cope with the instable authority of your authorship? Was there any joy in being a "spook" for the syndicate, or was it, as I imagine, one long process of giving birth only to grieve?

Dear Mildred,

I bet you didn't like Harriet Adams. I found a snippet of an interview in which you report that Adams instructed you to "make the sleuth less bold.... 'Nancy said' became 'Nancy said sweetly,' 'she said kindly,' and the like, all designed to produce a less abrasive more caring type of character" (qtd. in Kismaric 28).

So I have to ask: did you ever fight for Nancy?

Did you ever sit down at your typewriter and invent a parade of picketing characters? Nancy, George and Bess dressed all in black, circling the sidewalk in front of Grosset and Dunlap, hoisting signs with the slogan, "No characterization without representation!" You'd mask their faces, of course, to symbolize the insecure and contingent nature of their identities, and they would march silently, an indication of how Adams had colonized their voices. Hannah Gruen would sit on the sidelines, handing out flyers, gathering signatures on a petition, serving the girls coffee and an occasional handful of trail mix to keep their energy up. Carson Drew would rush between the inner offices of Grosset and Dunlap and the action on the street, reporting on his progress with the publisher's attorneys, generally feeling more helpful than he actually was.

If I had access to your private papers, would I find this sketch, hidden, left behind like a *Clue in the Diary* or a *Clue in the Old Album*? Evidence of your attachment to Nancy, of your commitment to me, a girl in the future who yearned for less caring and more abrasive role models.

❏

I wonder if I always suspected there was another version, a note composed in secret and hidden in a hollow space in the wall. The real Nancy was on the run, picking up her mail in dark glasses and a trench in some dusty courtyard, a foreign country.

❏

Bess Marvin on Food

> Bess asked haltingly, "Would you mind if I concentrate on dessert?" She hesitated a moment, then said, "Just a small hamburger and a large fudge nut sundae with a piece of cake?" (*Crooked Banister* 57).

Dear Bess,

Thought of you last night as I made a batch of No Pudge Fudge Brownies. Thought of you again when I went back for a third and another handful of pecans from the freezer. What is it about food and dessert in particular? What do we seek beyond nourishment?

> Bess Marvin. George's pretty, slightly plump cousin.
> Bess Marvin. The pretty, slightly plump blonde.
> Bess Marvin. A slightly plump blond with delightful dimples.
> Bess Marvin. Blond and pretty, slightly plump.
> Pretty Bess Marvin. She has been reducing to get a part in the Footlighter's play.

Dear Bess,

In 1935, Carolyn Keene introduced you in *The Message of the Hollow Oak* as "pretty, lady-like and sedate." She described you thus: "She took pride in her person and gave particular care to her luxurious locks" (6). Keene did not mention the size of your figure.

In that very same adventure, it's George — not you — who first mentions hunger. And when Pete, your friendly guide through the Canadian wilds, fries up some bacon and potatoes, Keene does not single you out. Nancy and George are equally famished. "The girls were ashamed of the amount of food they were able to consume. At home they might have scorned such simple fare, but after the morning's paddle even coarse bread tasted delicious" (91–92).

So what happened, Bess? How is it that you wound up the sole character obsessed with appetite?

> At Nancy's outcry Bess looked into the box. She gave a little shriek. "What! No food?"
>
> "Those little boys I saw running away," Burt remarked, "must have taken everything." He dashed off in the direction the children had taken....
>
> Bess sat down on the ground, disconsolate.
>
> "Oh, don't be silly!" George chided her cousin. "It wouldn't hurt you to go without a meal."
>
> "You're a good one to talk," Bess replied. "You eat all you want and stay slim. I can't help it if I get hungry" (1972 129).

Dear Bess,

Please. Smack. George. Just. Once.

> "This is our cook Mattie," said the captain.
>
> The woman chuckled. "I'm everything," she said. "Housemother, nurse, too. If you want anything let me know. And help yourselves to cake and fruit anytime." She pointed to the food on the side counter.
>
> "Oh, my diet!" moaned Bess (*Hollow Oak* 1972 96).

Dear Bess,

I have to confess, I inwardly scoff at people who speak of dieting. Last night on NPR, I heard a plug for an upcoming show on health. The guest will be an author whose new book includes recipes that allow us to "eat more food with fewer calories." My immediate response? Only privileged Americans would eat more in the hopes of weighing less.

But let me further confess that I operate on this same logic. I just don't talk about it. When I watch my weight, count my calories, eat a light salad for dinner so that I can go back for that third brownie, I do it in silence. When I go to the gym, simulate outdoor activity on the Arc Trainer, hit the mats to "develop my core strength," I tell people I do it for the exercise. I use euphemisms like "develop my core strength" to mask the fact that I care what my abs look like.

I don't want to diminish your own struggles with body image, Bess, but I will say this. That no matter how often George upbraided you for your generous appetite, no matter how thoroughly the 50s saw a shift in attention to the dimensions of a woman's body, you never edited your desires like I did mine. If I wanted food, I stifled the impulse till I could feed it in solitude. If you wanted food, you announced it boldly. I admire that.

> A little later Nancy was introduced to Madame Paray. Nancy complimented the dressmaker on Diane Dight's clothes.

"Her figaire ees slim and easy to fit," said the dressmaker modestly. "But I'm afraid she diet too much — and ze diet, eet keep you happy or else eet make you cross when you do not eet enough" (*Old Attic* 1970 46)

———

Dear Bess,

Did you know obesity is being criminalized in the U.S.? No one says so directly, of course. They all disguise it in a concern for health. CNN seems to have a weekly update. Obesity: Killing Our Kids. Obesity: Taking Four Years Off Your Life. Obesity: Not a Behavior — A Disease. CNN always accompanies their reports with shots of a busy city sidewalk. The camera, careful to cut the heads out of the frame, chooses one or two obese people to pan walking down the street. To protect their privacy, right? Well, in effect it robs them of all their subjectivity worth protecting. Instead they become objects, and as objects stand in for all obese folks everywhere. Whatever disgust or horror is cultivated in the viewers will now be projected onto every obese person they encounter. And they'll feel justified in their disgust and horror because it's for *their* own good, you know, *those* people, the one's who've "let themselves go."

Tell me, Bess. How did what's good for us become a measure of how good we are?

"Before we do another speck of sleuthing," Bess spoke up, "we're going to have lunch. I'm starved."

George began to laugh. "It would be good for you to go without it. How else can you lose those twenty pounds you've been talking about?"

Bess made a face at her cousin, then marched straight for the refrigerator. The first thing she pulled out was a large jar of mayonnaise (1962 157).

———

Dear Bess,

You go girl.

❏

Hannah Gruen, a Character Sketch

I see you, Hannah Gruen, like I've been back at the whiskey: double vision. In both images, you're the trusted housekeeper, a kind of domestic Shiva: above the white apron tied about your waist, six whirling arms bearing a feather duster, a hot water bottle, a broom. A truncheon, a bowl of broth. One is hidden inside an oven mitt. Here's where the visions diverge: in the 1950s, you're a Jane Austen–esque governess. You're always fixing "luncheon," suggesting that Nancy rest awhile on the divan. Advice giver, surrogate mother. In the 1930s original series, you're a maid. You're working class. You drop the g on the ends of all of your gerunds, you have bad grammar: "she and I knew each other real well," you said. In *The Sign of the Twisted Candles*, for instance, you know all the gossip that only service workers know: "I'll begin at the beginning, and I'll tell you how I know all about it. I got it first hand from Katrina Henkel, who worked for old Mrs. Sidney until the day of her death" (1933 44–45). You're always there at the end of things, one of the women who take care of us, to whom we wish to be entrusted after it's over, one way or another.

❏

We will delegate tasks. We will get dirt beneath our manicures. We will darn our gloves. We will work for the good of the team.

❏

Nancy was a daddy's girl, raised by Carson and the housekeeper. In our house across the street from a vacant lot, I used to imagine my mother was dead too, that I was the capable lady of a house, that I had a den. I was sure Nancy's street looked nothing like mine. Was there a row of dissolute rentals, a born-again church on the corner? I think I reckoned not, even then. I'd wrap a towel around my head in the bathroom mirror, the nun disguise, and lip sync Nancy Drew in *The Mystery at Lilac Inn*: "I only hope my masquerade will bring results" (1961 113). I could coax my grief to a crescendo, become an orphan who lived by her wits, upsetting myself until my mom's arrival home from K-Mart, worn through from stockroom duty. No matter when she got home, we had reading time in her bed: her, James Jr., and me, each child reading something slightly ahead of what was easy. We were rewarded by my mother reading at the end from Beverly Cleary or *The Lives of the Saints*. Clutched together in the frail cone of light that filtered through the wicker shade of her bedside table lamp, reading aloud at night in turn with my brother, I knew she would never die.

My father was a mechanic, and nothing like Carson Drew. If I were to provide a photo of my own father, it would have to be the Polaroid my mother took after a party circa 1979: my father is sitting on the toilet, drunk, with a blond curly wig, à la Carol Channing, slipping off, obscuring his moustache and his sad Cheshire smile.

For my seventh birthday, I asked for a detective kit and got it from my dad: a magnifying glass, a tube of talcum powder, a tube of graphite, and a white feather for dusting. I looked for a match to the thumbprint

my mother let me take from her on a piece of Scotch tape, dusted the door-
knobs and the China cabinet and the orange-painted wainscoting in the
kitchen. I couldn't find a clear match. Everyone who lived in the house
had touched everything so much that you couldn't find a clear mark from
anyone.

My father's fingertips were so soaked in motor oil that not even the
grainy soap he kept under the sink got them clean. His fingerprints were
permanently outlined in black, thin swooping whorls and ridges.

These were the years he worked at Tri-City Disposal fixing garbage
trucks. He used his breaks to smoke Kools and snoop around the dump
for treasure. I have a clear blue glass vase, an ancient chair upholstered
with a fragment of Oriental rug. I remember him falling asleep in the tub,
creeping in to watch him, his head tipped back and chest hair afloat, sleeping with his mouth open.

When he kidnapped us, I narrated it to myself like a Nancy Drew
story.

> *A stocky man in an army coat and handlebar moustache beckoned to the chil-*
> *dren. With trepidation, they approached his stationary vehicle. Kidnapped!*

My dad kidnapped me, along with my brother, from the edge of the
playground, in January of my seventh year. He took us to my aunt Mary
Kay's. Dad was twitchy, his moustache moved in his silences. He was talking to himself in the cab of the pickup.

My mother, frantic, doesn't call the cops. She drives to her mother's
house.

Grandma had decoded the police radio code for various crimes, and
obsessively listened to the hissing police scanner my grandfather had traded
someone a rifle for in a bar parking lot. On the night we were missing,
my wizened, unhappy grandmother had a shining moment of maternal
glory: she called everyone my father worked with, each of his bar buddies
she could find in the phonebook, every surviving member of his family.

> *Relentlessly, she pursued every trace of a clue.*

She had untreated scoliosis and uncannily unchanging black hair; her
left shoulder blade ran parallel to the ground. When she got to Mary Kay,
she broke through: defiantly, Mary Kay announced, "Yeah, they're here."
Grandma made a disparaging remark about Mary Kay's sexual proclivity
and assembled her sons.

> *Surely, she cried, we cannot leave the children in the clutches of their captors!*

It was a commando operation — I don't know where my dad was at the time. My brother and I awoke on the couch to a sound you'd never mistake for anything once you've heard it, the front door being kicked in by my uncles. I remember looking for my pink coat while my mother had a fistfight with my aunt, the only time I ever saw her do anything ugly, my uncle Tom breaking it up, my aunt Mary Kay screaming at him, "Don't hit me!" as though he would have. He did beat up her husband some, big man, so it was okay, a fair fight.

The brave young man struck his assailant to the floor.

Uncle Joe gathered us up, carried us out into the scrubby yard to uncle Tom's car, a dark green seventies Nova uncle Tom's girlfriend Michelle was gunning. I hadn't found my coat. Michelle gave me her navy blue cable knit cardigan with wooden Paddington buttons about a million sizes too big for me. Six of us in the little car, me wrapped in this fantastic perfumed sweater, smashed together in that confinement of a moment that would never be repeated, no one talking, the heater on full-blast and the radio a faint backdrop.

The young woman skillfully maneuvered the powerful roadster.

The ride seemed to take forever, and I wished that it would. I had never felt so loved, I had been rescued by my family. To this day, the smell of beer on a man's breath makes me feel safe, is almost enough to make me feel in love. My heroes did not go to Choate or Emerson College. They fixed their own cars on the weekend. They had a lot of girlfriends, and bad grammar, this is not what defined them.

❑

Mom: "So what's your point then, talking about all of this?"

"I don't know. I guess I wonder to what extent we were into the mysteries, and to what extent we were into the fantasy of living like that — upper middle class, a stable household, no chaos. Could you be a teen detective when you had so much else to worry about? Were we not supposed to notice that Nancy was rich? Was all that supposed to be incidental? Are there discoveries we weren't supposed to make? Where's the girl detective who's like David Copperfield, the detective orphan who lives by her wits? How would that be different? Didn't we need someone like her?"

❏

Heroine Worship

I. Heroine

Fear never stops her.
She opens the door to strangers
with no second thought.
She hits the hallways at night, alone.
She manages a household without a mother
and without doing housework.
She never has to dust
    or vacuum
    or scour the bathtub.
She never worries about money
    or date rape.
She never ages!
She doesn't diet. People admire her beauty,
but they celebrate her brains.
She keeps her wit and charm
no matter how difficult the person.
She never doubts herself
or questions her motives.
She loves the Midwest, appreciates its conventions —
    the social calls, the protocol,
    the industry of upright people,
    the relish for tradition.
She benefits from the privilege they confer,
yet always defends the underdog.
Her father loves
    and
    adores
    and
    trusts her.
For God's sake, he listens to her.
She convinces him to let her do anything.
Sometimes, she proves him wrong.

II. Worship

Nancy Drew, it was so easy
to be you on the page.
Real life became the test.
There, I failed.

❏

We will examine the soil for footprints. We will learn how to blaze trails. We will note our fear and press forward. We will peek in at the window. We will follow our hunches. We will painstakingly cover our tracks. We will keep our wits about us. We will carry waterproof matches. We will never be caught napping.

Works Cited

Keene, Carolyn. *The Clue in the Jewel Box.* New York: Grosset and Dunlap, 1943.
_____. *The Clue of the Dancing Puppet.* New York: Grosset and Dunlap, 1962.
_____. *The Clue of the Velvet Mask.* New York: Grosset and Dunlap, 1953.
_____. *The Crooked Banister.* New York: Grosset and Dunlap, 1971.
_____. *The Message in the Hollow Oak.* New York: Grosset and Dunlap, 1935.
_____. *The Message in the Hollow Oak.* Revised ed. New York: Grosset and Dunlap, 1972.
_____. *The Mystery at Lilac Inn.* 1931. Bedford, Mass.: Applewood, 1994.
_____. *The Secret in the Old Attic.* Revised ed. New York: Grosset and Dunlap, 1970.
_____. *The Secret of the Old Clock.* Revised ed. New York: Grosset and Dunlap, 1959.
_____. *The Secret of the Old Clock.* 1930. Bedford, Mass.: Applewood, 1991.
Kismaric, Carole, and Marvin Heiferman. *The Mysterious Case of Nancy Drew and the Hardy Boys.* New York: Simon and Schuster, 1998.

About the Contributors

Glenna Andrade is an assistant professor in the Writing Studies Department at Roger Williams University in Bristol, Rhode Island, where she teaches science writing and literature and philosophy. Her scholarly interests are in classic psychoanalytic theory, program assessment, and cultural studies, most recently focusing on the Harry Potter series. She earned her Ph.D. in English at the University of Rhode Island. She shares her cottage in Portsmouth, Rhode Island, with her partner Gerry and with a freckled cocker spaniel named Colby who enjoys digging in the garden, especially after seedlings are just planted.

Michael G. Cornelius is the chair of the Department of English and Mass Communications at Wilson College. He has authored and edited seven books, including two novels. He received his Ph.D. from the University of Rhode Island and specializes in early British literature along, of course, with Nancy Drew and other girl sleuths. He has published in numerous academic journals, including *Fifteenth-Century Studies, Studies in Medieval and Renaissance Teaching, The Delta Epsilon Sigma Journal, Magazine Americana,* and *SCOTIA: A Journal of Scottish Studies.* He has an article on Chaucer's ploughman in the anthology *Black Earth, Ivory Tower* (University of South Carolina Press, 2005) and another on spatial identity and the tale of Bluebeard forthcoming. He has also published prose and poetry in numerous journals, magazines, and anthologies, including *Velvet Mafia, The Egg Box, Lachryma, The Spillway Review, Future Mysterious Anthology Magazine, CreamDrops,* and *Encore.* Visit him on the web at michaelgcornelius.com.

Fred Erisman is the Lorraine Sherley Professor of Literature Emeritus at Texas Christian University in Fort Worth. Trained in American studies, he has a special interest in aviation technology in fiction. His book *Boys' Books, Boys' Dreams, and the Mystique of Flight* (2006) examines how aviation series books communicated aviation lore and information to American youth. He is currently at work on a companion volume dealing with girls' aviation stories.

Melissa Favara and **Allison Schuette-Hoffman** met in the hallways of the Pennsylvania State University and were soon comparing notes on their disparate investigations of Nancy Drew and her authorship. One of them teaches creative writing at Valparaiso University; one of them adjuncts as a writing instructor at several colleges in the Pacific Northwest. One of them has a one-year-old daughter and a dog; one of them has two cats. Both live in old houses full of mystery, which they are both working hard to restore. Both write creative nonfiction and dream of Nancy nightly.

Leona W. Fisher is an associate professor and past chair of the English Department at Georgetown University, and co-founder and first director of the Women's and Gender Studies Program. She has published on Victorian theatre, children's literature, and feminist topics, and is working on two long-term projects: one on Nancy Drew, the Girl Scouts, and constructions of American girlhood in the twentieth century; the other on genre and narrative voice in English and American children's and young adult novels.

Anita G. Gorman earned a B.A. in English from Queens College, City University of New York; an M.A. from the University of Wisconsin, Madison; and a Ph.D. in English from Kent State University. She recently retired from teaching at Slippery Rock University of Pennsylvania.

Melanie E. Gregg's research is focused primarily on French women writers of the Early Modern period and the twentieth century. Her publications include a bilingual edition of Gabrielle de Coignard's *Spiritual Sonnets* (1594) and an annotated edition of Madame de Lafayette's masterpiece *La Princesse de Clèves* (1678). Recently, she has turned her attention to Francophone women writers of the Belle Époque and has begun research for a two-volume project that will comprise an annotated translation of the collected works and correspondence of the poet, essayist, and novelist Renée Vivien (1877–1909). Gregg is currently an associate professor of French at Wilson College in Chambersburg, Pennsylvania.

Marla Harris is an independent scholar with a Ph.D. in English and American literature from Brandeis, where she wrote her dissertation on eighteenth-century British women novelists. Her current research interests include children's literature, detective fiction, and the graphic novel. She has published articles in *Children's Literature Association Quarterly, Children's Literature in Education, African American Review, The Lion and the Unicorn,* and *The Journal of Popular Culture.*

Linda K. Karell is an associate professor and chair of the English Department at Montana State University in Bozeman, where she teaches courses in American literature, literature of the American West, and literary theory. She's working on a book on literary revisions and their implications for the understanding of authorship, and Nancy Drew fit naturally into the project. She firmly believes the first Nancy — composite, multiply-authored character though she is — is the best.

James D. Keeline has been researching the Stratemeyer Syndicate for about twenty years, with special emphasis on series book illustrators, ghostwriters, and especially Edward Stratemeyer. He has presented annually at the Popular Culture Association conferences since 1992 on series book topics. He has four projects underway related to series books, including a *Series Book Encyclopedia* and a biography, *Yours Truly, Edward Stratemeyer*, which draws insights from the letters at the Stratemeyer Syndicate Records Collection at NYPL. Professionally, he is a web developer and has taught web technology courses for adults. Before that, he was an antiquarian bookseller, specializing in children's books for a dozen years. He is also a volunteer steam locomotive engineer for the Poway-Midland Railroad.

Leslie Robertson Mateer earned a B.A. in English from Bryan College in Dayton, Tennessee, and a master's degree from Slippery Rock University of Pennsylvania. She is currently a lecturer in English at the Pennsylvania State University.

H. Alan Pickrell is an Emory and Henry College professor emeritus of speech and theater. He holds a B.A. from Belmont University in Nashville, Tennessee, and an MAT from Vanderbilt University. He has studied additionally with the RSC at Wroxton College, a British extension of Farleigh-Dickinson University, the University of North Carolina at Chapel Hill, and the University of Georgia. He has been active in professional, amateur, and educational theatrical productions, and has worked in radio, film, and television as well. He and his wife, Ellie, live in a historic house in Abingdon, Virginia. A past chair of the Dime Novel, Pulp, Series Book division of the Popular Culture Association, two of his major interests are L. Frank Baum and his Oz stories and H. Rider Haggard and the Allan Quatermain tales. He has written numerous articles for *Dime Novel Round-Up*, *Newsboy*, and *Yellowback Library*.

Allison Schuette-Hoffman *see* **Melissa Favara**

Steven J. Zani is an associate professor of English and modern languages at Lamar University, in Beaumont, Texas. He has recent publications in a number of journals and books, including *The Byron Journal*, the *Lovecraft Annual*, and *James Bond and Philosophy*. He is also co-author of the freshman literature anthology *Inside Literature*. His teaching accolades include an "Outstanding Commitment to Teaching" Award from Binghamton University and a listing under "Best Classes" in *Texas Monthly*.

Index